MANAGING THE WATER ENVIRONMENT

MANAGING THE
WATER ENVIRONMENT

Edited by
Neil A. Swainson

Published in association with
the Westwater Research Centre

UNIVERSITY OF BRITISH COLUMBIA PRESS
VANCOUVER

MANAGING THE WATER ENVIRONMENT

Canadian Shared Cataloguing in Publication Data

Managing the water environment

"The papers ... were discussed at a seminar
sponsored by the Westwater Research Centre and
held at the University of Victoria in March 1973."
Includes bibliographical notes and index.

1. Water quality management — Canada — Addresses,
essays, lectures.   2. Decision-making in public
administration.   I. Swainson, Neil Alexander.   II.
Westwater Research Centre.
TD226.M35   354'.71'008232
ISBN 0-7748-0041-0

International Standard Book Number 0-7748-0041-0

Printed in Canada

Contents

Preface

A major function of a society is the development of institutional arrangements that will aid its members in realizing the goals to which their values lead them to aspire. Since both values and environmental conditions continually change, the search for such institutional arrangements is an unending task. In North America and Western Europe the private enterprise system, functioning through the medium of the market and a form of government which has consciously sought to reflect the values of each member of society, has been central to our conception of how institutions should be designed to achieve social goals. Although these concepts have remained central to our perception of what are desirable institutions—in spite of the success of Marxist thought in some parts of the world—developments in recent decades have made us increasingly uncomfortable with the adequacy of our political and economic institutions to reflect the values we hold. While this is not the place to assess in a complete or comprehensive way these institutional deficiencies, it is appropriate to recognize their essential character, inasmuch as this book addresses some of them.

It is evident that the private enterprise-market system has departed substantially from the theory on which it was based and with its domination by large units—both corporate enterprises and labour organizations—the stability of the system and its ability to reflect social preferences have become greatly impaired. This development has led in turn to increased governmental intervention in an effort to use publicly controlled governmental institutions to compensate for the evident limitations of the private enterprise-market system. As populations increased, economies became more productive, and values changed, it became evident that this system was deficient in another important respect. It would not achieve by itself an efficient allocation of common property resources—the air, the oceans, the inland waters, the landscape, and associated resources. This recognition, especially over the last thirty years, has resulted in still further governmental intervention into the economic system, and it is this intervention with which this volume deals.

While the papers published herein are concerned with governmental intervention to compensate for the limitations of market forces in allocating the use of common property resources, these governmental processes must be considered in the context of what has happened to government in general. As the result of a very large governmental effort to compensate for evident limitations of market forces combined with the growth of military establishments, the character of governmental institutions has been transformed. In particular, because of the size and complexity of governmental organizations and the pattern of relationships they evolve, a serious question arises about their capability to reflect faithfully the preferences of the public they are designed to serve. This concern lies at the heart of the demand for more direct public participation in governmental decisions, for the employment of ombudsmen, and for other means of making governmental organizations more responsive to social preferences.

Throughout North America and Western Europe we are struggling to remedy these deficiencies in our economic and governmental institutions. We are searching for major organizing conceptions to modify and supplement those to which we have long adhered, so that the kind of technology we have produced can be harnessed to lead us to the fulfilment of our aspirations instead of creating frustration and destroying features of our environment which we value. Although some feel that a peak of concern about such matters was reached a few years ago, especially with regard to environmental matters, no fundamental solutions have been found, and the search continues for governmental institutions that are better suited to dealing with the kinds of problems we now face than those we have inherited from the past.

This is the context in which we view this volume. Water is an important common property resource. Governments have sought to regulate the use of this resource because of the self-evident limitations of market forces. While much has been accomplished, it is fair to say that we have not yet arrived at a set of conceptions about the organization of governmental activities and their relationship to private individuals and organizations with which we are fully satisfied. Many still feel that existing processes fail to reflect public preferences in the balanced way we should expect in a democratic society. A significant aspect of this concern is the widespread feeling that the system only functions to reflect social values adequately when the public becomes aroused and a special effort is made to assure consideration of public preferences, that the system does not function automatically to achieve this kind of result, and that it is not yet a system with built-in controls and stabilizing mechanisms that operate to achieve social goals in a fully reliable fashion on a continuing basis. This is the nature of the problem addressed by the papers in this volume. By focusing upon water quality, we have sought to narrow the number of issues and thus achieve a greater depth of understanding of the problem we face than if we had considered common property resources in general. The paper by John Graham departs from this limited focus because we felt that his case for direct participation by members of the public in the resolution of environmental issues was better stated than any that we could find limited to water quality management.

The papers and the issues they raised were discussed at a seminar sponsored by the Westwater Research Centre and held at the University of Victoria in March 1973. This seminar was attended by the authors and a number of knowledgeable individuals from government, industry, and academic institutions. Subsequent to the seminar, revisions were made in some of the papers by the authors and Professor Neil Swainson, the editor, prepared an initial and a short concluding essay.

This volume certainly does not provide a definitive solution to the problem of allocating the use of common property resources efficiently in accord with public preferences. The essays included in it, however, probe deeply the nature of this problem and, as the result of careful analysis, indicate some alternative courses we should be considering in our search for a solution. This is not the first time some of these ideas have been examined, but we do feel that no previous effort has brought them together within the type of integrating framework provided by Professor Swainson's initial essay. Furthermore, in my judgment no other work has succeeded so well in relating the issues addressd to Canadian institutions and Canadian environmental problems.

The Westwater Research Centre is grateful to the authors for their individual contributions to this volume and to the participants in the seminar whose stimulating ideas helped the authors in strengthening and sharpening their analyses. We are particularly appreciative of the rich contribution made by Professor Swainson in editing this volume and in preparing the introductory and concluding essays. We are indebted to the Inland Waters Directorate, Environment Canada, for grants to the Centre which supported both the conference and the publication of this volume.

Irving K. Fox
Director
Westwater Research Centre

Acknowledgements

It is appropriate to recognize the efforts of a number of people who have helped make possible the publication of this volume. The preface notes our indebtedness to the authors of the six substantive papers which the reader will find sandwiched between the introduction and conclusion provided by the editor and to the participants in a Westwater seminar who helped refine the thinking which the papers advance. Mrs. D. Robertson has provided highly competent stenographic assistance in the preparation of the manuscripts. We are much indebted to Mr. Itsuo Yesaki for preparing the charts and diagrams incorporated in several of the papers.

I must record my own indebtedness to Rosemary Fox for her painstaking and subtle contribution to the editing process and to her husband, Irving, not only for his writing of the preface but for much additional assistance.

N.S.

1

Defining the Problem

The Institutional Arrangements for
Water Quality Management

Neil A. Swainson

The serious observer can hardly fail to be impressed by the complexities of both modern technology and the institutions that have evolved to function in modern society. These complexities, together with the degree of individual specialization so characteristic of our time, make it difficult for one to see any given problem in its broader perspective. This is true not only of large national and international issues relating to such matters as war, peace, economic development, and population growth, but also of more mundane problems such as those associated with preserving or restoring the quality of our inland waters.

While we have to deal with this complexity (and while beyond some stage in the policy-making process further consideration of it appears to become self-defeating), in the light of the analytic capabilities available to us today and the potential benefits to be derived from their intelligent use, it is not at all clear that we have approached the limits in our ability to deal with complex policy problems. Even when due allowance is made for all the difficulties involved, a strong case remains for improving our understanding both of what our problems really are and of the implications of potential solutions to them. It is with this conviction in mind that the authors of the following six papers direct attention toward some of the intricacies associated with a seemingly simple question—the significance of the institutional arrangements required if water quality is to be controlled intelligently. The papers have been written from a variety of perspectives. They are not intended to add up to a "whole," and this introductory essay does not attempt to synthesize them. Rather it is designed to put them in context, to provide a setting for the issues which they raise and the arguments which they advance.

The institutional arrangements which a society invokes as it seeks to respond to any clearly identified problem are the resultant of a balancing or synthesis of many forces and considerations. As Professor Hodgetts has pointed out so clearly with respect to the infrastructure of Canada's federal government, they inevitably reflect the impact of the physical environment itself, its size, its barriers to transportation, its range of climate, and other geographic differences.[1] They reflect also the economic setting in which they evolve, especially the weight attributed or not attributed to the importance of generating policies which are economically efficient in their allocation and utilization of resources. Technological change, especially in the processes of communication, clearly has a major, albeit hard-to-predict, impact on the form of institutional arrangements utilized. So has the cultural setting, which makes relevant a host of additional considerations, ranging from the weights attributed to non-material values through current perceptions of the right and proper roles for members of the public bureaucracy to the implications of a participation ethic, and in some cases, to linguistic matters.

Nor does the list of strategic considerations influencing the selection of institutional arrangements stop here. They will reflect to a considerable degree the past institutional experience of those making the selection and, perhaps, a social "tolerance level" for the utilization of certain types of institutional mechanism. The need to prevent the appearance of some possible consequences of pursuing basic policy objectives under certain circumstances will rule out some arrangements. A most important consideration will be the extent to which perceptions of anticipated "solutions" involve significant conflicts between highly prized social goals and hence are perceived to require mechanisms whereby the values involved can be aggregated in mixes and traded off. In addition, there may be some relationship between the stage in the "issue-attention cycle" through which most policy issues pass and the institutional mechanisms most appropriate at any one point in time to their resolution.[2] Issues which are currently the subject of high visibility political activity and relatively recent arrivals on the political agenda, in other words, may well require different institutional "treatment" from those concerning which rather clear-cut and straightforward solutions have already emerged.

There is, of course, still another major determinant of the institutional arrangements which we deliberately create for the resolution of complex policy problems. We start with the assumption that these arrangements do bound or limit, on the one hand, and facilitate, on the other, identifiable forms of behaviour. The formation of complex policy in Canada will commonly involve much bargaining, much collegial judgment, some sheer inspiration.[3] It may incorporate the insights from extensive analytic effort as well. Some of these forms of strategic behaviour—such as bargaining—will be utilized in any institutional arrangement, albeit to varying degrees. Some, such as the use of analysis, require specific provision if they are to be utilized at all. It is a matter of elemental rationality that a major test of an institutional design is the extent to which it permits, assists, even requires, recourse to certain types of desired behaviour and perhaps inhibits recourse to others on the part of those responsible for the generation of public policy. Normally, institutional arrangements will reflect operative perceptions of the relative importance of certain types of strategic behaviour, or if one will, those which it is felt should be dominant at any one stage in the policy formation process.

Now, it is a truism that the design and redesign of institutional mechanisms is one of the hallmarks of the political process of our time and an exercise which is becoming increasingly difficult. Institutional arrangements established in response to rather precise perceptions of desirable mixes and orderings of strategic behaviours today find themselves required to respond to situations in which no one strategy is dominant, or in which the dominance has changed, or in which a variety of strategies must be invoked concurrently. Time thresholds seem to be descending on us, partly as the outcome of rising expectations, and inhibiting our capacity to generate institutional innovations. Still further complications arise because our institutional arrangements are being viewed as much more than mechanistic means-to-ends; increasingly today values and costs inhere in them as ends in themselves and have to be taken into account when the merits of these arrangements are being assessed. To repeat, institutional design is not easy; we may well be living in a time in which, as Sir Geoffrey Vickers suggests, there is a growing disparity between the least "regulation" the situation demands and the most it permits.[4] But it is not clear yet that this is beyond the wit of man to resolve.

Against the background of this brief survey of some of the factors which bear upon the design of public decision-making processes, a three-component framework may be useful when examining the institutional arrangements associated with water quality management. One of these components may be designated as *technical*. The reference here is to the physical and biological characteristics of water which are related to quality management, the causes and nature of quality degradation, the technologies available for preserving and enhancing water quality, the economic characteristics of the water quality management task, and the technical uncertainties associated with some kinds of water quality management decisions. The second component is concerned with what will be referred to as the *normative* considerations. By these we mean the standard that we view as applicable in judging whether a given set of decision-making processes is in accord with certain pragmatic as well as some very basic ethical norms of our society. The third component will be referred to as the *performance* aspect. It is concerned with the relationship of the operation of the decision-making system, in the context of its technical constraints, to the "demands" of the normative requirements.

The next three sections of this paper describe these three dimensions of our framework. They are followed by a section which summarizes the framework, relates it briefly to the structure of government in Canada, and then uses it to examine briefly the nature of the contribution of each of the six papers.

THE TECHNICAL COMPONENT

For our purposes it is not necessary to review in any detail many of the facets of the technical aspects of water quality management. This has been done by engineers, economists, biologists, and other specialists with evident competence. Our task instead is to identify those technical features of water quality management which in logic have significant implications for the design of appropriate decision-making arrangements.

The Measurement of Water Quality

The term "quality" with regard to water refers to energy or materials contained in the resource. Energy may be in the form of heat or nuclear radiation. Materials may be dissolved or in suspension. Inasmuch as water is a ready solvent which carries quantities of different kinds of materials in suspension when in motion, the quality of the water is measured in terms of its constituents. Given the large number of possible constituents, water quality can be measured in terms of dozens of parameters. The relevance of any of these depends upon the use that is being considered. The salinity of water may be important if the water body is to be used for drinking or irrigation but less important if it is to be used only for navigation. The temperature may be important if the water is to be used for swimming or for the propagation of fish, but it may be of little importance if the water is to be used for some kinds of industrial processes. Substantial quantities of dissolved oxygen are desirable for water used as a fish habitat, but zero dissolved oxygen is preferable for some industrial uses to minimize corrosion. Water quality can be objectively measured in terms of the constituents it contains, but the desirability of a given quality depends upon the use to which the water is being put.

Physical-Biological Interrelationships

An important feature of the water quality management problem is the fact that water quality is one variable in a complex set of physical and biological interrelationships which have important consequences for the values derived from water and its use. This has led to the characterization of water quality management as a task which concerns the operation of a system. The size of the water body and the velocity of its movement influence the quantities of materials it can absorb. Such factors as temperature, the rate of re-aeration, the quantities of nutrients in solution, and the penetration of sunlight will influence the nature of biological processes. Sunlight penetration in turn is dependent upon quantities of materials in suspension. Thus, if one wishes to achieve a given water quality characteristic, the system relationships must be taken into account.

In view of the need to understand or adapt to these interactions, models have been developed to assist with the management of water quality. This has been a difficult exercise, and the models generated to date all have limitations which, from the perspective of institutional design, it is important to keep in mind. For example, the interactions which influence some parameters such as salinity and dissolved oxygen can be modelled quite effectively. Other interactions, particularly those involving biological processes, are much less well understood. Also, the stochastic nature of water quality situations must be taken into account. Since quality is a function of quantity and since quantity is dependent upon factors that govern the hydraulic cycle, it is impossible to predict with certainty what quantities and therefore what qualities of water will be available at a specified future time.

While it is essential to recognize that a water body is a system, it is equally important to be aware that the geographic location of actions upon that system is an important variable. For example, two waste discharges of specified sizes will have a different impact upon the system if they are in close proximity with one another than if they are widely separated. The system "assimilates" the wastes through dilution and/or degradation, and dispersed discharges make fuller use of this assimilative capacity.

Altering Water Quality

The quality of a given body of water can be changed in essentially two ways. One is by altering the discharge of materials or energy into it. The other is by action designed to alter directly the character of the receiving water body itself. The size of the receiving water body can be modified at critical times by storing flood waters and releasing them at times of low flow or by pumping water from underground sources. The ability of a water body to oxidize organic materials can be increased by pumping oxygen into it.

There are numerous ways in which material discharges to water bodies can be reduced or eliminated. Here it is useful to distinguish between *point* sources—such as municipal sewage outfalls and discharges from industrial plants—and *non-point* sources—such as run-off from urban and agricultural land. The nature of discharges from an industrial plant can be altered in a wide range of ways; altering the nature of its produce, reclaiming materials and altering processes, or introducing some form of waste treatment. Discharges from *non-point* sources can be altered by changing land use practices or collecting and treating the run-off.

The Technical Component of Water
Quality Management in Summary

The preceding comments should permit an almost equally brief characterization of the nature of the technical problem with which water quality management institutions must seek to cope. First, the institutional arrangements must facilitate the generation on a continuing basis of technical information concerning extant water quality conditions and the likely conditions associated with the anticipated/optional/sometimes alternative forms of future development. Second, the institutional arrangements for water quality management must deal with certain issues posed by the system character of water quality. What are suitable boundaries for subsystems to be used in management, since the water cycle is a world-wide system? As a practical matter, to what extent can the system be modelled so that the effects of altering a variable can be estimated?

Third, assuming that the objective in water quality management is to approach a result which is optimal, whatever one's evaluative criteria, institutions concerned with management must be able to avail themselves of the range of opportunities for influencing water quality. Fourth, the institutional arrangement must deal with certain economic problems which flow from the common property nature of water quality, such as the lack of market-determined prices for some services dependent upon water quality. Furthermore, they must be able to respond to the uncertainties associated with some water quality conditions and to the stochastic character of water quality itself.

THE NORMATIVE COMPONENT

Since water resources are for the most part common property, some type of control must be exercised to achieve the most socially desirable or best use of them. Society effects this control over individual and group actions via institutional arrangements, which minimally consist of a set of rules and often involve entities or organizations with a functional responsibility to implement them. Any conscious attempt to construct or reconstruct these rules, the organizations which generate, implement, and interpret them, or the relationships between such organizations and between them and the community at large leads directly to another question. How is one to identify a good institutional arrangement when one sees it? What are the evaluative criteria? The question is a fundamental one and in part raises considerations which have challenged political philosophers and men directly faced with the responsibilities and ambiguities of governing over the ages. This is not the place to examine in depth the philosophical foundations of alternative political theories. In the light of man's experience and reflection, however, it is possible to posit some simple norms which may be associated reasonably with desirable institutional arrangements in the modern democratic state. Some of these norms are advanced below, in no particular order.

First, a good institutional arrangement for the creation of public policy is one which ultimately facilitates social choice. However necessary it is to ensure that time thresholds not forestall the search for the innovative and that adequate provision be made for well-informed, reflective deliberation both in the policy-forming stage and as ongoing experience generates additional information, it can be argued that there is something fundamentally missing in the institutional arrangement which appears to inhibit or prevent the very act of choice or decision itself.

Second, it is imperative that institutional arrangements reflect in some reasonable way the dictates of what is often called political efficiency. As a general rule at least, they must not incorporate assumptions concerning the willingness of political actors to run risks and incur costs (to them) which are quite unrealistic.

Third, a good institutional arrangement is one which facilitates decisions based upon the maximum possible understanding of the consequences of the act of choice and takes these consequences into account in establishing the most desirable mix of social values. Some implications of this criterion, which is a difficult one to achieve, will be considered in the next section. It will suffice at this point simply to recall that this norm in no way assumes that individuals are likely to make maximizing their economic welfare the sole or overriding value in their lives. Individuals very much affected by and interested in water quality management decisions may in fact weigh other values above their own economic well-being. Whether they do so or not, in some circumstances raising taxes or product prices can be in the public interest, even though this action may have the effect of reducing the net material benefits of individuals in society. What this norm does take for granted is that individuals' perceptions of the consequences of various forms of action or inaction on others as well as themselves be as well informed as possible. Ultimately, this process of clarification will be limited by our analytic capacities, the costs of the analysis itself, and the resources which individuals are willing to devote to it.

Fourth, it is imperative that the decision-making process takes into account in some reasonable way the interests and the preferences of those clearly affected by policy decisions.[5] Note the distinction advanced here between interests and preferences; it is made simply to draw attention to the obvious, that interests need not be articulated as preferences and frequently are not so expressed. But to return to our main point, we take it as axiomatic that the interests and preferences of no group will be ignored because, for example, of the status of its members, of their lack of specialized knowledge, or of their sex. We assume surrogates will represent the interests of those, such as the young and the mentally ill, not competent to represent themselves.

Fifth, a good institutional arrangement encourages the derivation of policy decisions which, aggregating mixes of materials and non-material benefits and costs, move us toward rather than away from a maximization of social utilities. It does this while recognizing (1) that individuals have different sets of values to which they give different weights, (2) that individuals' values will be affected differentially by any one decision, and (3) that while individuals frequently have interests, often not reflected in explicitly held preferences, which they rely on representatives to identify and articulate, the existence of clearly expressed individual preferences, and the intensity with which they are held are significant indicators of individual interests, and these, quite properly, are considered to be influential in the policy-formation process.

Sixth, the ideal type of institutional arrangement has constraints on the losses it can impose on individuals. One of our operative ideals, for instance, is that it should not be possible to deprive an individual of his livelihood or his independence as a human being (except for criminal acts), even though in some cases such actions might provide greater benefits to society as a whole. In particular, there is widespread agreement that the least advantaged members of our society should not be further disadvantaged in the interest of enlarging the aggregate good.

Finally, a good institutional arrangement is one which educes decisions which are accepted in society as legitimate, as the end product of processes of decision widely viewed as acceptable. To a significant extent, of course, perceived legitimacy will be a function of the degree to which the institutional arrangements meet the six criteria already posited. But this is certainly not the whole story, for a widespread characteristic of our age is the fact that so many existing institutional arrangements, and particularly those associated with environmental decision making, are being challenged for a good many additional, if sometimes complicating and confusing reasons.

Once again we have to eschew here any examination-in-depth of a complex phenomenon. Many of the challenges to the legitimacy of traditional decision-making processes are associated with a strong demand for decentralizing the processes of government, with much anti-organizational and anti-bureaucratic sentiment, and often with a wholesale assault on the concept of efficiency itself. What we do have to recognize, in positing some characteristics of the good institutional arrangement, is the extent to which its *processes* as well as its *results* are viewed at the time as just and the fact that, for some today, institutional legitimacy is closely associated with the degree to which it incorporates mechanisms of direct democracy.

The author believes that this last perspective often involves an oversimplistic interpretation of reality. Frequently, as Robert Dahl points out, it unwisely ignores or discounts the emergence of factions and the role of leadership, the difficulties inherent in defining the "people" affected by any decision, and, perhaps most important of all, the implications of drastically increasing the number of decision-making units (while decreasing their size) which its logic would seem to entail.[6] This is not to suggest for a moment that a characteristic of the good institutional arrangement is that assignments of authority to jurisdictions never overlap. Nor is it to argue that large organizations have, overall, an inherent merit as opposed to small ones. What reservations of the sort just advanced do draw attention to is the phenomenon of the mass society. The watercourse with which at least one of the following papers is explicitly concerned flows through a metropolitan area which, with its adjacent rural hinterland, contains well over one million residents. Virtually all of these people have a stake in the quality of the water in question. Yet, whatever the institutional arrangement utilized, only a very small fraction of the population will become directly involved in detailed decision making concerning it.

The case for direct democracy on moral and philosophical grounds remains impressive, just as it is impressive for representative, referendum, and committee democracy, and, on occasion, for delegating authority to responsible agencies. As Dahl argues so well, no one of the forms of democracy is inherently superior to the others and hence a superior road to institutional legitimacy. Mixes of them, which may change for differing stages in the decision-making process, for differing levels of government, for the passage of time, appear to be necessary if public choices are to be made effective. We shall return to this consideration later but leave it now with the simple observation that the strength of the social commitment today to participative processes in decision making is such that, whatever the ambiguities it involves, it cannot be overlooked as one of the factors which significantly influence the legitimacy of institutional arrangements themselves.

Positing norms in this way in no sense is intended to imply that any one set of institutional arrangements can be expected to produce optimal decisions. Optimal decisions do not emerge in the real world. What the list does suggest is that we have accepted some broadly defined criteria to help us recognize the desirable both in the means whereby we arrive at collective decisions and in the decisions themselves. Advancing them, further, is not intended to suggest that there is no latent conflict between the assumptions or consequences associated with the norms themselves, for potentially, and often in practice, these conflicts do exist. The institutional requirements, for example, of the need not to disadvantage further the disadvantaged, to generate reliable highly technical data, to utilize this data to illuminate public and private dialogue and hence to influence preferences, to economize in the use of resources, and to associate a widespread public perception of equity and fairness with the entire effort are not easily reconciled. Fortunately, most organized forms of human endeavour demonstrate an extraordinary capacity both to live with and to thrive on conflict and ambiguities of this sort.[7] And, of course, much of the fascination of institutional design stems from the belief that, given the wit and the will, man often can reconcile the seemingly irreconcilable in desirable packages of accommodation. It will be appropriate now to turn our attention to some features of this reconciliation as it concerns the water quality management problem.

THE PERFORMANCE COMPONENT

In reflecting on the types of institutional arrangement most suitable for water quality management, we are seeking arrangements which, adapted to normative conditions prescribed above, are capable of dealing with the kind of technical problem that has been defined. Arrangements which reasonably meet or satisfy these requirements will depend upon the interrelationships among a number of factors. These include the resources brought to bear upon the management task, the rules that determine the relationship among individuals and organizations and their respective power and authority, and the motivations and perceptions that determine the response to the pollution problem, to the established rules, and to the actions of the various entities by the individuals involved in one way or another with the decision-making process. Resources are of two kinds: information-generating resources and technical resources to achieve changes in water quality. Let us examine more fully the nature of the problem of designing arrangements that meet the technical and normative requirements of the management task.

To repeat a point made already, the importance of reliable information about the consequences of alternative courses of action is taken as self-evident. And to repeat still another earlier emphasis, this does not imply that individuals are expected to act in accord with what might be termed "economic rationality." Instead we assume that individuals will choose courses of action within the context of their own constellations of values and in the light of their perceptions of the consequences of these alternatives to themselves and others. Since the normative conditions anticipate that decisions will be taken in the context of a genuine sensitivity to public preferences and reflect these preferences reasonably, it is only logical that these preferences be not blind hit. When derived, they should take into account information about the consequence of what appear to be the best available courses of action.

Also, in proceeding, it will help to differentiate, even if somewhat arbitrarily, between two categories of behaviour which may be labelled the taking of *policy* decisions and *implementation* actions. Policy decisions are concerned with the courses of direction to be pursued. As the term is used here, implementation actions are those directed to the carrying out of policy. The distinction is important even though experience has demonstrated that there frequently can be substantial and often unanticipated differences between policies adopted and programmes implemented. The interplay of forces which precedes the taking of a policy decision seldom disappears during the stage of implementing action. Further, logic frequently makes it wise to modify policies during their implementation as new insight emerges with reference to ends as well as to means. There is, in other words, a policy component to implementation action. Probably, to date, we have not devoted enough resources to reconstructive effort of this sort. Our point remains, nevertheless, that the need for a reasonable degree of consistency, responsibility, and predictability in our actions dictates that beyond some point the policy component in implementing action be cut off.

The technical considerations make it clear that because of the common property nature of water resources and the difficulty of pricing some services associated with water quality, some decisions (but not all) must be socially determined if our normative standards are to be met. Furthermore, since most individuals neither can nor will want to participate in the making of most decisions that affect them, provision must be made for the faithful representation of numbers of individuals by a single individual. The system must have the capacity to develop highly technical information about the opportunities available for altering water quality and their likely consequences and to communicate this information in such a manner that it can be "received" by those affected and their representatives.

It also follows from the normative specifications that the "representatives" in some sense must be able to bargain with one another and agree to trade and hence to synthesize mixes of preferences to achieve maximum utilities for society—within the constraint that overall the more disadvantaged will not become worse off as a result of these interactions. While many of the offsets and accommodations just referred to might be effected within what may be narrowly defined as the water quality sector, a question arises as to whether it is not desirable to expand the trading arena to incorporate other perspectives and transactions involving other public goods so as to enrich the trading opportunities. The need to provide for this expansion is all the more imperative, of course, when one realizes that water quality management is not a discreet policy issue to be resolved in isolation. It has to be viewed, ultimately, in the context of larger policies concerned with the general direction of the environment and with land-use planning.

With the foregoing considerations, the technical aspects and the normative specifications in mind, we can sketch the basic features of simplified decision models. For policy decisions the essential components are shown in figure 1:

If these models are to be elaborated to function to meet the normative specifications and to ensure that those who make and must sustain the water quality management decisions have the required technical capabilities, it would appear that a set of institutional arrangements must be established with the necessary capabilities. Rules must be adopted and enforced which distribute power amongst the public and private entities and govern their actions in a manner that will achieve the desired result. The development of such institutional arrangements requires that individual motivations and perceptions, individuals' ability to communicate and receive information, and the manner in which these factors influence the behaviour of groups and organizations all be taken into account. Let us elaborate more fully the nature of the requirements for suitable institutional arrangements, first for arriving at policy decisions and then for the derivation of implementing actions.

Policy Decisions

First, a decision must be made as to which individuals are *primarily* affected by the problem at hand and thus are *primarily* concerned with its "resolution." For example, if institutional arrangements for managing water quality in the Lower Fraser River are being considered, are we to include in our definition of those affected the residents of the entire Lower Fraser Valley or just the residents of the Lower Mainland area, or should the "problem-shed" be broadened to include the residents of the entire province or even of Canada as a whole? A quite reasonable answer might insist that the people of the entire nation have an interest in the water quality of this area, and, indeed, such a viewpoint is reflected in current institutional arrangements. But clearly the nature of the problem and the degree of interest in it will vary from region to region, and within the region, the province, and the nation. A basic task in institutional design consists of deciding what is the relevant population around which to structure what might be described as the primary decision-taking apparatus and how, and at what stages, the interests of the broader population are to be introduced into the calculus. For this watershed, reconciling the roles of three, indeed

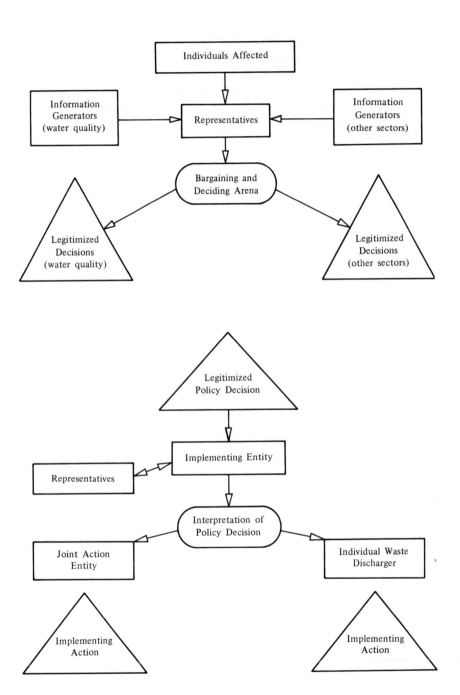

Figure 1

four levels of government, all of which have valid perspectives from which to approach this set of policy problems, remains an essential question for federal-provincial and provincial-local government relations.

Second, it is at this stage of decision making notably that the institutional arrangements have to identify the interests and preferences of all the individuals most affected. In other words, it is when basic objectives are being agreed upon, basic data are being gathered and assessed, and basic lines of action are being set that the operative system of representation has to try to weight individuals' values as equally as possible. This is a complex and difficult exercise, which subsumes many specific questions such as the following—

1. Since it makes no sense to assume that every individual is fully informed on every public issue which affects him, how can a system of representation for individuals be constituted in which they will have confidence? In this century we have placed increasing emphasis on the capacity of organized interest groups to augment the roles of formally elected representatives. Doubtless we shall continue to do so, although increasingly we need to ask about the adequacy of their "coverage" of the interests of the entire population and about the significance of the pluralists' conception of government as a broker.[8] Precisely the same question concerning the adequacy of interest "coverage" needs to be asked with reference to the contributions of career civil servants. And much of the challenge inherent in raising it in the first place focuses our attention on the real and the prescribed roles of the members of our elected legislatures and of our responsible political executives in Canada. Here still remains our primary mechanism for identifying, weighting, indulging the interests and desires of individual citizens.

2. For those individuals who have formed preferences, how can they be communicated with fidelity to appropriate representatives?

3. On the assumption that, whatever our models of politics turn out to be, our society will remain significantly pluralist and recognizing that there is a widespread variation in the resources available to groups and individuals wherewith they can influence the decision-making process, how can a set of rules and perhaps of entities be devised which meets our normative requirements? Specifically how can individuals and groups enjoy access to the policy-forming process without acquiring undue influence over the policy output? This last question is particularly relevant in view of the consideration which follows.

Third, if our model is to be effective, it is at the policy formation stage that the capability to generate technical information of the type essential to water quality management is important. Obviously, this calls for analytic expertise, but a problem arises the moment one concedes this, as producing "technical information," pursuing analytic effort, is anything but a "value free" effort. Technical specialists inevitably, and properly, have their own views as to what the problems are and where the most likely roads to their solution lie. Their perceptions have a major impact in determining the kinds of data produced, the alternative forms of action or behaviour assessed, the quantum of resources allocated to this assessment, and the division of the resources between the assessments. If it be imperative, as we assume it is, that the goals sought be those of the general populace affected, early in the policy-formation process institutional provision has to be made to ensure that a variety of perspectives be brought to bear upon the insights of the specialists in order that, wittingly or otherwise, they do not skew or misdirect the information-generating process. Central to this question is the relative power of civil servants and elected representatives in the making of final decisions. The former, as specialists, often produce the technical information themselves, or invoke its production, and significantly influence its interpretation. Deciding upon the extent to which the generation of information needs to be replicated in order to validate its findings is another continuing question for institutional designers.

A further consideration stemming from the relationship of technical information to intelligent water quality management is that while, normally, its production is initially associated with a comparative evaluation of means to ends, as has been noted already, in time its emergence must logically affect evaluations of ends. Periodically also new goals for public policy emerge during the analytic process. The end result, in any case, frequently is the reconstituting of the public's and decision-makers' perceptions of what the policy problem was in the first instance. Much of this desirable circularity in the policy-formation process may be provided outside first order or primary decision-making mechanisms. But not all of it will emerge in this way. Indeed, there is a good deal of evidence to suggest that deliberate provision has to be made in the design of institutional arrangements if reasonable attention is to be directed to the relevance of technical information for the reassessment of policy objectives and if the benefits to be derived from an ongoing and reciprocal refinement of ends and means are to be attained.[9]

Fourth, the institutional arrangements concerned with the generation of policy decisions must foster a reconciliation of interests and preferences. Two orders of value conflict, at least, must be dealt with. One, the one we normally think of, involves the differing sets of values of differing individuals as they pertain to water quality and its management. The other involves the conflict, equally inescapable and only to a degree even recognized in advance, between the values of each individual. Traditionally in Canadian government much of the reconciliation to which we refer has been effected within executive government. A great deal of the process has been internalized, becoming the object of highly visible political activity only in the final stages preceding the act of decision and not always then. Frequently, it has involved what may be designated as appellate recourse to superior levels of authority within governments and to "superior-level" governments, with the higher levels concerning themselves with a broader range of interests and publics, although much of the governmental authority involved, while overlapping, has been fundamentally co-ordinate and complementary.

The extent to which, above the local level, the trading process is extensively concentrated in the executive branches of government in Canada is well recognized and in marked contrast to the more overt and diffused recourse to such practices as log-rolling and coalition building in some other political systems. There is no denying, however, that, even with strong executive leadership, bargaining, plenty of it, does take place within the Canadian context, that there are cases to be made for and against it as a mechanism of accommodation, and thus that it is not clear to what extent it can or should be excised from any complex exercise in public policy formation. It is also apparent that the more significant or important the values a polity has to reconcile, the more difficult it usually is to change the institutional arrangements within which the reconciliation has to take place. This is notably true of Canada. Thus for Canadians the incentive appears to be all the greater to search hard for hitherto unrecognized opportunities to innovate within the context of existing arrangements. In any case, a number of difficult questions will face Canadians as they wrestle with water quality management. A significant one involves harmonizing the now widespread demand for making more "open" the trading-off process with past practices of cabinet government. Another question involves deciding at what level or in what arena, or arenas, and at what stage in the policy making, the necessary reconciliation of interests and preferences should be effected. All sorts of efficiency considerations appear to require that not all of the accommodation be pursued within the institutional arrangements primarily concerned with water quality management. At the same time, it is not entirely clear what arenas the varying stages of policy making should embrace.

Our simplified model does recognize that the reconciliation of conflicting values is pursued differently in different political systems and differently for different issues at different times and at different places in the same system. It does not suggest that the policy process has to end up in the single discrete decision; it recognizes that policy may be the resultant of many decisions.[10] But it does insist that however the final direction in which public policy is going to move is determined, it does involve a balancing or reconciliation of claims or values, benefits, and costs—in short, an act of choice.

The Implementation Process

There are numerous considerations which bear upon the shaping of institutions primarily designed to implement decisions. One is the operative perception of the capacity or the will of government (the two are by no means identical) to manage a complex regulatory process. Approaching water quality management via the definition and enforcement of water quality (ambient) standards, or of effluent standards, assumes a capacity to manage comprehensively via comprehensive administrative mechanisms. As several of the authors whose papers follow point out, this fact is not widely appreciated. On the other hand, at least in theory, if the route to implementing water quality objectives involves a concentration on damage functions, the definition of thresholds, and the utilization of market mechanisms via some system of effluent charges or market trading in discharge rights, it is arguable that·a much more modest assumption concerning necessary capabilities to manage comprehensively can be lived with. The institutional mechanisms designed to utilize these approaches may be expected to differ.

A second basic consideration might be categorized as the determination of the polity to ensure the fidelity of the implementation of its water quality management decisions. It is obvious that this fidelity will depend upon (1) the accuracy with which the public policy is relayed to any implementing agency or agencies, (2) the accuracy with which these agencies reflect original intent—or better induce desired response and action—in their communication to waste dischargers and to those responsible for the operation of joint action agencies (such as those providing for low flow augmentation), and (3) the resources available to take the desired action.

It is important to recognize here that this process can fail at all three points. If, for whatever reason, the initial policy decision is unclear or ambiguous, there is by definition no real reference point against which to assess its implementation. Even if the transmission of decisions is quite clear, however, difficulties can still emerge. Members of the implementing agency staff inevitably have their own perceptions of the water quality management problem, which may cause them to interpret the adopted policy in a manner which varies from what was intended. Further, however close their understanding of the policy in question to its designers' intention, staff personnel at the implementing level are frequently subject to the representations of individuals and groups seeking interpretations of the policy in question favourable to themselves. Again, the joint action agency may not act as desired because of a lack of resources. An additional complication is often rooted in the rivalry of public agencies, in the extent to which as organisms they build up patterns of expectation concerning their own and other agencies' responsibilities and acceptable forms of behaviour. Effective water quality management may require that for a number of them these expectations be thoroughly shaken up. But if this be the case, those responsible for this institutional re-arrangement will want to guard against possible dysfunctional consequences on policy outcomes when the existing "domain-consensus" is upset. Finally, ambiguity in official communications, inaccurate perceptions of the costs involved, or a failure to appreciate the complexity of human motivation may mean that waste dischargers themselves fail to act as desired. All the way down the line, the fidelity of the responses sought will be a function of the authority of the communications utilized to some extent. Presumably the authority will have to be associated with penalties or sanctions, which will have to be certain and costly for non-compliance.

Some requirements which must be met if our implementing entities are to be faithful in interpreting adopted policies are self-evident. Decisions must be unambiguous; and communications, as clear and authoritative as possible. In addition, provision may have to be made to facilitate an effective monitoring of the implementing process by the individuals and groups affected by the policy itself. Once again we have to recognize, but largely sidestep, the hazards and problems associated with the application of elements of direct democracy to this stge of the policy process. Our point is an elemental one. To the extent to which individuals and groups do have the capacity to generate influence and relay it to public officials during the implementing process, great care must be taken to ensure that "external" influence, if exercised, is equalized. And to legitimize the end product, it is important that this be seen to be done.

The argument advanced to this point may be summarized in three propositions. First, the measurement of water quality, let alone the management or deliberate control of it, involves an extraordinarily complicated process—far more complicated than is widely realized. In this connection, the prospects for misdirected effort, or inefficient effort, are correspondingly great. Rational decision making in this context requires a comprehensive knowledge of the variations and interdependences which exist in the natural environment, the effect of modifications in the quality of water on life in all its forms, and an understanding of the consequences of a broad range of actions open to man. Secondly, the importance of the intelligence function in this category of decision making and the existence of some thresholds relating to water quality and its consequences which society, today, feels ought not to be crossed require that policy formation make heavy use of certain specialized decision-making strategies. These in turn appear to require specialized institutional arrangements, designed in the context of a set of social norms, which are important both for the types of behaviour which they attempt to stimulate and for those which they seek to proscribe. Thirdly, the institutional arrangements applied to water quality management have to reflect in a reasonable way the interests and preferences of the Canadians most directly interested and in some manner and at an appropriate stage the interests, where relevant, of a wider Canadian public. In addition, they have to ensure that water quality is being managed, and managed ultimately in the light of decisions taken by those directly responsible to the publics concerned and in such a way as to command widespread public support.

Now an obvious characteristic of these arrangements in Canada is that they involve an exercise in co-operative federalism. As J.W. MacNeill very properly observes, both the federal and provincial levels of government have capacities and responsibilities related to the research, general information gathering, planning, regulatory and financial strategies which this type of policy formulation and implementation involves.[11] Federal and provincial roles overlap both with respect to the determination and regulation of water quality itself and, indirectly, with respect to the spillovers associated with almost any conceivable form of regulatory action which can be undertaken. In addition, it is obvious that for some of our most significant watercourses, the decisions of two additional levels of government—the regional and the local—often have a direct bearing on water quality; thus these two may also assume a significant management function.

The fact that responsibility for water quality management has to be so widely shared creates a number of well-recognized problems. For example, the investment in resources required simply to integrate the efforts of up to four levels of government can be very significant, especially in a country as large as this one. And to complicate matters, securing desired intrajurisdictional co-ordination is frequently made all the more difficult by the tendency of many governments to create functional agencies committed to the preservation or enhancement of single or of a few environmental values, in short by the difficulties associated with securing intrajurisdictional co-ordination as well. Secondly, there are attributes of policy making and administration under conditions of shared jurisdiction which, as Professor Corry suggested in a classic memorandum a generation ago, Canadians could well do without.[12] Decision-makers and their supporting staffs, under such circumstances, are always tempted to allocate to another level of government responsibility for programme failures, for unanticipated costs and delays in programme implementation, for visible and unpopular (to some) allocations of costs—even though the costs, if not the incidence of their allocation, be inescapable. Behaviour of this sort has two great difficulties associated with it. It may serve not just to diffuse but also to attenuate the overall level of responsibility associated with the policy making in question. And it may encourage decision-makers to distort, by unduly simplifying, the complex issues at stake. Thirdly, overlapping in federal-provincial jurisdiction is not necessary to produce large scale recourse to partisan mutual adjustment, or if one will, to bargaining in Canada. Most of our provinces are large enough to permit a very wide range of interactions within them. Indeed, a very real problem associated with divided federal-provincial jurisdiction is that it may pave the way for two-party contests between the federal government and a single province or indeed between two provinces, which contests, in turn, may lead to deadlock rather than to the integration of viewpoints so widely associated with partisan adjustment.

There is, of course, another side to this coin. As the public choice theorists and Professor Corry himself continue to remind us, there can be real merit in overlapping jurisdictions in seemingly untidy institutional arrangements. Three may be cited here briefly. One is the well known argument for bargaining, broadly defined, especially as it has been developed by Charles Lindblom. There are limits to the capacities of individuals and governments to appreciate the complexities of major policy issues. Overlaps, even when associated with competitive costs, may be the only means of uncovering important insights. Even when the national interest clearly is at stake, and the national government properly involved, we always have to keep in mind, for example, that a province rather than a national government may be the first to hit on a new concept of great value to the whole polity. Just the reverse, of course, may happen with respect to provincial interests. A second reason for welcoming a sharing of responsibility is that it is possible to perceive a strengthened capacity to handle it in some welcome manifestations of advancing maturity in the Canadian federal system. There is no denying the existence of stresses during the first two decades after World War II associated with the marked changes which took place in Canada apropos the absol ute and relative capacities of the federal and provincial governments to be innovative in policy formation and implementation. But it is possible to argue that a good many of the uncertainties of this period have been clarified. The strengthening of the analytic capacity of public bureaucracies, especially at the provincial level, has been a wholly beneficial development. And to some extent an appreciation of the merits of classic federalism has helped; we may be seeing less trenching now on the fields of jurisdiction of other levels of government and, to a degree at least, an appreciation of the thesis that by respecting the competence of other levels of government, one heightens the competence of one's own.

A third reason for being prepared to welcome overlapping jurisdiction is that requiring successful exercises in consultation and co-operation may strengthen the capacity of the Canadian federal system to respond to challenges which certainly lie ahead of it. Obviously these are going to be serious, and maintaining a reasonable balance between the forces of unity and disunity in Canada is not going to be easy. But we need to be clear about whence our major difficulties are likely to come. When Professor Smiley perceived what he called the structural crisis of Canadian federalism in 1972, he located it in an unwillingness on the part of the provinces to allow the federally governing parties to "speak authoritatively" for all Canadians on matters clearly within parliament's sphere of competence.[13] Today, some of our most acute difficulties seem to be rooted in an overt conflict between the prerogatives associated with provincial resource proprietorship on the one hand and a federal regulatory power on the other. In any case, our point is a simple one. There is no fundamental reason why, with respect to water quality management, the association of Ottawa and the provinces need fall into either of these categories. Both levels of government have clear-cut allocations of authority concerning it; to some extent each can frustrate the other, but there is no reason why they need do so. Nor, fundamentally, is there substantial evidence to suggest that they want to. In short, Canadian federalism may well be host to the compounded crisis of which Professor Smiley writes, and it may well get worse, but it is not one to which problems associated with the management of our water's quality need contribute. Happily there is a good deal of evidence to suggest that this is widely appreciated. There is no reason to suggest that the federal government should—or is likely to—give up its responsibilities, for example, with respect to the nation's fisheries or that it should opt out of a more direct managerial role when domestic water quality has major international significance. But while reserving a latent capacity to serve as a prod, it appears to be quite prepared much of the time to play a basically facilitative role, assisting the provinces in the derivation of approaches to water quality management which reflect local conditions and sets of values.

If the provinces are to play a key role in this policy formation, it is only reasonable to expect that the institutional arrangements involved may differ from province to province and within provinces. A good deal of institutional logic would suggest that for the larger parts of many provinces which are very sparsely settled, the primary decision making may have to be pursued at the provincial level itself. To transfer responsibility for it to regional or other agencies under these circumstances would seem to limit unduly the range of interests which ought to be brought to bear on the decision making. On the other hand, when watercourses cut through densely settled areas, some such devolution may be very much in order. Here, as elsewhere, the intergovernmental/agency co-operation required will call for some jurisdictional modesty and common sense, but without making unrealistic assumptions in this direction, the prospects are favourable that the required co-operation can be attained and that effective ongoing water quality management can be one of the success stories of latter-day Canadian federalism.

While the six papers which follow range widely over the issues raised on the preceding pages and each naturally has its own distinctive thrust, they may be usefully grouped, via their central themes, into three pairs. Although written from quite different perspectives, the first two papers are concerned with the institutional "setting" wherein Canada and British Columbia approach the management of water quality and seek to examine this setting in the context of at least three of our normative criteria. Indeed, the more general of these two papers (that of Professor Anthony Scott) raises questions of direct importance to almost all environmental, and much other, decision making in federal Canada. Both Professor Scott and Professor Robert Franson (with his colleagues) are interested in determining how our policy making might reasonably reflect the preferences of those directly concerned (criterion 4) and the extent to which it is informed or intelligent (criterion 3). Professor Scott in addition directs much of his attention to the costs associated with the decision making itself and the case to be made for minimizing them (in essence, criterion 5). He leads off, in a sense, by turning directly to the allocations of environmental decision-making authority in Canada, to the extent to which they overlap, and to the identification of the level in the hierarchy of governments at which primary responsibility for decision making may be concentrated most wisely. He suggests that the allocation will vary with functions but that the preceding sentence really misstates the question. He believes that the evidence is not yet available to enable us to answer the "optimum level" question definitively with respect to environmental matters or, perhaps, with respect to some others of major importance also, such as the problems of income stabilization and stabilizing the economy. The crucial question to ask, he suggests, concerns the sum total of the costs associated with allocations to any one level or mix of levels. These he perceives as involving the direct cost of producing, per citizen, each unit of the public good in question, the cost of related intrajurisdictional bargaining/accommodation which is the stuff of the political process, and the cost of interjurisdictional transactions which inevitably must occur when authority is shared.

Much of his attention is devoted to demonstrating, as he sees it, the simplicity of many of the perceptions of government held by his fellow economists. His thesis, briefly, is that attention should be directed first to minimizing the aggregated costs of policy formation. Identifying the appropriate level or levels to which to allocate authority should follow this determination, he suggests. With Canadian circumstances very much in mind, he stresses the reality of variations in Canadian regional tastes and standards and the degree to which research and data-gathering roles may be pursued by governments which do not assert direct jurisdictional competence.

Mr. Scott is worried about a penchant for associating superior levels of government in a hierarchy with superior decisions.[14] He emphasizes the merits of small jurisdictions—their social and environmental closeness to individuals, their capacity to reduce intrajurisdictional accommodation costs, and their facilitating certain types of dialogue—as he advances the interesting argument that the capacity of small jurisdictions to bargain is, to some extent, a function of the range of functions for which they are responsible. And he suggests that environmental management is likely to be most successful when pursued as far down the hierarchical scale of governments as concurrent adaptations to individual tastes and to aggregated costs permit.

The basic objective of Professor Franson's essay is to identify clearly the allocations of authority which relate to the management of water quality in Canada and the rules and institutional arrangements which have been created in part to pursue this managment function with reference to the waters of the Lower Fraser Valley in British Columbia. An additional concern of his is with the legitimacy of the decision-making processes being utilized (criterion 7). The picture which emerges from Professor Franson's review has some distinctive characteristics. First, it reveals just how long water quality has taken to arrive as a discrete and major objective of comprehensive public policy formation on the public agenda in Canada. Many of the more than twenty statutory enactments bearing on this question in Canda have been responses over an extended period of time to very narrow subsets of the problem as it is now envisaged. Secondly, as has been noted earlier in this section, this is a policy area to which the aspect doctrine so hallowed in Canadian constitutional interpretation is directly applicable. From differing perspectives both the national and the provincial governments, and their creations, may initiate and sustain policies which directy bear on water quality. Thirdly, many of the most important statutory enactments passed to date in Canada have been highly general and have involved extensive delegations of authority to executive government, with respect both to the setting of goals and to the definition of the means, or the routes, to be utilized in seeking these goals. Furthermore, to date the enforcement of a good many of the rules and regulations promulgted under these statutes has been sporadic and intermittent.

If, as Professor Franson indicates, much incrementalism and lately a good deal of uncertainty have marked the responses of Canadian governments to water quality management in British Columbia and to the watershed of the Lower Fraser in particular, it is interesting to speculate why this has been so. Part of the answer appears to rest with two simple facts: the weights we attribute to many values change, and the density of population in the area in question has built up gradually. There seems to be little doubt that there is now a widespread public desire to preserve water quality and to restore it where it is impaired. But part at least of the measured pace with which Canadian governments have reacted to their perceptions of this desire or demand may well be the result of uncertainties, already referred to, which exist concerning the present state of the water resource, the technology of improving and preserving it, and the most appropriate institutional mechanisms to utilize in this process. Public decision makers and their staff advisers appear to be more aware of these difficulties than is the public at large in Western Canada. Additionally, they are cognizant of the unpleasant reality that the management of water quality involves generating costs with respect to other highly prized social values.

Actually, Professor Franson does not seek to account for the current state of the institutional arrangements for managing the quality of the water in the Lower Fraser River. After explicating the constitutional and legal frameworks through which governments currently operate, he examines the capacity which they possess to acquire the information which they need to arrive at sound decisions (especially when viewed in the context of criteria 3 and 4). And he ends perturbed at the permissive rather than prescriptive character of current institutional arrangements—for example with reference to formal public consultation, early-stage interagency and intergovernmental consultation and co-ordination.

The second two papers concentrate on the extent to which current institutional practices do or do not adequately take into account the interest and preferences of those most affected by environmental decisions (criterion 4) and today, as decision-making mechanisms, are or are not widely regarded as legitimate (criterion 7). These papers directly address the question: Who should be primarily involved in establishing the goals of our "environmental" policy making and how should these goals be attained? Both reveal their authors' conviction that the current set of institutional arrangements leaves much to be desired. Both reflect at length on the difficulty manifest in any attempt to arrive at policy decisions which have a significant environmental impact. Both acknowledge the need for the utilization of specialists' insights. Neither would agree that fundamental acts of choice should be made by analytic personnel. From this point on, however, their prescriptions for remedial action differ sharply.

As Mr. John Graham sees the problem, much of our former approach to the making of public policy is no longer adequate. It has generated an authority crisis, he avers, because of its unilateral reliance for acts of decisions on elected representatives and, often, on employees of none-too-responsible public agencies. This crisis, he suggests, applies both to the decision-maker and the decision-making process. He perceives at least two other major explanations for it. One, which he views as a correlate of traditional practice, lies in a thoroughly unsatisfactory assumption concerning a passive citizenry. And the other he finds in the extent to which traditional decision-making arrangements have directed far too little attention to a scanning and critical examination of basic objectives.

As he sees the situation, there are three basic variants of the existing situation which we can pursue. One, which is inherent in our criterion 3, but which he finds inadequate, would involve an emphasis on generating better information for the decision-makers. A second, which he notes is widely endorsed, involves the introduction to the decision-making arrangements of an environmental impact agency, or its equivalent, and often a quasi-judicial adjudicatory board. His thesis is that this approach will also fail to solve the problem as he perceives it, not least because it tends to educe win-lose zero-sum situations, when we so badly need new incentives to find integrative solutions with positive-sum characteristics. Finally, he opts for planning based on public participation, which holds out, he believes, the promise of greatly reducing the tension and the coercive aspects of traditional decision making and promises thus to answer the legitimacy question inherent in criterion 7. Implicit in his scheme is the structuring of small temporary groups within which conflict resolution and—what is even more important—an attitudinal revolution can take place. He concedes that his formulation incorporates major assumptions concerning the reasonableness of man and the practicability of variations on direct democracy but affirms that the approach he endorses must be tried if we are to engender the mutual understanding and trust which he finds so lacking today.

Mr. Edwin T. Haefele, on the other hand, has great difficulty with Mr. Graham's conclusions. He is convinced that the attempt to articulate large-scale citizen participation in the decision-making process is doomed to failure and that, far from resolving a legitimacy crisis, it will serve only to heighten it. How, he wonders, is the system in practice to weigh conflicting claims advanced by individuals and groups and to reconcile those whose claims are rejected? Where, he asks, does the approach to legitimacy by involving interested citizens stop? He suggests that this procedure cannot stand up to the claims for representative government, which he views as a mechanism with a unique capacity to determine and aggregate individual preferences (criterion 4), and to transform them, via bargaining and vote trading, into viable social choices. He is very concerned that our institutional arrangements measure up to the requirements of criterion 1, that is, that they actually facilitate rather than deadlock the process of social choice.

Mr. Haefele's theme is that we have created great problems for ourselves by cutting and specializing the decision-making process on functional, issue lines and by abandoning in such traditional instrumentalities as parties and legislatures the basic social need to reconcile individual interests. He perceives much of the current legitimacy problem, at least in the American context, as stemming from an unworkable attempt to fill the gap via executive action. But he believes that there is no real substitute for the general purpose representative who is able to serve on a multitude of decision-making bodies with varying jurisdictional responsibilities and spatial boundaries. By reconstituting what he understands to have been an earlier concept of the role of the general purpose legislator, he suggests that for a range of environmental decision-making we may be able to associate some of the efficiency characteristics of the technical alternatives to water quality management which are already recognized with some of the equity characteristics which may be latent and often unrecognized in executive and legislative behaviour. Thus, to repeat, he maintains that when legislators trade votes and build bargains, in a significant sense they also aggregate value preferences and move in the direction of increasing social utilities (criterion 5). And this, in view of their expertise at winning elections, is what he perceives them to be pre-eminently qualified to do.

Our final two papers deal rather more explicitly with problems directly, and in some cases uniquely, associated with water quality management. Both are written by economists who direct much of their attention to the merits claimed for, and the likely consequences of using, various orders of pricing in pollution control and abatement policies. But, although these papers vary greatly in length, both move well beyond these options and seek to assess a comprehensive range of alternative institutional arrangements and mechanisms. Read together, they do this in the light of virtually all our normative criteria. In addition, both are much concerned with some of the difficulties associated with the implementation process and particularly with the manner in which governments can respond most effectively to the truly complex.

Professor John Dales, who is already very well known for his incisive writing on this subject, approaches it with a number of very specific concerns. One is his belief that many of the pricing suggestions advanced by economists to this point have been of very little use. Another is his conviction that modern man is overloading the agenda of governments. As will be noted in a moment, he sees no alternative to governmental action at a number of crucial stages in handling this problem, but he does suggest that this action can be taken while the problem remains "manageable" if use is made of private ordering derived from the price system to allocate that crucial and scarce resource—the capacity of water to accept waste and to cleanse itself.

Professor Dales himself identifies what may be called the basic principles or hallmarks of his argument. One is that deciding upon the *capacity* of the natural system to absorb waste and the *distribution* of this capacity are two quite discrete and distinct problems. A basic criticism of governmental behaviour to date which he advances is that, while in logic the capacity decision should be arrived at first, for a whole series of reasons, which he enumerates, governments have avoided it and have concentrated upon varying approaches to the second, or distributional, exercise. They have got the matter backwards, he contends. Secondly, he is convinced that for water quality management purposes it is desirable to split large national/provincial areas into regions, which he believes must be arbitrarily established by government. In this way, he believes, the management task will be facilitated, and it will be possible both to adapt to the existing variety of ambient standards and to increase them.

The reader should appreciate that Professor Dales disagrees with extant Canadian federal government policy, which envisages the implementation of national standards with respect to effluent discharges. Indeed, he argues that the broad-spectrum approach reflects great respect for economic growth but little, in practice, for water quality. When he turns to the range of institutional arrangements most seriously considered for water quality management, he finds great shortcomings in reliance on exhortation, on judicial determination, on point-by-point administrative decision making, on the promulgation of effluent standards, or on the use of tax breaks and similar incentives to reduce waste loadings on the natural system. He concedes that there is not likely to be a single ideal set of institutional arrangements and that any set utilized is likely to contain a mix of approaches. Thus he agrees that some responsible administrator must be able to prevent the discharge of substances known to be hazardous and to build into the system suitable allowances, probably of an uneconomic nature, when the risk or uncertainty associated with discharges is great. But his fundamental proposition, of course, is that, used on a zonal basis, effluent fees and what he calls discharge warrants are incomparably superior management tools—because either is likely to minimize the direct economic costs of effectively limiting or reducing the waste loadings on the natural system. A further merit to a discharge warrant scheme, he believes, is that it ought to minimize the transaction costs of which Professor Scott writes.

If there is one overriding theme to Professor Marc Roberts' extremely comprehensive analysis, it is the complexity of the real policy issues raised when we seek to protect the environment. Early in his paper, and repeatedly thereafter, he develops the case for an iterative, incremental approach to the "problem," for he emphasizes that neither theory nor data supports the proposition that we know how to derive from "the system" optimal solutions. He develops at length what we have called the technical component of the decision making, emphasizing, for example, such considerations as the costliness and still very imperfect nature of helpful information, the variability of the natural environment, the degree to which natural systems may be irreversible, and the existence of thresholds. And he expands at length on some major explanations for the imperfect nature of the bargaining or trading currently associated with environmentally significant public policies and related externalities.

When he turns his attention to the fundamental objective, he concedes that it is some level of ambient standard, but, in company with Professor Dales (and possibly Professor Scott), he has his doubts about uniform standards nationally. He insists that, at best, the standard will be a crude approximation and that it provides a setting within which society has to pursue a series of choices involving operations on the ecosystem itself or options in production, in pricing, and on operations directly bearing on supply and demand in the market.

After identifying a series of criteria against which to assess the merit of choices (his normative component in the decision making, if one will), Professor Roberts proceeds to offer a detailed comparison and critique of the merits, absolute and relative, of a reliance on effluent charges and effluent standards. Not surprisingly, he finds that both approaches have strengths and attendant problems. Interestingly, he suggests that some of the assumptions which have led economists to favour fee systems over effluent standards are vulnerable and that the implementation of either approach in practice involves differing sets of penalties which, for cultural considerations, may become strategic factors in the ultimate decision making.

Readers will note that he shares Professor Dales's scepticism apropos the effectiveness of such forms of public action as the offering of tax concessions and cost-sharing grants directed at input modification and also some of Mr. Dales's reservations about the transaction costs likely to be involved in attempts to decentralize the process of damage assessment and remedial action via a combination of liability rules and private bargaining. And they will want to note particularly his assessment of the case for the utilization of transferable pollution rights. After examining at length the deficiencies of the most widely endorsed decentralized approaches to waste treatment and environmental enhancement, Professor Roberts assesses the consequences of the direct public provision of these services. He discusses the case for controlling the inputs to pollution. Before concluding he faces up to the equity considerations at the heart of our normative criterion number 6 as they pertain to the policy proposals he has examined.

Professor Roberts ends his extensive analysis emphasizing the extent to which problems of environmental policy making are those of democracy.

Action has to be taken, here as elsewhere, in the face of imperfect information about the state of the environment, the state of public preferences about it, the consequences of choice, and the impact of institutional arrangements themselves. Useful conceptual and analytic approaches exist, and much helpful data can be derived analytically, although he insists that none of it leads to definitive answers.

But this is to go on too long. It is high time that the reader was turned loose on the contributions of our six authors. After he has read them he will find, in a short concluding statement, some reflections on the implications of their arguments for further research in this field. This introductory paper will have served its purpose if it has identified the perspectives of our contributors and has drawn attention to some of the major considerations which serve to emphasize both the importance and the complexity of the linkages between institutional arrangements and water quality management. Our stress on complexity is re-emphasized by Professor Roberts' final observation, in which he draws attention to our oft-neglected responsibilities as fiduciaries for protecting the range of choices and weighting of values which succeeding generations may wish to exercise. The extent to which public choices, even with respect to operational institutional arrangements, are to be bounded by this normative consideration remains an inescapable and challenging question for each generation to decide.

Notes

1. J.E. Hodgetts, *The Canadian Public Service: a Physiology of Government, 1867-1970* (Toronto: University of Toronto Press, 1973), chapter 2.

2. Anthony Downs, "Up and Down with Ecology: The 'Issue-Attention Cycle,'" *The Public Interest* 28 (Summer 1972): 38-50. Mr. Downs suggests that most American public policy issues pass through an "issue-attention cycle"; my hypothesis is that this generalization applies to Canadian experience as well.

3. Cf. Charles Perrow, *Organizational Analysis: A Sociological View* (Belmont, Calif.: Wadsworth Publishing Co., 1970), chapter 3; J.D. Thompson and Arthur Tuden, "Strategies, Structures and Processes

of Organizational Decision," in *Comparative Studies in Administration,* edited by J.D. Thompson *et al* (Pittsburgh: University of Pittsburgh Press, 1959), chapter 12. These essays probe the relationship between the nature of policy problems, the internal structure of organizations which have to deal with them, and the decision-making strategies to which these structures are most clearly attuned.

4. Geoffrey Vickers, *Value Systems and Social Process* (New York: Basic Books, 1968), pp. 77-78.

5. The reader interested in some recent incisive thinking on the relationship of individual preferences to governmental decisions in a democracy is referred to John Plamenatz, *Democracy and Illusion* (London: Longman, 1972), pp. 183-84.

6. Robert A. Dahl, *After the Revolution: Authority in a Good Society* (New Haven, Yale University Press, 1970), chapter 2.

7. R.M. Cyert and J.G. March, *A Behaviourial Theory of the Firm* (Englewood Cliffs, N.J., Prentice-Hall, 1964), pp. 117-18.

8. Some students recently have assailed our latter-day adaptation to interest group pluralism in extreme terms. Theodore Lowi, for instance, maintains that it deranges and confuses public expectations about democratic government, weakens individuals' capacity to live by democratic norms, and demoralizes government and renders it impotent. Theodore Lowi, *The End of Liberalism: Ideology, Policy, and the Crisis of Public Authority* (New York: W.W. Norton, 1969), chapter 10.

9. Charles Schultze, *The Politics and Economics of Public Spending* (Washington: The Brookings Institution, 1968), p. 74.

10. Charles E. Lindblom, "Tinbergen on Policy Makings", *Journal of Political Economy* 66 (December 1958): 536.

11. J.W. MacNeill, *Environmental Management* (Ottawa: Information Canada, 1971), chapter 16.

12. A.W. Corry, *Difficulties of Divided Jurisdiction: A Study Prepared for the Royal Commission on Dominion-Provincial Relations* (Ottawa: King's Printer, 1939).

13. D.V. Smiley, *Canada in Question: Federalism in the Seventies* (Toronto: McGraw-Hill Ryerson, 1972), p. 185.

14. He joins company here with some sensitive political scientists. Cf. Corry, *Difficulties of Divided Jurisdiction,* and E.R. Black and A.C. Cairns, "A Different Perspective on Canadian Federalism," *Canadian Public Administration* 9 (March 1966): 27-44.

2

The Economist and Federalism
in Environmental Management*

Anthony Scott

In this paper I first deal with the economist's blindness to the diversity and complexity of government levels and jurisdiction. My point is that his training in the market's powers and failures had induced him to regard "government" as a mere residuary sector for carrying out those functions beyond the scope of property rights and the profit motive. This point is then amplified by referring to the oracular and supernatural powers imputed by the economist to the concept of the "organic state." In the last half, these ideas are applied to environmental problems.

WHY DOES THE ECONOMIST BELIEVE GOVERNMENT TO BE MONOLITHIC?

We begin formally, with an individualist point of view. The aim of economic policy is to provide goods and services to individuals in accord with their tastes. These goods and services are provided by firms within the private sector and by jurisdictions in the public sector. The locale of their actual production is another story, to which we shall return.

Within the private sector, the market place and a system of property rights are responsible for distributing incomes and choosing goods and processes of production. The usual way of thinking about the matter, rather one-sided, is that when this market "fails" to produce certain goods in the amounts desired by individuals or when it brings about a distribution of income or wealth that is different from that socially desired, there is revealed a residual task to be performed by government.

* Portions of this paper repeat remarks delivered at the December 1972 meetings of the American Economic Association, to be published in *The American Economist*. I am grateful for comments from Melville McMillan, Marc Roberts, Jim Wilen, H.F. Angus, Peter Pearse, Ron Shearer and Neil Swainson.

Economists have long recognized this regrettable danger of market failure and have, of course, accepted the implied necessity for government "intervention" in what would otherwise be the private sector, leading to government provision of goods, services, and redistributive policies. But the economists' theory falters here. There is no fully developed approach to "government." What is it? The theme of this section is simple. It is that economists' individualist traditions, contrasting the complexity of the market with the simplicity of "government," have beguiled them into a centralist position which is no part of their discipline. A transplant from jurisprudence and political science of the concept of the nation-state, this position deserves profound scepticism. Just as economics deals with the rich diversity of corporate forms and institutions that make up a market, so it should comprehend the complex, overlapping, and complementary system of jurisdictions that constitutes "government."

It is not difficult to understand how economists got themselves into this tangle. Like many aspects of our science, it can be traced easily back to Adam Smith. For it is to Smith that most of us owe the idea that an invisible hand, working through market arrangements that we now stylize as perfect competition, harmonizes the self-interest of unlike persons and induces them to co-operate in serving the social interest. Consistent with this outlook, Smith saved most of his fire for an attack on the unjustified obstacles placed by the state in the way of free trade and the division of labour between men, regions, and nations. Indeed, as several commentators on Smith have noted, his influential obsession with the harmfulness of governmental interference with commercial and industrial progress was overdone. For in his time, the great structure of mercantilist regulations and navigation acts, dating back to the Tudors and Stuarts, had already been largely dismantled.

Whatever the explanation, the result for Anglo-Saxon economics is plain. Economists have followed Smith's lead in looking primarily to the unobstructed market to bring about maximum welfare for consumers. For the first hundred years they concentrated on showing that there was little that the forces of competition could not achieve; the residual "duties of the sovereign," while obvious enough, were few in number and could be safely neglected by all save specialists in public finance. In the second hundred years, following Sidgwick, Marshall, and Pigou, they have extended somewhat the list of types of "market failure" to perform the wonders attributed to the hidden hand. Consequently, with the economists' fuller understanding of the intricacy and beauty of the competitive model, their list of government functions began to resemble the set of problems with which real-world politicians and voters are actually concerned.

But this recognition of a larger role for government was a triumph for common sense, not for economic analysis. Analytically, economics still had its back turned on government. The typical micro-economist continued to think of the market as being *the* organizing principle that systematized and channelled the otherwise anarchic and wasteful activities of individuals. Thus, the diverse working of markets was most worthy of study—in international trade, labour and industrial relations, banking and finance, concentration and monopoly, population trends, and business cycles. The actions and reactions of economic actors were infinitely various and worthy of examination and classification. Government, on the other hand, was at best a braking force on the excesses of the market and at worst a source of distortion and obstruction. In general, it was not worthy of study for its own sake. While government was indeed to be observed everywhere, the task for analysts was to show how "economic forces" determined each industrial structure and market pattern. Since "economic forces," by definition, did not work through government channels, they could not help to explain the structure of government. This, therefore, was not on the economists' agenda. There was little that Smith's tradition could contribute to the understanding of government and politics, except perhaps distrust.

Thus, while economists might understandably have regarded government as a system of institutions for performing those functions left undone by the private sector, a system having its own characteristics and predictable responses to opportunities and constraints, they eventually found themselves regarding government as external to the system, as performing "non-economic" functions, and as unsuitable for the systematic theorizing to which the market place has been found susceptible.

This bias in the economists' agenda naturally led to indifference to and neglect of the many possible forms and levels of public activity. However, in its historical context, this neglect led economists to views quite inconsistent with those that had emerged from their more expert interpretation of industrial development. On the one hand they had shaped their own clarifying quasi-historical theory about the progress of mankind from early tribal autarky, which satisfied them that the nineteenth century trend toward the variety and individuality of the market place was an optimum expression of basic human forces. But on the other hand they borrowed quite uncritically the prevailing literary, constitutional, and historical approach to the origins of *the* government. This was simply that *the* modern state was a consolidation of fragmented antecedents—especially the medieval state—entities built around monarchs, who in their uniqueness, in the system of land tenure, in their military command over their vassals, and in their judicial and even religious supremacy, anticipated many of the elements of modern government.

In explaining how the monarch and his political successors established the self-sufficient unity of the modern state, economists concurred with the political historians in imputing the consolidation of medieval units to such material conditions as the improvement of transportation facilities, the rise in the average standard of living, the emergence of large cities, and above all the improvement of communications.[1] The modern state, it was agreed, with its government, was here to stay. Few writers were left who argued instead for the power and wealth of a regional peerage, local popular decentralization, or, at the other extreme, "international" groupings. Furthermore, because the destiny of any national state was eventual undivided sovereignty against outside forces, so its internal organization required a self-government that could embody and direct this national integrity. This government had to be able to command all parts of the country and (in the democratic versions) be legitimate in the sense of representing them. In serving all interests and regions, it must be wary of divisive, parochial, or separative forces. In short, in accepting the historians' and philosophers' account of the growth of the political state, economists had been induced to accept also the idea of the *centralized* state.

One example of this centralist view can be found in the literature about the arguments against free trade and laissez faire. After decades of contention, economists have recognized that "optimum tariffs," if they worked, would be more advantageous to a nation than free trade. Likewise, they have conceded that barriers that achieved other "non-economic," national objectives were acceptable (although believing that these same ends could be better achieved by other means). In brief, they have joined non-economists in a search for that set of foreign economic policies that would be to the "general good" of the economy as a whole. But they have not shown the same eclecticism in domestic matters. As a profession they have been critical, if not contemptuous, of "discriminatory" protection policies when introduced by smaller regions *within* the nation. While they might, that is, reluctantly find that a protective tariff on chemicals was the best available means of achieving some national end, they would be quick to agree with the chemical executive who argued that: ". . . we should discourage with all our influence the fragmentation of production that would be brought about by a persistent policy of discriminatory purchasing by provinces and municipal governments."[2] To hold this centralist view has not been easy for economists. But it has been staunchly held in the face of strong evidence to the contrary: that in most countries, especially in federations, there are many jurisdictions, some having powers over many functions and some specialized to a very few; some stretching over vast areas and some confined to a village or a few acres of a city.

Among the results has been an unfortunate tendency for economists to perceive only national economic issues as worthy of their study. This is revealed in two ways. First, there is a blindness to local or regional applications or illustrations of economic analysis that tends to be self-perpetuating. Second, there is a tendency, when local problems are forced on economists' attention, to recommend their promotion to national status under the jurisdiction of central governments.

Macro-economics, in which many economists are specialized is an example. The facts of geographical mobility and of trade have made it almost impossible to apply aggregative theory to small or specialized jurisdictions. Therefore (at least until the recent wave of interest in urban problems), most economists have simply neglected the problems of less-than-national areas. It has been assumed that first priority should be given to aggregate income or demand at the national level, that "structural problems" and "imperfections" could not be tackled first. Once the problems of the broadest jurisdiction have been solved, those of the smaller regions might then be cleared up.

To this observation should be added the possibility that aspiring economists find the variety of regional activities and procedures lacking in data suitable for econometric study, difficult to generalize about, and lacking in potential for widespread policy changes at the stroke of a single pen. Thus, unlike sociologists, lawyers, and political scientists, they rarely venture the slow scholarship that is necessary for local studies. They rarely recognize that the lack of regional data is the result of their own demand for ever more frequent and precise national aggregations.

Whilst they are often to be found as paid consultants to local bodies, their quickest professional pay-off comes from grasping the fewer apparent intricacies of some national issue. Where necessary, they are often to be found advocating that a mosaic of non-uniform systems be tidied up by being switched to the jurisdiction of a senior government. (Witness the usual assumption that when or if welfare programmes are transformed into a guaranteed annual income the latter should be moved from local to national administration.) A second result of the centralist obsession among economists faced with the reality of the governmental mosaic is a strengthening of their misunderstanding, almost contempt, for the actual proceedings of any jurisdiction in coming to decisions. Economists are schooled in "rationality," which is to say they believe that both individuals and collective groups should scan and clarify their objectives; order or weight them; determine their interconnections and their opportunity costs; and choose those that will make as much headway as possible in the public interests or in the interest of the individuals affected. But when they observe provincial and local government, they see that various legislatures and councils are consistently behaving otherwise. They are behaving "politically," with an eye to TV and an ear to any interest group that may complain. Their decisions seem destitute of strength, purpose, or principle. They behave inconsistently from meeting to meeting and year to year. They seem responsive to interest groups, however illogical their presentations, and unresponsive to logical or rational plans, however attractively presented. Worse, they not only prefer votes and re-election to ideas and plans, but indulge in horse-trading, log-rolling, mugwumpery and, if they get the chance, gerrymandering. Much of the time they appear simultaneously ignorant, perverse, and corrupt.

Now the relevance of this to our theme is that the smaller the government, the more evident is its "political" procedure. Large and central governments conduct some of their decision-making behind closed doors, at the airport, or over the telephone, but smaller and more regional jurisdictions keep much of their activity open to the public. Thus it is easy to believe that local governments are particularly stupid and corrupt.

Furthermore because local and provincial governments rarely have large staffs of experts who are professionally trained, the economist rarely finds anyone at the local level with whom he can, or would wish to, conduct a conversation. Any economist depending on a rational approach to convince decision-makers that some part of the economic system should be altered could be pardoned for steering clear of local and even provincial governments.

WHICH GOVERNMENT IS IN CONTROL?

There is a second view of government. Each jurisdiction is presumed to have "allocational" and "distribution" branches,[3] overseeing the performance of the private sector and making up for its deficiencies by appropriate laws, taxes, spending, and transfers. Endowed with these functions, "government" is no longer the despised residuary man-of-all-work described in the foregoing section but now becomes the delphic repository of all virtue and wisdom. Economists critical of economic trends blame "the government" for its failure to predict, prevent, or remedy. Clearly, to be blameless, the government must not only be well-informed and powerful but also endowed with a will of its own that can direct its actions correctly.

The theme of this section, the idea that government has a mind of its own, serving the public interest under its own steam, is difficult to reconcile with the revealed diversity and complexity of government institutions. The contradiction can best be seen by examining an extreme form of public-interest doctrine, the concept of the organic state.

Beyond the unquestioning identification of "government" with the actual national central government lies the tendency to confuse this jurisdiction with an actual "organic" or collective personality having motives and constraints that are different from the sum of individual wants and means. This is not the place to debate the merits of this collective approach to public-sector decisions. More in fashion among political scientists than the rigorous and abstract individualist approach, it is intended to be more descriptive of the actual decision processes, the interplay of interest groups, and the emergence of personal leadership. For our purposes, what is important is that in its tendency to describe the decision-making process as a comprehensive balancing among interest groups in search of a higher "public interest," the organic approach provides an opportunity to locate the economists' "social welfare function," public conscience, or the maximizer of general welfare, within the government itself. Much of Pigovian welfare economics can be, and indeed has been, interpreted in this way.

Both Pigou and Lerner convey an impression of an ideally paternalistic government controlling the allocation and distribution of resources within an uncertain and imperfectly competitive economy. Note the corollaries of this organic approach:

1. There can be only one wise, paternalistic authority. Neither these authors nor their readers can imagine a whole spectrum of organic governments each judicially balancing and correcting the imprecise, selfish, and short-sighted allocations of the market place. Because the real world is multidimensional, with many governments, the logic of the organic approach is to regard one of them as supreme, and the rest as juniors or agencies.

2. The structure of government is placed beyond scrutiny. In being given the task of ensuring the efficiency of the economy as a whole, the "government" may be pictured as applying the principles of welfare to the private sector. But there are two reasons why it cannot apply them to the public sector. Either this government *is* the public sector, with all parts and agencies regarded merely as branches, in which case it can hardly be expected to police or censure itself; or, there are other governments, which are not junior to it. In this case their performance cannot be effectively scrutinized by a government that has no jurisdiction over them.

The upshot of these two points is that the actual existence of diversity and independence among governments indicates the extreme weakness of the organic, or paternalistic, approach to the role of government. It strains credulity to assign the role of disinterested allocator and mediator to a *set* of governments. Which, or which set, is the embodiment of the "public interest"? In brief, how are we to identify wise government policy until we have learned not only to satisfy ourselves which agencies are in control of particular problems, but also to build a government structure that can, under changing circumstances, best make new controls and follow wise policies?

Some writers, noting all this, then redirect the enquiry. Evidently it seems to them to follow from what has been said so far that the task is to find the "right" size of jurisdiction. If the economist has unthinkingly assumed that today's central governments are the vantage point from which economists must examine the allocation and distribution of resources, has he been wrong? What level of aggregation should he adopt? Where should the all-knowing economic observer stand when he pulls out his copies of Pigou, Musgrave, and Arrow, his telescope, his charts and his tables and assumes "an economic point of view"?

My own belief is that this is the wrong question because there is no single point of view from which the Paretian optimum, or any other optimum, can be seen to be satisfied. It is true that the broader the jurisdiction, the more individuals and the more opportunities will be included; but this is a truism. It tells us nothing about how many points of view *should* be taken into account. Instead, we should search for the optimum *structure* of governments and jurisdictions. The analogy with our studies of the private sector is complete. Applied economists do not, any more, ask themselves "How big should all firms be?" Instead, recognizing that different products, processes, and markets dictate different sizes of establishment and of firm, they attempt to discover that organization of each industry most conducive to overall efficient allocation under consumer sovereignty.

The implication of this analogy for government is that we must accept and work with many sizes of jurisdiction, at various levels of aggregation over population and area, each jurisdiction providing products or policies appropriate to the spread and technical conditions of production and decision making. Government should not be seen as a single, residual, non-market institution but as an intricate complex of geographical and functional jurisdictions, having potential static and dynamic equilibria among its components analogous to the static and dynamic private components within the market place. Government is both local and national, just as factor and product markets are both local and general. And it may have transactions and make agreements at all its levels, both with other governmental jurisdictions and with the diversity of persons and firms in the private sector.

Recognition of the diversity in "government" will, I think, serve us well in attempting to reconcile the economists' two extreme views. On the one hand, the bewildering image of contradictory government edicts, decisions, and allocations should be seen as the product of a system of government actions and decisions, a system having a micro-structure, ecology, and macro-tendencies parallel to these characteristics of the private sector.

This diversity shows that the organic view is completely misleading. "Government" is no more the repository of Paretian discrimination and wisdom than printers of Bibles are, inherently, a fount of religious guidance or the criminal-law system a source of understanding of the problems of marriage, divorce, and population control. Being heterogeneous, overlapping and interacting, governments can originate policies and standards and reflect demands and ambitions. But the diversity of their electorates and the incompleteness of their jurisdictions means that, far from applying knowledge and welfare criteria to the private sector, they themselves must be simultaneously with the private sector the subject of the *same* type of scrutiny. Government is not above the market place; governments and firms, in interlocking systems, are part of a single, extended "market."

My colleague at the University of Toronto, Albert Breton, has for several years shared a view about the diversity and segmentation of government. One of its aspects is federalism, government with many geographical jurisdictions assembled at three or more "levels" into units that have only one "national" jurisdiction at the highest level. While my remarks should not be taken as representative of Breton's views, I must acknowledge my debt to him for discussion of most aspects of all the questions I am raising. We both hope to systematize and clarify these aspects in our joint work.

Breton and I have recognized, of course, that the diversity of governmental jurisdictions is not merely geographic. People living side by side, or even in the same building, can belong to, and have policies provided by, different groups, "clubs," districts, councils, or governments. While it would be idle to deny that federal government is made up of units that lie side-by-side on the map, this tells us more about the limitations of maps than about the possible diversity of government. But in the final sections of this paper, I will concentrate on geographical diversity alone, as exhibited in the federal and municipal systems of government.

DIVERSITY IN SIZE AND LEVEL

Let us resume the formal argument commenced early in this paper. If "market failure" means that there is much for the government to do, if many levels of government can exist, and if economists have unduly neglected this diversity, what should be advised by some detached observer, given the responsibility for reforming a structure of government? Should the diversity be tidied up by consolidation?

The key to the whole matter is that *none* of the argument from "market failure" implies that jurisdiction must be large. There must be collective provision, redistribution, and regulation. But does anything follow about size?

The most obvious criterion is scale of the production function. If government intervenes to deal with poor private performance or to provide public goods that may easily serve millions of persons, must not the jurisdiction be at least as large as the number served? And if a policy or public good can serve only a few people, must not the jurisdiction be appropriately small? Reflection will quickly show that this does not follow at all. The physical conditions of production need not determine the scale of decision making. Transportation provides many examples of "indivisible" goods that are in fact provided and administered by separate small firms and jurisdictions. For example, the "Orient Express," a train running from France to Turkey, ran over the rails of many countries, yet carried passengers efficiently all the way. And at the other extreme the Canadian National Harbours Board runs many small ports that are scarcely even connected by water with one another.

In general, there are three ways of dealing with economies of scale. We may organize ourselves into jurisdictions that have the same scale as the productive process or the number of customers. Or, secondly, we may divide ourselves into many smaller jurisdictions which can share among themselves the provision to their members of goods and services produced on a larger scale. Instead we may produce the large-scale good (at higher cost) many times over at the small jurisdiction level. Thirdly, we may organize jurisdictions that are larger than the scale of the public good and produce it in several locations.[4] A fourth possibility, similar to the first, is to produce a small-scale good in many small jurisdictions.

All these jurisdictional possibilities exist and are in use at the present time. None of them is obviously the best. No jurisdiction ever has exactly the scale implied by its productive process, its sources of labour or finance, or the number of its owners or clients. As Coase pointed out in 1937 and E.A.G. Robinson even earlier, the whole trick of firm organization is to decide when to produce things internally and when to depend on external transactions and contracts.[5] So it is with jurisdictions; costs dictate when goods should be produced internally, rather than being procured (using transactions and contracts) in the market place.

The theme of the present piece is that costs also determine the ideal scale of a political jurisdiction. The relevant costs may be classified into three categories. We may get some feeling about their influence by asking how they alter when the number of members of a jurisdiction is increased.

The first type of cost is the very one we have been considering thus far: production costs. What is important is production cost per citizen. As the number of citizens in a jurisdiction increases, we may expect to enjoy something like the economies of mass production. Furthermore, the fixed production costs of indivisible public goods may be split among more persons.

The second type of cost stems from the need to reach agreement within the jurisdiction. Collective decision requires time, understanding, and compromise. Yet, if the public services to be provided are indivisible, members of the jurisdiction must eventually agree on a single course of action. And divisibility may not help: the process of agreeing on the provision of a number of qualities or amounts of a diverse and dispersed good or service may be prolonged by the very variety of possible alternatives. Such costs can be expected to increase as the number of persons who must communicate and agree within a jurisdiction increases. (Alternatively, if the costs of reaching agreement do not increase, the burden of coercion or exploitation of unhappy minorities must increase with the number of persons included.)[6]

The third type of cost is least familiar: it stems from the time and trouble required in bargaining and agreeing with other jurisdictions. Such costs will arise whenever the scale of a jurisdiction differs from the area affected by the goods it provides or that its neighbours provide. The resulting spilling-over of services is merchantable (as is the prevention of disservices). These costs are obviously the governmental equivalent of interfirm transaction costs. For a given jurisdiction, they can be expected to increase with the number of neighbouring jurisdictions with which it must trade and the differences between their preferences; obviously, it will decrease with increases in the size of typical jurisdictions.[7]

Two observations may be made. First, it is obvious that type two (agreement costs) and type three (transaction costs) are substitutes for one another. The growth of a jurisdiction reduces its dependence on external transactions but increases the internal difficulties of agreement. There will be some least-cost total of these two costs, for each grouping of people, for each public service. Second, it is also obvious that there is no particular reason for this least-cost total to be found at that size of jurisdiction for which type one (production) costs are least. It is inevitable that, taken together, the three types of costs will determine a least-costly scale of jurisdiction that differs from that best able to "produce" a certain service.

Hence, the best system of governments will be one in which the assignment of functions to jurisdictions has minimized the total cost over the entire system. Given that there are many functions to be performed and many tastes to be catered for, the ideal system will therefore tend to have more than one "level" and at the lowest "level" it will be divided into many adjoining jurisdictions. Furthermore, because agreement-and-transaction-cost minimization will dictate that most jurisdictions provide more than one good or service, it is inevitable that the typical sizes of jurisdictions will be compromises that lead to spillovers everywhere and call for continuous bargaining and transactions between jurisdictions.

It should be noted that our emphasis on costs has made it unnecessary to refer to "responsiveness" separately, or to "diversity of tastes," which, it is often rightly observed, call for as many small governments as there are groupings of tastes needs or demands. As Stigler has written:

No one can doubt that the individual citizen gains greatly in political dignity and wisdom if he can participate in the political process beyond casting a vote periodically. It is also generally conceded that a good political system adapts itself to the differing circumstances and mores of different localities, or, as I would wish to rephrase it, the system should allow legitimate variations of types and scales of governmental activity to correspond with variations in the preferences of different groups of citizens.[8]

Such "participation" and "correspondence" clearly call for the creation of numerous jurisdictions, close both geographically and socially to each person. In the present essay, this need is already implied in the individualistic context of the analysis. The question here posed is not whether it is desirable to have governments that are sensitive to local and minority wants, but simply how much of such local government can be afforded. To recapitulate, the gains from reducing the size of jurisdictions are seen as a reduction in the costs of agreement (or of exploitation and coercion) offset by an increase in the costs of transactions and production.

Once the matter of variation between regional tastes and needs is admitted to the calculus of ideal jurisdictional size, it must be recognized that just as expansion may smother varied localized demands, so diminution also may deprive local decision making of the moderation and interdependence that stems from variety. There is some best amount of diversity. In general, however, the cost of coercion in large groupings seems more to be feared than that of petty factionalism and vindictiveness in small ones. We might well begin by asking how *small* we can make a collective decision and still keep down transaction costs of making agreements with neighbouring jurisdictions and internal costs of producing small amounts for local consumption alone. No argument from transactions, scale, or planning works overwhelmingly toward large size.

JURISDICTION OVER THE ENVIRONMENT IN CANADA

We may now attempt to connect these ideas to the problem of jurisdiction over environmental control and investment. Before turning to this application of our ideas, we must survey the present division of rights and responsibilities in Canada. It can best be described under two headings.

Proprietary rights

Unlike the situation in the United States or the United Kingdom, most powers over the environment in Canada stem from ordinary proprietary or ownership rights. Most natural resources (land, water, forests, minerals, wildlife, and airspace) within most provinces belong to the Crown in the right of the province. The rest are divided between private owners and the federal Crown (the territories, some tidal waters, national parks, canals, and other purchased or acquired properties).

Legislative powers

The provincial power to tax is limited to "direct" levies; otherwise the federal and provincial governments both have extensive freedom to tax or impose charges.

> "Environmental management" is not recognized as a distinct category of constitutional jurisdiction; indeed it is so broad a field that it touches many areas of constitutional authority. . . . Some aspects of the subject fall within the exclusive authority of the provincial legislatures (e.g. most problems of urban transportation) and others are entirely within federal jurisdiction (e.g. pollution that crosses the international boundary). In many cases, however, the legislative powers of the federal and provincial governments overlap, with the result that either may make laws on the subject, but the federal laws will prevail in the case of conflict, which is rare. . . . [9]

On balance, it is unlikely that the federal government would seek to act where the provinces are already on the job. As MacNeill points out, most spillovers from economic activity are contained wholly or largely within a province; most pleas for environmental management can most easily be drawn up using the provinces' proprietary powers; and most environmental damage is suffered in relatively uninhabited rural areas under direct provincial administration. Indeed, since MacNeill wrote, it is clear that most federal activity stems either from the federal territorial, boundary, and maritime responsibilities; from the spillover from federal responsibilities (railways, public buildings, defence installations); and from the extraordinarily wide application of fisheries and agriculture powers.[10]

What powers are needed? At the macro-economic level, consideration of population control and output restriction are implied. If such sweeping measures are to be used effectively, they would, under today's constitutions, be national or even global responsibilities.

At the more specific or micro-economic level, there seems to be wide scope for choice of jurisdictional size. Regulation of discharges into rivers or the air, for example, can obviously be the subject of private, local, provincial, or national transactions, taxes, and regulations of land use, emissions, production methods and so forth. Automobile noise and exhaust are hardly susceptible to control by private transactions, but they are, and will be, the subject of policies at all three public levels. The same spectrum of measures is available for other environmental damage and can be implemented by each or any combination of jurisdictions.

It is of course very likely that interjurisdictional transaction costs would be very high if it were proposed to administer national policy by bargaining between local jurisdictions (although the idea is not absurd and needs further investigation). On the other hand, it is likely that decisions and policies dealing with specific services that affect a more limited area are much more amenable to local or regional jurisdiction, even if the area does not "map into" the jurisdictions. Let us examine the costs of local jurisdiction over pollution programmes.

At the outset, confusion may be avoided if two points are made. First, the scientific need for environmental research or investigation at a national (or global) level does not automatically imply a need for national (or global) jurisdiction. One may concede that river-flow or microbial problems are best looked into by some task force or laboratory that transcends the boundaries of local government without conceding that this same broad perspective is either capable or suitable to consider or implement the research findings. Similarly, the need to "co-ordinate" atomistic local jurisdictions in environmental or other spillover-creating activities does not imply that some senior government must impose its wishes on them. One may agree with Stein that the "consideration of environmental interrelationships" may call for the "creation of an agency that is capable of maintaining an overview, in a broad sense, of all environmental planning..."[11] without agreeing that this agency must have *political* jurisdiction or that "consolidation," or "integration," is necessary. It is obvious that adjoining small authorities cannot know all the facts, nor can they even trust their neighbours to give an objective account of the water quality benefits or damages that they are experiencing. Some agency must be entrusted with collecting this information. But, as with research, it does not follow that this "co-ordinating" role calls for senior *government*. The "agency" may well be a medium by which local jurisdictions reduce their transactions costs.

Production cost

The analogue of "production cost" is the burden of reducing the amount of pollution or the harm it does. This may include everything from changing the activity or even the location of dischargers to changing the location or even the tastes of pollutees ("victims"). Between these extremes lies a range of potential large-scale projects for changing river or air flows or absorptive capacities, public sewage systems, private abatement technology, and various social and private means of reducing the harm to downstream consumers or users at their own locations or compensating them.

While the choice of which, or which combination, of these measures should be chosen is a matter of efficacy and cost in each case, it is fairly clear that the location of the whole range of possible measures lies within a geographical region which may be described as lying on the receiving medium, the watershed, airshed, or more generally, problem-shed.

The usual argument for *regional* water quality management, for example, is that management of a smaller area than the region (i.e. smaller than the watershed) will preclude the managing agency from considering the whole range of abatement and harm-reducing measures and confine it to localized techniques. These may be sub-optimal technically: either more expensive or less effective.

It should be realized from what I have said earlier that this should not be seen as a conclusive argument for regional management but simply as a statement of one of the kinds of costs that will accrue: the cost-curve of abatement (using the word to include measures of mitigating harm to individual victims) as a function of the area included may have its lowest level when the area is very large: when, for example, the abatement works or measures are distant from the beneficiaries.

What are the implications of this? There are two possibilities. First, the best technology, while chosen from a list that includes the large-area techniques, may in fact not be as broad as the "problem-shed." It may be highly localized, and the actual force of abatement costs may not favour large-scale operational agencies. (However, it must be noted that if small jurisdictions are eventually chosen, there must be research organized on a scale broader than the jurisdiction to investigate all alternatives. Such broad initial and continuing study, however organized, does not dictate that eventual management itself must be on a broad scale.)

The fact that the list of potential measures is as wide as the problem-shed is not particularly compelling, any more than the fact that one's spouse may potentially be chosen from half the human race indicates that jurisdictional power over marriage and divorce must be assigned to the United Nations. It is the likely, rather than the conceivable, area of technology that should influence the optimum size of managing unit.

The alternative possibility is that the area of least-cost technology is in fact extensive, stretching from upstream storage for maintaining discharge dilution in dry periods to the locations of stream-purification and intake filtration plants far downstream. In this case, the influence of technology favours broad, problem-shed-sized managing agencies.

But these two cases merely imply something about costs. If the technology is not entirely contained within one jurisdiction's boundaries, then the jurisdiction must incur the transactions costs of agreeing with neighbouring jurisdictions or management regimes and investments.

Internal and external costs of government

If the jurisdiction is expanded to cover the breadth of the abatement technology, it must incur the increased internal costs of agreement of lumping together more and more persons with different ideas about water quality and about all the functions (education, health, roads, parks, welfare) that come under the expanded jurisdiction. These costs will increase with the number of persons and locations included and will be a force to prevent the jurisdiction from expanding to the full scale of the problemshed or of the breadth of the least-cost abatement technology. In principle, these costs can be reduced in five ways:

1. A higher-cost technology, less extensive in space, can be chosen.

2. The least-cost technology can be operated ("supplied") by a non-jurisdictional agency responsible to a number of jurisdictions, involving new internal costs of agreement.

3. The least-cost technology can be operated ("supplied") by one or a few jurisdictions that agree (bargain) with others. In effect, they are marketing their spillovers. This way of compromising the non-correspondence of technology and internal costs involves transactions costs.

4. The least-cost technology can become the responsibility of a higher or senior political jurisdiction. This is the original Breton solution (*Canadian Journal of Economics,* [May 1967]: pp.165-88).

5. A specialized political jurisdiction, specific to this technology, can be created. A school board is a traditional example. The various types of water management districts and boards described by Kneese and by political scientists fit here (although some of them are actually not "jurisdictions" but joint management agencies such as would be included in 2 above).

Ideas on this matter change rapidly. Today we observe prominent American economists who in the last five years urged a "regional" basis for discriminating fees or charges slipping into another camp and campaigning for a *national* basis for a charge on effluents and wastes poured into rivers and lakes.[12]

Their change of mind[13] may be more apparent than real. For some who were advocating "regional" water quality management have turned out not to have been against central government management, but against overly localized management. Their position has already been dealt with in this paper. To the extent that "regional management" simply means regional fact-finding and co-ordination, it is an efficiency goal that involves searching for the least-cost (or highest-rent) system of water quality, without necessarily choosing region-wide decision making.

But to the extent that it requires a special regional political decision-making body, in default of the assignment of water quality decision making to a high-level arm of government, it is an administrative target that, because it ignores the possibility of transactions concerning spillovers between neighbouring jurisdictions, neglects an alternative source of economic efficiency.[14]

Others who favoured "regional management" may actually have favoured mostly the effluent fee or charge that such governments were supposed to levy. Economists' conversion to national implementation may therefore be better explained by a desperate desire to get the principle of a charge accepted somewhere than by any belief in the superiority of a nationally uniform law. A *national* tax, for example, imposed on each industry using a standard process and paying similar wages and interest rates is bound to produce nearly identical amounts of pollution abatement per plant. Thus it is bound to produce *too much* abatement in some waters and not enough in others. Furthermore, while it may reduce a factory's incentive to relocate in less polluted sites, it will increase the peoples' and towns' incentives to move. As a charge for a natural resource to carry off waste, a uniform tax is similar to a uniform rent. We all know that rent control gives the wrong signals and brings about misallocation of labour and capital to land. Similarly, a centrally imposed maximum or minimum pollution charge will bring about misallocation, yielding homogenous individual abatement practices in heterogeneous locations and densities.

The heart of the matter obviously is that such economists have long abandoned the local government as adequate for environmental matters. Just as geographers have for years been urging multiple purpose river basin planning, so economists in their turn have been impressed that single purpose water quality services and upstream-downstream externalities militate against relying on the decision of small local units. Their interest in the Ruhr, the English water districts, and the Great Lakes Treaty is good evidence of this search for a larger unit. Recognizing that the basin or watershed must be perceived as a unit, they have not only taken the next step, of advocating basin-wide management, but also have apparently plunged ahead to advocate basin-wide political jurisdiction.

But such basin-authority orthodoxy does not, and should not, call for a full political jurisdiction. Research and co-ordination are, after all, simply preliminary to both transactions between governments and agreements within a larger government. They do not necessarily imply that taxes, effluent restrictions, subsidies, treatment works, or even property rights need be of broad-scope jurisdiction.

A second theme permeates economists' distrust of local taxing or pricing of local resource uses: a feeling that poor regional governments will cave in under big business pressure and underprice their water quality, especially when businesses threaten to play one region off against another. Alternatively, such economists may be swayed by their distrust of the naked politics of local bodies. They may believe that local legislatures are helpless—they lack the power or isolation—to withstand local pressures and impose controls in a convincing way.

Such views, indeed, are like most other arguments against local assumption of important governmental responsibilities: that it is bound to fail. In crude terms it is that, in the absence of central compulsion, regional or local governments must always yield to demands to lower water quality. Such beliefs are so implanted that any discussion of local government jurisdiction must pause to broaden the discussion of environmental policy. Many conscientious environmentalists (who have come into frequent contact with local decision making but who have only a reading familiarity with central government) believe that the latter is more immune to "political" considerations and compromises.

The citing of recent pollution decisions in Congress and the House of Commons on the handling of pipeline and tanker problems, the presidential denial of full funding for the implementation of the Great Lakes' Treaty, indecision on water responsibility, compromise on lead in auto exhaust and sulphur in coal and oil can easily indicate "politics" at the highest level. "Politics" is not really a criticism anyway. The question is not whether politicians should act politically, but whether their jurisdiction, when they make environmental decisions, should be national or local.

We must therefore return to the more specific charge that local jurisdictions are likely to buckle under pressure. This could be serious if it meant that localities could not rely on their neighbours to deliver any particular level of environmental quality. Bargains between neighbours would be valueless except at very high agreement costs and a *prima facie* case would be created for replacing external deals with internal high-level enforcement of national environmental standards.

Do they buckle? We get evidence on this from the attempts of local governments to attract industry by proffering lower tax rates, weaker safety or health regulations, and other incentives, practices that may lead to interlocality competition. The evidence, however, is that these incentives are rarely very attractive because firms rightly suspect that for example, low initial taxes may mean poor local services or higher taxes later on. In any case, the actual competition is not nearly as fierce as the publicity which accompanies it.

Evidence about these practices suggests that localities will be firm on environmental standards if firmness pays. There are two good reasons for them not to be firm since their neighbouring jurisdictions may be unable or unwilling to offer payment or reciprocal benefits for clean-ups that benefit outsiders. (Agreement costs again.)

First, there is the matter of preferences. People in some regions have different "preferences" for clean environments. Some of them already set very stringent standards or have refused permission to polluters to locate in their region. Others are less interested. They will not prevent industry from degrading the local environment because they do not care. If their degradation does not spill over, should there be national standards?

Second, there is the matter of differing local incomes. Here the economist comes closer to the heart of the matter. Regional taste for environmental quality is apparently income-elastic, the poorest regions being more permissive than the richest regions. Should such permissiveness be allowed? Those who favour national standards say no. They appear to depend on one of two arguments. Some say that poor regions are forced to yield on environmental questions because they are poor and so would welcome a national standard that would strengthen their bargaining position, making it impossible for them to prostitute their environment for employment and industrialization. We must ask whether there is any evidence that the poor regions would welcome being deprived of this power to bargain. I believe there is none.

Alternatively, those who favour national standards might advocate national redistribution of the GNP so that the poor regions would not feel compelled to offer easier environmental standards. The weakness with this argument is that it depends completely on a thorough going, egalitarian, nation-wide income redistribution. Few western countries appear to favour such a policy. If we do not, then it probably follows that we must allow the poor regions to get along as best they can, leaving them the right to attract or hold industry by any means open to them: low wages, low taxes, or low environmental requirements.[15]

These points suggest that the fear of bad or weak local decision making is not well founded from a "political" point of view. What then is the *strength* of the argument for local environmental decision making?

First, regional government is responsive to the tastes, constraints, and alternatives as they impinge on those affected by policy. Second, the region may well be the "natural" management unit corresponding to the scale of the environmental or ecological aspects to be protected. This point has been well argued by Kneese, Fox, and others. (However, as I have argued in connection with economies of scale, the optimum technical unit for one function need not *determine* the size of the political jurisdiction.)[16] Third, the region, even when it is smaller than the natural geographical environmental unit, may be the least-cost environmental management unit. Just as with efficient provision of public goods and redistribution, there is presumably some optimum size of environmental jurisdiction, such that as one attempts to "internalize the externalities," the marginal costs of centralizing are just equal to the extra transaction costs of agreeing (or contracting) with neighbouring jurisdictions about shared environmental quality. The internal environmental marginal costs of expansion are not only the costs of administration but also the costs of forcing citizens over an ever-wider area to accept common environmental policies or standards. These can be very high.

The alternative to these costs of centralization is the cost of interjurisdictional negotiation and transactions on environmental or ecological policies. It is not clear that these costs must be high. Some *nations* have, indeed, agreed to abate pollution internationally to standards that are more stringent than those they impose on themselves domestically. The same ease of agreement may also be true of smaller jurisdictions. What is more important is that within-jurisdiction agreement has opportunity obstacles and costs that are not *removed* by increasing the size of jurisdiction, but merely concealed.

Of course, this paper is exploratory. There are not only costs of interjurisdictional transactions but also obstacles that may be very difficult to remove. In the market place these obstacles would be described as "imperfections," not only preventing "fair" bargains from being struck but, even worse, preventing some transactions from taking place at all. The different size, wealth, or tastes of one jurisdiction may prevent it buying from or selling to its neighbours, and the absence of many-jurisdiction competition may shelter it from having to compromise. These imperfections need study: how serious are they and how can they be minimized? Here are a few suggestions:

    1. the smaller jurisdictions are, the more they will have to deal competitively with their neighbours and the more routine such bargaining will be on environmental, traffic, health, or educational issues;

    2. the larger the number of services each small community provides for its citizens, the more rarely will it be purely a buyer or purely a seller of spillovers with its neighbours and the more willing it will be to negotiate;

    3. the rarer the intervention of senior governments, the more local units will be forced to bargain rather than "appeal to the minister," for a better bargain;

    4. when large jurisdictions bargain over only one spillover, the weaker will need the support of some presumption that the stronger must bargain in good faith. The assignment (constitutionally) of property rights is one possible route (see my proposal to the OECD). Another would be the sort of declaration that has emerged from IMCO or from the Stockholm declaration.

CONCLUSION

The economist must resist the urge to entrust the most interesting problems to the most conspicuous government. Assuming that a diversity of jurisdictions is already in existence, there are strong reasons for revising our uninformed theories of "government" and seeing its diversity and complexity.

The management of the environment, in particular, is likely to be most successful when it is administered as locally as costs and tastes will permit. This does not indicate that the parish or the village is always right; very small units have high transactions costs in bargaining with their neighbours. Indeed, a whole spectrum of management levels and overlaps may well emerge. Larger jurisdictions lead to higher internal agreement and administrative costs.

While it is easy to make catchy slogans about the desirable scope and reach of central government, the more detailed examination of the pros and cons of regional provision of public goods and regional decisions about redistribution in cash and in kind bring to light many disadvantages of national rules and regulations. Just as the argument for a common market is a specious application of arguments for freer trade, so arguments for an all-transcending national writ are misleading extensions of the concept of market failure.

Economists who breathe a sigh of relief when the national government is induced to take an interest in a local environmental problem are probably invoking an erroneous idea of the role of government. For the national government is not the landlord and has no abiding interest in the optimum combination of local resources with other inputs. In action it is swift and general, but in policy decisions it is inaccurate and indiscriminating. To appeal to the national legislature is to abandon the efficiency argument for environmental management and rely on the political power of the environmental mystique in circumstances where the national parliament is, literally, irresponsible.

Notes

1.   See, for example, Henri Pirenne, *Economic and Social History of Medieval Europe,* trans. I.E. Clegg (London: Kegan, Paul, Trutch,

Trubner, 1936), p. 220; and Harold Innis; *Empire and Communications* (Oxford: Clarendon Press, 1950).

2. Robinson Ord, Deputy Chairman, Chemcell Ltd., commenting on statements in Albert Breton, *Discriminatory Government Policies in Federal Countries* (Montreal: Canadian Trade Committee, Private Planning Association of Canada, 1967), p. xiii.

3. R.A. Musgrave, *Theory of Public Finance* (New York: McGraw-Hill, 1959), chapter 1.

4. Number three, I think, the suggestion of J. Weldon, "Public Goods (and Federalism)," *Canadian Journal of Economics and Political Science* 32 (May 1966): 230.

5. R.H. Coase, "The Nature of the Firm," *Economica* 4 (November 1937): 386-405; E.A.G. Robinson, *The Structure of Competitive Industry* (Cambridge: Cambridge University Press, 1935).

6. For the pioneering discussion of the effect of these first two types of costs, see J.M. Buchanan, "An Economic Theory of Clubs," *Economica,* 32 (February 1965): 1-14.

7. Transactions costs among jurisdictions are mentioned by many writers but are thoroughly discussed by few. See particularly R.M. Bird and D.G. Hartle, "The Design of Governments" in *Modern Fiscal Issues,* ed. R.M. Bird and J.G. Head (Toronto: University of Toronto Press, 1972), pp. 46-62. They cite Robert Warren, "A Municipal Services Market Model of Metropolitan Organization," *Journal of the American Institute of Planners* 30 (August 1964): 193-204.

8. G. Stigler, "The Tenable Range of Functions of Local Government" in U.S. Congress, House of Representatives or Senate, Joint Economic Committee, *Federal Expenditure Policy for Economic Growth and Stability,* (Washington, D.C.: Government Printing Office, 1957). See also C.M. Tiebout, "An Economic Theory of Fiscal Decentralization." in *Public Finances: Needs, Sources and Utilization,* ed. J.M. Buchanan (Princeton: Princeton University Press, 1961), pp. 79-97.

9. J.W. MacNeill, *Environmental Management,* A Constitutional Study Prepared for the Privy Council Office (Ottawa: Information Canada, 1971), p. 9.

10. Ibid., p. 137.

11. S.B. Stein, "Environmental Controls and Different Levels of Government," *Canadian Public Administration* 14 (Spring 1971): 129-44.

12. The obvious example of advocacy of the regional approach has been A.V. Kneese's famous *The Economics of Regional Water Quality Management* (Baltimore: published for Resources for the Future by the Johns Hopkins Press, 1962). For a typical recent example, see R.M. Solow, "The Economist's Approach to Pollution and its Control," *Science* 171 (August 1971): 498-503.

13. Kneese and R.H. Havemann have recently advocated a national effluent tax. For a discussion, see the papers by J. Stein, A. Kneese, and Veldman and Tidemann in the *American Economic Review*, June 1971 and December 1972. A.M. Freeman and R.H. Havemann, in another article, "Residuals Charges for Pollution Control, A policy Evaluation," *Science* 177 (28 July, 1972): 322-29 (especially p. 329 and footnote 33), seemingly seek national control of any effluent tax.

14. See Marc Roberts, "Organizing Water Pollution Control: The Scope and Structure of River Basin Authorities," *Public Policy* (Winter 1971): 79-141.

15. This argument refers to the case for national standards. However, if national standards have been adopted for *other* reasons, nation-wide distribution is not indicated. Grants to help poor regions implement the national standards will suffice.

16. See Irving Fox, "The Institutional Framework for Regional Environmental Management" (mimeographed). I feel this excellent paper depends too much on "state and federal" intervention. (See page 27 of Fox ms.)

3

The Legal Framework for Water Quality Management
in the Lower Fraser River of British Columbia*

R.T. Franson, D. Blair, R. Bozzer

INTRODUCTION

British Columbians are fortunate. They live in a province that is still relatively unaffected by the severe environmental deterioration that exists in much of the rest of North America. Thus they are afforded a unique opportunity to avoid the loss of their beautiful surroundings and abundant resources by the implementation of wise resource management policies. While this opportunity is clear, the techniques that may prove useful are not. For this reason, Westwater Research of the University of British Columbia has undertaken a study of the institutional arrangements of water quality management in the lower Fraser River basin.

The physical area covered by this study is the Fraser Valley, which lies parallel to the International Border and stretches from the Fraser's delta to Hope, about ninety miles upstream. Lakes and tributaries are plentiful in this region of fertile agricultural land, much of which is still farmed. However, urbanization is extending south and west from Vancouver and gradually taking over much of the Fraser's delta.

The Fraser is the principal river of the province, draining two mountain ranges and 91,000 square miles of land. In total it is 1,000 miles in length and supports a large salmon run of importance to the economy of British Columbia.[1] Generally, knowledge of the hydrology and ecosystem of the river is limited; especially information about the specific locations where the river is used by salmon fry, either for rearing or acclimatization to the salt water habitat.

The quality of water flowing the lower reaches of the Fraser River is best summarized by the following quote taken from a recent report reviewing Westwater's findings:

* This paper has been brought up to date as of 1 January 1974.

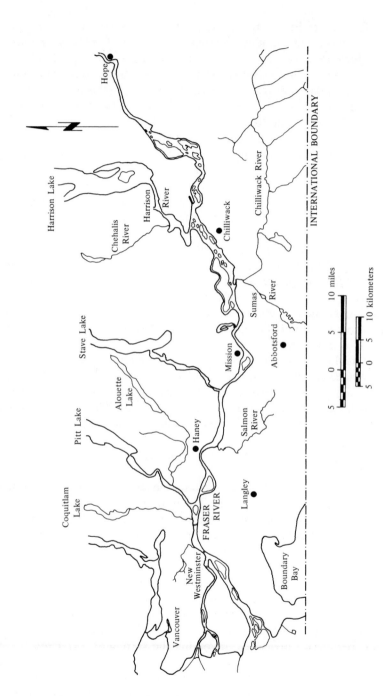

The Lower Fraser River Basin

The Lower Fraser River does not suffer from the kind and degree of pollution that produces dramatic newspaper headlines and arouses widespread public concern. Instead it poses a different kind of problem and one that is representative of so much environmental pollution in our urban-industrial society. The aquatic environment of this great and valuable river is receiving quantities of toxic materials that are building up in the tissues of the aquatic organisms and the sediment not only of the river itself but its tributaries and estuary. The quantities discharged are not acutely toxic, but what will their effects be over time? Today no one can do more than hazard a guess and in the meantime the public's representatives must decide how much to invest in trying to answer this question and whether control measures should be instituted to reduce the risk that such discharges pose.[2]

In other words, the Fraser is still relatively unpolluted. British Columbians have the opportunity to keep it as clean as they wish. But how? A river is affected by all the activities that take place within its watershed, and in the case of a great river like the Fraser thousands of individuals, often acting independently, determine what will take place. Society can act only by controlling individual behaviour through laws or by taking direct actions through its governments.

Just as the outcome of a game is determined by the skill of the players and the rules of the game, the success British Columbians have in managing the Fraser will depend on the skill of their decision-makers and on the legal framework within which decisions must be made. The way we choose to make a decision often imposes constraints on the result. Today, for example, governmental review of the water quality aspects of a major project takes place after design, approval in principle, and, in some instances, site development.

Clearly, it is necessary to understand the legal framework within which water quality decisions are made. The purpose of this paper is to describe this framework with particular reference to the Lower Fraser. While this paper is mainly descriptive, some preliminary observations about agencies, based on exploratory field research[3] and the analysis of statutory and published material have been made. These observations are, of course, tentative and subject to further empirical validation.

The constitutional constraints will be discussed first, followed by a discussion of the legislation that has been enacted by both levels of government. The latter heading has been subdivided further into the following topics: regulatory measures, involving the setting of water quality standards by governmental agencies and the enforcement of these standards by a system of inspections, fines, and so on; waste collection and treatment by government; financial incentives, including tax deductions and similar measures; and planning measures, including land-use controls and other measures aimed at controlling the initiation of activities that might lead to pollution.

Two aspects of these legislative schemes have been singled out for special study: the manner in which information is generated and the degree of public participation in policy development. The importance of the first seems self-evident—the quality of decision making must depend in part on the knowledge of the decision-maker.

The importance of public participation in policy formulation may be less evident. It is often forgotten that legislation usually depends for its success upon the consent of those whose conduct it regulates. Water quality objectives must be acceptable to a wide segment of the community if they are to meet with any success at all. An agency that sets about enforcing unpopular objectives would soon lose public support. Without it, budget cuts and other forms of legislative interference with its activities become likely. Information and communication play a vital role. Not only must the agency know where and how contaminants enter the water, their impact on water quality, and how to deal with them, but it must also know how the public feels about these contaminants and whether it is willing to pay the price of eliminating them.

For long-term success the agency must avoid viewing public attitude as a static thing. Public attitudes change with time, and, in some circumstances, the agency may have a duty to foster such changes. Consider, for example, the agency that knows that a particular pollutant will prove very harmful through long-term effects but also knows that the public is unaware of the problem and certainly would not support closing down plants that discharge the pollutant. What should it do? If it keeps quiet all will go smoothly for a time, but the public will ultimately discover the damage and will then be enraged. The agency cannot act unilaterally without public support in most cases. Consequently, it has only one viable alternative: it must educate the public.

Thus, successful implementation of a legislative scheme depends on good communications between the enforcing agency and the public. The agency must often go beyond mere information gathering. It must often exercise leadership by embarking on positive programmes to educate the public. It must play the leading role in developing the consensus upon which effective implementation of the legislative scheme will depend. To be effective, legislation should encourage the development of these attitudes by its agents.

THE CONSTITUTIONAL FRAMEWORK

The investigation of the legislative framework of water quality management in the lower Fraser River must begin with an appreciation of its constitutional foundation. Much effort has been devoted both to arguing the merits of provincial versus federal authority and to attempting to isolate the boundaries of their respective jurisdiction.[4] In this survey our purpose is solely to present the main conclusions of this work, understanding that many of the nuances of this subject are obscured by such a brief summary.

The British North America Act,[5] the primary constitutional document of the Canadian federation, distributes the right to legislate on various subjects or "heads of powers" between the provinces and the federal government, chiefly in sections 91 and 92. Not surprisingly, issues of water management and pollution control were not foreseen by the drafters in the 1860's when the document was negotiated. As a result there is no head of power in the British North America Act which assigns exclusive jurisdiction to either level of government, federal or provincial. Neither, it should be noted, have there been any fundamental changes in the British North America Act, although unsuccessful attempts have been made to re-negotiate the basic division. The heads of power which bear on water management are summarized in the following pages.

The most important heads of federal legislative authority for water management are Navigation and Shipping (s.91[10]), the Sea Coast and Inland Fisheries (s.91[12]), and the Criminal Law (s.91[27]).

Commentators agree that the navigation power allows the federal government to regulate any project that affects navigation, such as a power dam or a bridge. However, there is disagreement concerning the extent to which this power can be extended to authorize federal legislation dealing with water quality. The better view seems to be that regulation of the dumping of deleterious substances or refuse from ships is clearly exercisable by the Dominion under this power.[6]

The scope of the fisheries power is easier to define. It authorizes legislation for the regulation, protection, and preservation of the fishery resources.[7] Preservation of the river's flow and of the quality of the habitat also clearly falls within federal legislative competence.

The criminal law power reserved to the federal government is "the criminal law in its widest sense"[8] and encompasses the ordinary ends of "public peace, order, security, health, and morality."[9] Two restrictions on this power have been suggested. The first is that there must be danger to the public health before the power can be invoked. This restriction would probably not bar federal jurisdiction over water quality management because of the close relationship between health and pollution control. The second restriction relates to the management techniques used. Traditionally, the criminal law power has been applied to situations where certain conduct was prohibited and jail sentences or fines were imposed upon violators. It has been suggested that more esoteric regulatory schemes, for example, ones involving prior approval of developments or effluent charging schemes, are not authorized under this power. While the better view seems to be that this restriction is not severe, it seems to be conceded that the range of sanctions available may be somewhat limited.[10]

In addition to these three primary heads of federal authority, two limited powers might also buttress federal water quality legislation. Jurisdiction over Trade and Commerce (s.91[2]), an area once confined to legislation over interprovincial trade, has been expanded in the case of *Re The Farm Products Marketing Act*[11] to encompass intraprovincial commerce. Little agreement can be found on the extent of this federal jurisdiction. Laskin suggests it adds little to the powers to legislate respecting water.[12] More in point is the concurrent jurisdiction over Agriculture (s.95), which makes federal legislation paramount in this field. This federal authority should sustain legislation aimed at regulating the use or discharge of agricultural pollutants.

Finally, two other bases of constitutional authority are useful in upholding legislation by the Dominion. The first is the federal spending power. Monies raised by any authorized federal system of taxation (s.91[3]) become the property of the Dominion and may be disposed of in any manner (s.91[1]). This power has been used to support various programmes that disperse grants-in-aid and would, if tested, likely support such federal activities as the making of sewage treatment grants and loans under the National Housing Act.[13]

Secondly, attention ought to be drawn to the general or residual power. The preamble of section 91 gives the Dominion the power to make laws for the "Peace, Order and Good Government of Canada." It has been interpreted to give the Dominion jurisdiction in areas not covered explicitly by sections 91 and 92. Recently, this residual power has been used to support federal legislation establishing a National Capital Region as being for the general advantage of Canada.[14] A more recent lower court decision in *Regina* v. *Lake Ontario Cement Limited,* [15] rejected the argument that jurisdiction over environmental management was reserved to the Dominion under general power. The extent of this power is a continuing source of controversy in constitutional law.[16]

The provinces draw their power over water management from the exclusive provincial jurisdiction over the management and sale of the public lands belonging to the province (s.92[5]), local works or undertakings (s.92[10]), property and civil rights in the province (s.92[13]), all matters of merely local or private nature in the province, except those reserved to the Dominion (s.92[16]), and from their ownership of all the natural resources within their boundaries.[17] So far we have mentioned only legislative jurisdiction. But each province owns all lands and resources within its boundaries that are neither alienated nor owned by the federal government. A result of this provincial ownership of crown lands and resources is that the water rights which are appurtenant to this land are "owned" by the province, though water itself is, of course, incapable of ownership until reduced to possession. Also, because provincial legislative jurisdiction extends to property and civil rights, the province has legislative jurisdiction over water rights within its boundaries.

Commentators agree that these sweeping powers give the provinces completely adequate authority to manage water quality within their boundaries. Naturally, there is little they can do about pollution coming from outside their boundaries. In addition, their powers are effectively limited by the existence of concurrent federal powers over the same subject matter.

If a direct conflict should arise between otherwise valid enactments of these two levels of government, by the doctrine of paramountcy the federal legislation would prevail. However, it should not be assumed that the federal government can entirely pre-empt the field of water legislation. On more than one occasion in the past, courts have held that federal legislation was invalid where it appeared that its purpose was to oust provincial governments from a field where they had legislative competence. Thus, for example, if the federal legislature stretched the fisheries power by enacting a complete regulatory scheme for water quality management, the legislation might well be held invalid as dealing essentially with property and civil rights within the provinces.

In conclusion, while both levels of government have the jurisdiction to enact measures relating to water quality management, neither has the freedom to act without regard for its own jurisdictional limits and the interests of the other. There is nothing to prevent both governments from acting concurrently, as long as their enactments are within their own legislative competence and do not directly conflict. However, the practical effect of such concurrent power appears to prevent either government from enacting a truly comprehensive scheme of water management. The federal government, for example, might have great difficulty sustaining a system of water management based on effluent charges because it could not be supported by the criminal law power, leaving only the very specific powers like the fisheries and navigation powers to provide a foundation for the legislation, subject to possible support under the peace, order and good government clause. Since a great deal more than the protection of fisheries and navigation is involved in any comprehensive water management scheme, there is a substantial risk that such legislation would be held invalid. This may serve to explain federal reticence to move under the 1970 Canada Water Act, the constitutional validity of which has not yet been challenged. On the other hand, the provincial governments could well enact schemes depending on effluent charges, but they could not prevent regulation by the federal government under the fisheries power.

THE LEGAL FRAMEWORK

A wide variety of techniques exists for controlling water quality. Undesirable discharges could be reduced by the establishment of an agency to collect and treat such discharges. This approach is traditionally used in dealing with domestic wastes. More unusual methods involve acting upon the receiving water body itself, by augmenting flows, by enhancing natural assimilative processes by the use of mechanical aeration, or by treating an entire river. Alternatively, property rights could be established in the assimilative capacity of the receiving waters together with a system of allocation of rights among users.[18] Other techniques involve economic incentives to encourage treatment and recycling or direct regulation of the kinds of materials that people or manufacturers use.

Regulatory Measures

Despite this wide variety of techniques, Canadian legislatures have placed reliance primarily on two: the collection and treatment of municipal wastes by governmental agencies and the direct regulation of the discharge of manufacturing effluents that are not discharged to municipal treatment systems. The latter approach is best exemplified by the provincial Pollution Control Act and the federal Fisheries Act. These are discussed below.

The province of British Columbia has established a permit system to deal with water quality problems. Under the Pollution Control Act, 1967,[19] "no person shall discharge sewage or other waste materials on, in, or under any land or into any water without a permit or approval from the Director." In addition, discharges that existed before January 1970 must have been registered with the Director of Pollution Control before March, 1972 (s.5[1a]). The director is empowered to order these registered dischargers to bring their operation under permit (ss.5[1a], 5[b])[20].

The Pollution Control Act is administered by the Pollution Control Branch of the Water Resources Service, consisting of a staff of more than 190 under the direction of the Director of Pollution Control. The Branch has grown very rapidly, having numbered only 85 in 1971. Although it consisted entirely of engineers in its earlier years, it has been broadened to include, among others, biologists and chemists.

The act also creates a board known as the Pollution Control Board which hears appeals from decisions that are made by the director. At the present time the board is made up primarily of civil servants, especially representatives from departments which have some interest in water management. Under the act both the director and the board have the power to prescribe standards concerning what shall constitute a polluted condition and the quality and character of effluents that may be discharged (ss.4,10). The act is, however, silent about the legal effect of these "standards" and the use that is to be made of them.

In defining standards under the act, the branch proceeds on an industry by industry basis. Separate public inquiries are held for each industry group by the director, together with an advisory panel. Objectives are formulated and recommended to the Pollution Control Board. These objectives are considered by the board and, if accepted, form the criteria on which future permit applications are evaluated. The branch anticipates that within five years of the issuance of objectives in a particular industry further public hearings will be held and standards will be finally adopted as their end result.[21] Between August 1970 and July 1973 public inquiries were held with respect to Forest Products, Mining and Milling, Food Processing and miscellaneous industries, the Petro-Chemical Industry, and the disposal of municipal wastes, thus completing the first round. At present, board-approved objectives exist for only the Forest Products Industry, but the director has also submitted proposed objectives to the board for the Mining and Petro-Chemical Industries. Prior to the adoption of objectives, it appears that the director's decisions concerning whether or not to permit a particular discharge were made on an *ad hoc* basis. Currently, while objectives are used in evaluating permit applications, it is not known whether or to what extent receiving water characteristics are known or considered.

While the Pollution Control Act deals with the right to put materials into the waters of the province, complementary legislation, the British Columbia Water Act[22] deals with the right to divert or make consumptive use of the waters of the province. Under the Water Act, a license is required before any water is diverted or any consumptive use is made of water. The act is administered by the Water Rights Branch of the province, also a part of the Water Resources Service and under the deputy minister responsible for the Pollution Control Act. While the Pollution Control Act recognizes the interests of water licensees by giving them a right to object to the granting of a pollution control permit (s.13[2]), permittees under the Pollution Control Act are not given any right to object to the granting of a water license, even though the assimilative capacity of the stream would certainly be affected by any withdrawals.

Two different aspects of implementation of the Pollution Control Act must be considered: first, how compliance with its provisions is achieved; and, second, what discharges the director approves during his day-to-day administration of it. There can be a world of difference between the legislation passed, the standards adopted, and the result achieved. Bargaining can occur at any stage in the enforcement process, and, if it does, we may expect standards to be eroded.[23]

The history of section 5 of the act, which deals with registration, illustrates some of the difficulties involved in enforcement of legislation of this kind. When the act was first passed in 1967, it required all discharges existing before January 1970 to be registered by 31 December 1970. However, by October of that year the branch had received only 125 applications for registration.[24] Branch officials had estimated that between 8,000 and 10,000 dischargers would be required to register. The act was not amended to alter the deadline in 1971, but during that year a branch survey indicated that 999 effluent and 1,106 solid waste discharges were unregistered.[25] No prosecutions were undertaken during this period. The act was finally amended in 1972[26] extending the deadline for registration to March 1972 and instituting an intermediate approval stage between registration and issuance of a permit.

In addition to difficulties involved in the registration of discharges, the branch has been slow in bringing all discharges in the province under permit because it is relatively new and has been short-staffed. In the entire province in 1972, 332 applications for new permits and 38 amendment applications were received. Of these and the applications carried forward from the previous year, 227 new permits, amendments, and appendices were issued, 24 were refused, 36 voluntarily withdrawn, and 321 remained pending. At the end of the year the total number of valid permits issued and outstanding in the province stood at 641,[27] considerably less than the branch's estimate of the total number of discharges cited above. While these statistics do not *per se* measure the success of regulation they are illustrative of the "catch-up" stage in which the branch is currently involved.

The foregoing history illustrates that a time-lag often occurs between enactment of a regulatory scheme and its effective implementation owing to the lack of information about the industries that are being regulated. Before control could be exercised, the points of discharge had to be located. However, the government did not have sufficient staff to locate all pipes in the province, and even if it could find them, all the discharges could not be analyzed and brought under permit immediately. Consequently, it established a registration system. Registration carried no onerous conditions, and, in theory, the dischargers were expected to come forward and register their effluents to establish their status as one whose discharge predated the act. When this did not happen, the branch had to decide whether to prosecute offenders or to seek to achieve co-operation through less forceful measures. It is clear that the latter course was chosen.

The policy adopted by the branch might be better understood if the need for co-operation is appreciated. To begin formulating standards for pollution control in the province, the branch required a great deal of information from industry concerning its processes, the methods of waste treatment that might be used, their costs, and the economic situation faced by the plants. It might have been thought that too stringent enforcement policies would substantially interfere with the branch's ability to get both the information and the compliance it needed. Moreover, it might also have been feared that in a resource based economy like British Columbia's, such an enforcement policy would be unpopular. When the New Democratic Party came to power in the fall of 1972, it early announced that violators of the Pollution Control Act would be prosecuted, and since then a number of prosecutions have been launched.

The second aspect of implementation of the act that should be considered is the practice of the director in granting permits. Does he stay within the objectives established? Are the conditions in each permit arrived at by a bargaining process between the director and the applicant? And, if so, what opportunity has the public to participate in the bargaining process?

Until recently, there was very little information available on these questions. The permits are matters of public record and could have been examined; however, they are not very informative. In the past, more detailed information was filed by the applicants, but the director treated this information as confidential. As a result of a recent court decision, such information must be provided to anyone who has a right to file an objection to the granting of a permit.[28] Although this class of persons is very narrow the director has apparently opened all files to the public.[29] We hope this new policy will allow for future in-depth research on the administration of the permit system.

The federal government's principal legislation dealing with water pollution is the Fisheries Act.[30] This act makes it a crime for any person to deposit a deleterious substance in waters frequented by fish or to place such substances where they may end up in waters frequented by fish (s.33[2]). A substance is defined to be deleterious if it or its by-products render the water "deleterious to fish or to the use by man of fish that frequent the water" (s.33[11]). A fine of up to $5,000 for each day of a continuing offence is provided for. Other provisions seek to prevent destruction of eggs or fry (s.30) and to prohibit the deposit of ballast or ash (s.33[1]) and specified logging wastes (s.33[37]).

The act also authorizes the federal Cabinet to make regulations "prescribing

(a) substances and classes of substances,

(b) qualities or concentrations of substances and classes of substances in water, and

(c) treatments, processes and changes of water ...

that are to be included within the definition of deleterious substances (s.33[12]). By this section, government officials are given a power to regulate effluent quality but are relieved from the vagaries of having to prove in court that a substance is harmful to fish. They merely have to prove that the deposit exceeded the maximum permissible under the regulations. When a specific substance is covered by such regulations, its discharge within the limits set is not unlawful (s.33[4]), though it still may be contrary to provincial enactments.

Regulations have been issued under this section dealing with pulp and paper effluents[31] and the discharge of mercury or mercury compounds from plants that produce chlorine or sodium hydroxide by electrolysis of sodium chloride brine.[32] The pulp and paper regulations set standards for three categories of deleterious substances: total suspended solids, oxygen-demanding decomposible organic matter, and toxic wastes. At present the pulp and paper regulations apply only to plants that were either constructed or altered after 24 November 1971. In a more preventative vein, the minister is given wide powers to review plans for new installations and, with cabinet approval, to require modifications in the plans or specifications or to prohibit the construction outright if he is of the opinion that the deposit of a deleterious substance is likely to result if the construction is carried out as proposed (s.33.1).

Most of the provisions described above were newly enacted in the 1969-70 session of Parliament. Prior to that time, the act simply prohibited the deposit of various specific harmful substances and provided for criminal sanctions.[33] The blanket prohibition against discharging deleterious substances expands, but basically continues this approach. It is subject to a number of serious deficiencies. Among them is the fact that an individual who wishes to comply with the law cannot be sure of what constitutes a deleterious substance. Likewise synergistic effects arising from the mixing of an individual effluent with the receiving water can cause a prosecution even though the effluent by itself is non-toxic to fish. If enforcement agencies anticipate difficulties in attempting to prove that a substance is harmful, as is likely when the damage is cumulative or long term, they may be reticent about proceeding with the criminal sanction.

Enforcement of the Fisheries Act is the responsibility of the federal Department of the Environment. The department was created in June 1971,[34] partially in response to the increased public interest in environmental quality and partially to bring some co-ordination to the numerous government departments involved in managing renewable resources. One of the objectives of the department is to clean up and control pollution.

In order to attain this objective a new service within the department was created, entitled the Environmental Protection Service. This service is to inherit the responsibility of the enforcement of all federal anti-pollution legislation including regulations enacted under the Fisheries Act. Organizational difficulties delayed somewhat the assumption of this function by the service, but at the moment progress is being made in resolving the jurisdictional problems. However, as a result of the newness of the Environmental Protection Service, two agencies within the department enforce differing portions of the Fisheries Act. The Fisheries Service enforces the general prohibition against the deposit of deleterious substances. The Environmental Protection Service enforces the standards for the regulated industries, and it is also responsible for the promulgation of standards in other industries. The department's approach to standard setting seems to be clear. Nation-wide standards will be established for each separate industry.[35] Individual existing plants are likely to be brought up to compliance according to an individually negotiated schedule. The implications of this programme for public involvement are discussed below.

An interesting contrast is provided between the policies of the federal Fisheries Service and the provincial Pollution Control Branch. For some time the former has apparently not hesitated to prosecute offenders under the Fisheries Act;[36] yet, the provincial Pollution Control Branch did not until recently prosecute offenders. The difference between the two policies in the same place and time raises some interesting questions for further research.[37] For example, did the Fisheries Service experience more or less co-operation than the branch? And what differences between the two agencies contributed to the differences in policies?

In addition to the two primary statutes discussed above dealing with pollution control, there is a plethora of other provisions in federal and provincial legislation that aim at the objective of preventing the discharge of materials that may impair the quality of the receiving environment. A compilation of federal enactments would begin with the Canada Shipping Act,[38] issued under the aegis of the federal constitutional power over navigation and shipping. Under this statute the cabinet is empowered to make regulations "for regulating and preventing the pollution by oil, chemicals, garbage, sewage or any other substance from ships in any Canadian waters" (s.483[2][b]). Since the definition of Canadian waters includes all internal waters of Canada, this statutory instrument has wide application, including the waters of the Fraser River. Under the above and other empowering sections of the Canada Shipping Act (ss.737,739), regulations have been issued dealing with pollution by oil and by garbage.[39] Both regulations take basically the same prohibitory approach to regulation as the federal Fisheries Act, namely, preventing the deposit of the specific deleterious substances. Fines of up to $100,000 may be levied (s.761), and civil liability may be incurred (s.734). The act also imposes reporting requirements on the polluter for breach of the sanction (s.737[2]).

The federal Department of Transport, which is charged with enforcement of the Canada Shipping Act, also administers the Navigable Waters Protection Act.[40] Although this act is principally designed to prevent the obstruction of navigable channels by the construction of various works, it also prohibits the dumping of ballast (s.20) and sawdust-type wastes (s.19).

Further federal prohibitions have been proclaimed under the authority of the Migratory Birds Convention Act.[41] The Migratory Birds Regulations make it unlawful to deposit oil or other substances that are harmful to birds in waters frequented by migratory birds.[42] Penalties for breach of this regulation are small, ranging from a minimum of ten dollars to a maximum of three hundred dollars, with one-half of the proceeds payable to private prosecutors.[43] Officially, enforcement of this provision is the responsibility of the Environmental Protection Service.

Finally, two relatively unused water quality provisions exist in the bylaws of the two harbour commissions in the Lower Fraser. Under the bylaws of the Fraser River Harbour Commission it is an offence to drain, deposit, or spill any substance that may cause a nuisance or endanger health or property.[44] A maximum penalty of five hundred dollars is imposed (s.131[1]). A parallel section exists under the bylaws of the North Fraser Harbour Commission making it an offence to deposit refuse.[45] Penalties under the latter enactment are a maximum of fifty dollars in addition to liability for damage caused by the deposit (s.124[2]).

The majority of provincial statutes which serve to regulate the disposition and use of the provincial natural resources also contain provisions aimed at preventing pollution or empowering certain officials to order remedial action in certain situations. The British Columbia Water Act allows a Water Rights Branch engineer, or, alternatively, a water recorder, to order any person to refrain from putting into any stream "sawdust, timber tailings, gravel, refuse, carcass, or other things or substance, or to remove any substance" (s.37[1]). Failure to comply with such an order is an offence subject to a maximum fine of $250 or, in default, a maximum of twelve months imprisonment (s.41). The Pipe-Lines Act[46] imposes a statutory duty on companies to prevent, report, and clean spills from pipe-lines, and allows the Minister of Mines and Petroleum Resources to order further remedial action where, in his opinion, satisfactory measures have not been implemented to contain a spill (ss.39,39a). The Petroleum and Natural Gas Act, 1965,[47] contains much the same provision in relation to spills at wellhead or production facilities.

Permit requirements related to protection of land and water quality are found in the Park Act[48] and the Mines Regulation Act.[49] The Park Act prohibits the transportation or deposit of "any garbage, refuse, or domestic or industrial waste, through, over, in, or on any park" unless under the authority of a valid park use permit (s.16). The duties of reclamation and conservation imposed by the Mines Regulation Act in the case of surface mines involve the restoration of the mining area to the satisfaction of the minister and having regard to current and potential uses (s.11). Reports filed under this statute are mandatory prior to the commencement of work on the mine site (s.11[2]).

Prohibitory sections are contained in the Land Act,[50] the Litter Act,[51] and in the Sanitary Regulations[52] promulgated under the Health Act.[53] It is an offence under the Land Act to deposit on any crown land, including a waterway, any "glass, metal, garbage, soil or any other substance" (s.59) unless authorized by the Minister of Lands, Forests and Water Resources. The Litter Act also prohibits the disposing of litter other than wastes of primary industrial processes "on any land or fresh water or ice thereon" (s.4) excepting certain cases where other acts such as, for example, the Pollution Control Act, are complied with. The prohibition contained in the Sanitary Regulations deals with pollution of streams by assorted substances including poisonous liquids and certain sewage (s.66[1]). The latter regulations also prohibit discharge of solids into the Okanagan Lake system (s.66[2]).

One final provincial provision should be emphasized. The Municipal Act authorizes a municipal council to enact bylaws "prohibiting any person from fouling, obstructing, or impeding the flow of any stream"[54] or sewer and to impose penalties for such activity. However, few municipalities appear to have exercised this power.

During our research we attempted to discover how each of these provisions were enforced and how co-ordination was achieved between the various responsible agencies. Naturally, it is difficult to generalize about such a wide variety of provisions. Some were enforced vigorously, notably the wildlife and fisheries provisions which are enforced by provincial Fish and Game Branch and federal Fisheries Service field personnel.[55] These personnel often complain that enforcement is not pursued vigorously enough by other agencies.[56] Many provisions appeared to be enforced sporadically, with investigations usually occurring when complaints were received.[57] A notable example of this group are the anti-pollution provisions in the harbour commissions' bylaws. For the most part, officials responsible for enforcement of these many anti-pollution provisions tended to regard pollution as a matter for either the provincial Pollution Control Branch or the federal Environmental Protection Service to deal with.

Still other regulatory measures are intended to control the kinds of products that are in use. For example, the federal Pest Control Products Act[58] requires registration of all products for directly controlling pests.[59] If a product is not registered under the act it cannot be commercially manufactured or imported. The federal Hazardous Products Act[60] has also been used to regulate the sale of cleansers and polishes containing such substances as petroleum distillates or chlorine. The provincial Pharmacy Act[61] requires a license for the sale and application of listed pesticides.

While many of these measures are aimed primarily at health and safety, they have an indirect effect on water quality by controlling the use and manufacture of toxic substances that might ultimately find their way into receiving waters.

A similar use-regulatory measure is aimed directly at maintaining water quality. The Canada Water Act allows the federal cabinet to prescribe the maximum nutrient content of any cleaning agents or water conditioners.[62] This provision, aimed at reducing nutrient discharges, was included in the Canada Water Act in a last minute response to the wide publicity that phosphates in the Great Lakes were receiving at the time Parliament was considering the act.

Thus far only one regulation has been promulgated under this section. It makes it an offence to import or manufacture any detergent containing in excess of 20 per cent (by weight) phosphorus pentoxide of 8.7 per cent (by weight) elemental phosphorus.[63] Beginning on 1 January 1973, the phosphorus pentoxide allowable was reduced to 5 per cent (by weight) or 2.2 per cent (by weight) elemental phosphorus as a result of research conducted by the Department of the Environment.[64]

Waste Collection and Treatment

The collection and treatment of waste water has traditionally been a function of local government. Four kinds of local government organization are possible in British Columbia, and, although their powers vary in some respects, under the Municipal Act all have the power to operate sewage and surface run-off collection and disposal schemes (s.531[1]).[65]

Regional Districts, each consisting of several municipalities, have been created throughout the province to take over some of the municipal functions that are better organized on a regional basis. Regional planning is the only mandatory function assigned to all regional districts by statute (Municipal Act,ss.,794-98). Other powers of regional districts are determined in two ways: by statute and by the terms of their letters patent. New powers may be acquired by amendment of the letters patent at the request of the regional district board, a body composed of representatives of the member municipalities.[66] Consequently, no two regional districts have the same powers.

Sewage collection and disposal are generally considered to be regional rather than purely local concerns, and the provincial government is encouraging transfer of this function to the regional governments. The Municipal Act provides that a simple majority vote of the regional board is sufficient to allow assignment of the sewerage function to the district (s.766[4c]).

There are four regional districts in the Fraser Valley, two of which have taken over sewage collection and disposal. One is the Greater Vancouver

Regional District (GVRD), which recently absorbed the older Greater Vancouver Sewerage and Drainage District (G.V.S.D.D.),[67] and the other is the Central Fraser Valley Regional District (CFVRD) which acquired sewage disposal authority in 1970. A third, Fraser-Cheam Regional District (FCRD) appears to be considering the same action.[68]

Regional districts and municipalities, like other dischargers, must comply with the Pollution Control Act before discharging any sewage into surface waters (ss.5[1],5[1a]). In addition, sewage discharges must be purified and all menaces to the public health avoided.[69] Before construction or alterations can be commenced on sewage works, permits must be obtained from the Pollution Control Branch indicating compliance with both the Health Act (ss.24,26-28) and the Pollution Control Act (s.21).

Financial Incentives

Debt financing for sewage works is usually arranged through two acts: the National Housing Act and the provincial Municipal Finance Authority Act. The National Housing Act[70] provides the major source of assistance to municipalities for sewage treatment purposes (ss.50-54). Under this act the federal government will forgive 25 per cent of the principal amount of any loan if the project is completed before 31 March 1975, and 25 per cent of the accrued interest as of the project's completion. If the project is not completed by 1975, the government will forgive 25 per cent of the amount advanced up until that time including accrued interest.

The provincial Municipal Finance Authority was established in 1970 ostensibly for the purpose of assisting the smaller municipalities to obtain financing for sewage, water supply, and pollution control and abatement facilities.[71] Since that time an amendment to the act[72] has enlarged the object of this corporation to one of providing finance for all capital requirements of regional districts and member municipalities. Under the act regional districts and member municipalities must finance all capital projects funded by loans, including those for pollution abatement and sewage treatment, through the authority (ss.22-23). Member municipalities which, by written notice, opted out of the authority for water, sewer, and pollution control by 2 July 1970 are exempt from this requirement (s.21), but only Vancouver chose this course of action. Federal loans are exempt from these provisions, allowing unhindered financing through the National Housing Act.

The province has in addition passed the Municipal Treatment Plant Assistance Act[73] which allows the payment of a grant to a municipality, annually calculated as 75 per cent of the amount by which the annual principal and interest charge for a treatment plant and trunk collectors exceeds a levy of two mills on all taxable land and improvements within the municipality. In the Lower Fraser Valley to this time only the village of

Harrison Hot Springs has qualified for such a grant.[74]

In addition to loan provisions mentioned above, a number of federal and provincial taxation provisions affect both private and public pollution control systems. Federal incentives for the installation of pollution control equipment exist in both the Income Tax Act[75] and the Excise Tax Act.[76] The latter statute exempts pollution control equipment from the 12 per cent federal sales tax. The Income Tax Act grants a straight-line 50 per cent per year capital cost allowance deduction for pollution control machinery and equipment acquired prior to the end of 1974 and buildings commenced prior to the end of 1973.[77] This two-year rapid write-off applies only to property primarily acquired for pollution control.

Provincial taxation statutes merely exempt pollution control systems from municipal property tax[78] and from levies in unorganized areas.[79]

The Planning Approach

Most of the legislation discussed above is designed to deal with water quality problems by specifying how waste must be dealt with. It is not designed to influence the location of facilities that generate waste. For example, officials of the Pollution Control Branch state that their legislative mandate prevents them from any concrete input into the plant location decision.[80] In their view, their job is limited to assuring that an appropriate level of treatment is achieved. On the other hand, the federal Fisheries Service say they are free to challenge the location decision by virtue of their power to review plans under the Fisheries Act (s.33.1).

One of the alternative ways of managing water quality is by the general determination of land use in a region, and more specifically by influencing the location of effluent-generating establishments. This technique may be particularly useful in a province like British Columbia where water quality is still good and much of the land area undeveloped. Moreover, water quality decisions should not be made independently of other land- and water-use decisions. It would make little sense, for example, to maintain a quality of water in the Fraser River suitable for water-based recreation if land-use decisions made the area unsuitable for recreation in other ways (such as, by creating excessive industrial traffic).

The decision to locate an establishment has a number of consequences for water quality. The basic disposal decision—whether air, land, or water will be used—is affected, as are the costs of constructing and maintaining collection and treatment facilities. Care exercised in locating polluting activities may help to avoid synergistic effects caused by the mixing of diverse effluents as well as undesirable concentrations of oxygen demand in small areas of a water body. It must be recognized that it may often be desirable to concentrate industrialization to avoid impact on recreation, wildlife conservation, and dwelling areas, relying instead on waste collection and treatment. The point being made here is that land-use and waste handling cannot be considered independently. Biologically sensitive areas of a river and recreational areas can also be protected by regulation of land use. More general land-use decisions also affect the kinds of effluents that will ultimately reach particular areas of receiving waters since, for example, different effluents are generated by agrarian land-use practices than are generated by urbanized or industrialized land uses.

The jurisdictions which have power to attain these water quality planning goals and influence location decisions include all levels of government—municipal, regional, provincial, and federal. A variety of mechanisms can be used by these jurisdictions, including official regional plans, official community plans, land-use reservations, zoning control, and land-use contracts.

In the Fraser Valley land-use control at the regional level began formally in 1949 with the establishment of the Lower Mainland Regional Planning Board (LMRPB).[81] The efforts of the board, without any statutory authority to implement its proposals, culminated in 1966 in the acceptance of the Official Regional Plan by all twenty-eight member municipalities. However, with increasing resistance being encountered, especially from the city of Vancouver and the provincial government, the LMRPB was dissolved by order-in-council in April 1969. At that point, the duty to maintain the Official Regional Plan was assigned to the regional districts,[82] and amendments to the Municipal Act defined how their duties should be carried out.

The Official Regional Plan sets out twenty-year and longer range growth plans for the entire Lower Mainland under five land area classifications—urban, rural, industrial, park, and reserve. The plan itself is not a zoning bylaw and does not directly affect the right of property owners to use their land as they see fit. However, neither the regional district board nor any municipal council may "enact any provision or initiate any work" which would "impair or impede the ultimate realization of the objectives of the plan" (Municipal Act, s.797[1]). The municipalities need not enact any zoning bylaws. If they do not, development can take place without any control. But if the municipalities do enact or amend zoning bylaws, they must be consistent with the regional plan.

Co-ordination and communications between the regional districts and the other levels of government is provided by two institutions: The Lower Mainland Review Panel (LMRP) and the technical planning committees. The LMRP was created after dissolution of the LMRPB to maintain coherence of the lower mainland regional plan. It consists of two board members from each of the four regional districts in the Lower Mainland and functions in an advisory capacity to the regional districts.

Technical planning committees have been created in each regional district to provide liaison between regional board administration, the member municipalities, and the provincial government (s.798B[2]). Each committee is comprised of the planning director and medical health officer of the district, officials of each member municipality, and representatives of those provincial and federal departments that wish to take part. It also functions in an advisory capacity to the regional district. Further technical information for the planning process is provided by the planning staffs of the districts and the municipalities.

Even if the regional plan is implemented by the enactment of zoning at the municipal level, it is possible to put in developments contrary to the plan. The steps that the developer would have to take are these. First, he must convince some municipal councilman, and through him the municipal council, that his development should be undertaken. Second, the municipal council would have to apply to the regional board for an amendment to the plan. The proposal would then be sent to the Lower Mainland Review Panel and the technical planning committee for their comments (s.796), which are not binding on the district board. The third step in the process would be the amendment of the regional plan by a two-thirds vote of the regional district board. After that action has been taken, the municipality has the power to re-zone the area in question, but before it can do so it must hold a public hearing (s.703).

Also at the municipal level, council may, by a two-thirds majority and cabinet approval, adopt an official community plan (s.697). This plan is an overall, long-range scheme like the regional plan and may be for any or all of the municipality. It too is not a zoning bylaw (s.698[2]).

Municipal land reservation and dedication for public or municipal purposes may be accomplished with cabinet consent (s.467). Zoning (s.702) and land-use contracts (s.702A[3]), are the final control mechanisms at the municipal level. Zoning does not apply to crown land, Indian reserves, or private lands in tree farm licenses. Otherwise it is primarily used to preserve the cultural integrity of an area, while land-use contracts are employed to extract concessions from developers. Their use for water quality goals is undeveloped but potentially valuable.

Environmental management and land-use planning goals at the provincial level are the responsibility of the Environment and Land Use Committee. This committee was established by the passage of the Environment and Land Use Act in 1971[83] to achieve greater co-ordination between provincial departments. It creates a cabinet level committee composed of the ministers of eight departments dealing with local government, health, and resources. It has the duty, *inter alia,* to "establish and recommend programmes designed to foster increased public concern and awareness of the environment," and to "ensure that all aspects of preservation and maintenance of the natural environment are fully considered in the administration of land use and resource development commensurate with a maximum beneficial land use . . ." (ss.3[a],3[b]).

The committee has the discretionary power to hold public inquiries, "whenever it appears to the Committee that a proper determination of any matter within their jurisdiction necessitates an enquiry" (s.4[a]). In the first six months of 1972 four such hearings were held on various subjects, including the reclamation of a gravel pit, a proposed Hydro transmission line, hog fuel discharge, and the environmental impact of a proposed copper smelter.[84]

Under the act the cabinet itself is empowered to make orders respecting the environment that, on the recommendation of the committee, may be considered advisable (s.6). Such orders may be promulgated notwithstanding "any other Act or regulation" and may also be directed to a minister, government department or Crown agency. This power would appear to contradict a similar power in the Pollution Control Act which states that regulations, orders, approvals, or permits issued under the latter act which are in conflict with orders under other acts prevail (s.5[B][1]). Because the Environment and Land Use Act was passed later and because it evidences an intent to co-ordinate all control over environmental quality, it would probably take precedence over the Pollution Control Act.

Until recently the Environment and Land Use Committee had not embarked on a programme of planning on other than a minor scale. However recent additions to the staff available to the committee indicate that planning will become a major part of its activity, especially concerning the northern development of the province.

The passage of the Canada Water Act by the federal government in 1970 represented an innovative departure from existing water law. The act, which takes a basin approach to water management, is designed primarily to foster federal-provincial co-operation. It enables the federal government to participate in intergovernmental committees that may consult on water resource matters and advise governments on the formulation of water policies and programmes (s.3). The federal government is also empowered, with respect to waters of "significant national interest," to enter into agreements with the provincial governments establishing programmes for the conduct of research, the formulation of comprehensive water resource management plans, and the design of conservation or development projects (s.4).

In certain cases, where federal waters are concerned or where water quality has become a matter of "urgent national concern," the federal government may enter agreements with the provinces designating water quality management areas and establishing joint water quality management authorities (s.9). These agencies are given the power to develop and recommend a water quality management plan and, with the approval of the appropriate federal and provincial ministers, to take steps to implement the plan, including design, construction, and operation of waste treatment facilities, collection of effluent discharge fees, monitoring of water quality, inspection of treatment facilities, and so on (ss.13[1],13[3]). Discharge of waste of any type within a water quality management area is forbidden, "except in quantities and under conditions prescribed with respect to waste disposal in the water quality management area in question" (s.8).[85]

It is difficult to assess the degree to which the Canada Water Act is being used. While no water quality management areas have been designated yet, five study agreements have been concluded between the federal and provincial governments; however, several of these predate passage of the act.[86]

Also at the federal level, government policy requires environmental impact assessments to be made of any major projects before they are carried out.[87] This activity is carried on by the Fisheries Service under the general power available under the Fisheries Act and the Fisheries Research Board Act.[88] To date impact assessments have been concerned mainly with proposed federal government port developments, such as Nanaimo and Prince Rupert, and appear to be less concerned with private projects. These assessments, however, are the only federal control device of a planning nature where the Canada Water Act provisions do not apply.

Finally, the role of certain demand-oriented agencies in the Lower Fraser region should be considered. Chief among these agencies are the federal Harbour Commissions and the National Harbours Board. By their policies these bodies can influence both development within the river and its estuary and the planning and zoning of land adjacent to the river or the estuary.

Since these bodies are agents of the Crown, certain immunity attaches to them. Federal public property is not subject to provincial legislation.[89] Moreover, provincial legislation cannot restrict the rights of lessees or licensees of the federal Crown.[90] Zoning bylaws enacted under the Municipal Act do not apply to either Crown unless it has, by statute, waived its immunity.[91] This immunity, however, does not extend to nuisances existing on crown land and sought to be removed by properly authorized municipal bylaws.[92] Moreover, while a municipal building permit is not required for construction on crown land,[93] business licenses would be required for occupiers of that land.[94] As a result, the Harbour Commissions may develop any property they hold in the right of the Crown free from any planning or zoning controls.

The various federal agencies that operate the major harbours in the Lower Mainland have differing impacts on the Fraser River. These bodies, the National Harbours Board—Port of Vancouver, the North Fraser River Harbour Commission and the Fraser River Harbour Commission all operate under different statutory authority.[95] Only one of these, the Fraser River Harbour Commission (hereinafter referred to as the Commission) is considered because it has the greatest potential and current impact on the river.

The Commission has jurisdiction over the largest part of the Fraser system—the Pitt River and the South Arm of the Fraser from Kanaka Creek to its mouth. It is of particular interest because it is actively proposing the development of the South Arm as a major port to compete with the ports of Vancouver and Prince Rupert.

Basically the continuance of the New Westminster Harbour Commission created in 1913 (S.C.1913,c.158), the Commission is a corporate body with a long history. Its powers are specified by the Harbour Commissions Act,[96] and include the power to "regulate and control the use and development of all lands, buildings and other property within the limits of the harbour, and all docks, wharfs and equipment erected or used in connection therewith"(s.9).[97] In addition, it has jurisdiction over lands owned or leased to the Commission (s.11[10]). This power is not restricted to the harbour limits but includes the "immediate vicinity" of the harbour. The Commission may acquire land, purchase, construct, operate, and maintain such docks, wharfs, buildings, and other structures and equipment required in the operation and development of the harbour (s.10). There are more than 133 miles of river waterfront under the jurisdiction of the Commission (the figure excludes Langley and Maple Ridge), comprised approximately as follows: 76 per cent agricultural or undeveloped; 11 per cent industrial or port; 6 per cent recreational; 4 per cent residential; and 3 per cent transport.[98]

In addition to the general powers discussed above, the Commission may enact bylaws for the management of internal affairs, with the approval of the federal cabinet, for the following purposes (s.13[1]):

(a) Regulation of navigation and harbour use by vessels and collection of rates.

(b) Regulation or prohibition of constructions, works, operations, excavations, erections, and cable-laying.

(c) Maintenance of order and protection of property and imposition of penalties.

(d) Regulation of the movement of explosives and other harmful substances.

The revised bylaws approved in 1970 (SOR/70-440) deal with internal administration of the Commission (1-15), movement of vessels (28, 44-89), safety (22-25,39,125[1]), and dangerous goods (90-125). Flood emergency bylaws (127;128) give the Commission the power to pass orders and directions to protect persons and property from flood perils. Health and fire bylaws grant the Commission further regulatory powers to control many, if not all, noxious activities in the harbour.

Enforcement of bylaws is facilitated by regulations that prohibit anyone from hindering an agent, employee, or officer of the Commission (16) and that give officers of the Commission rights of full access over any part of the harbour or foreshore (17).

Under the provisions of section 5 of the Harbour Commission Act, the board of directors of the Commission is composed of five members, three appointed by the federal cabinet and the remaining two determined by consensus among the councils of the adjoining harbour municipalities that provide "normal municipal services" (ss.5[1][c],5[2]).[99] Tenure is during pleasure but not in excess of three years, and reappointment is permissible (s.5[5]). The intention of the split appointments was to ensure representation of local interests in the harbour while still maintaining federal government control.[100]

Unlike many of the other agencies that have some impact on the Fraser, the Commission appears to focus on the river and its banks as a unit. A recent study done for the Commission by planning consultant Norman Pearson evidences a concern for water quality and for other beneficial uses. He states as one of the objectives of his suggested plan "[to] protect conservation and recreation areas, maintain water quality, retain the salmon fishery, and provide public access to the water."[101]

Although there is no formal mechanism to co-ordinate the actions of the Commission with the municipalities, informal co-ordination has attained prominence with the discussion of the Harbour Development Study. Efforts were made by the Commission to seek approval of elected municipal officials for the plan proposed by the study.[102] However, no opportunity was made available for public input concerning the study.

THE ACQUISITION OF INFORMATION

The generation and communication of information is clearly an integral part of any successful regulatory or planning system. Despite the importance of this function, the legislatures have given it little attention.

Both the federal and provincial governments have chosen to deal with water quality primarily by creating agencies to regulate the conduct of clearly identifiable waste discharges. Under both legislative schemes it is clear that these agencies are expected to collect the information they need. Generally, both the Pollution Control Act and the Fisheries Act seem to confer adequate powers to enable officials to do so. However, while both acts provide extensive powers to enable officials to gather information, neither act requires them to conduct studies or, for that matter, even to establish water quality objectives. Moreover, neither act provides any guidance concerning the factors that should be taken into account in setting standards or granting permits.

The Pollution Control Act

The Director of Pollution Control is given the power to conduct public or other inquiries (s.14). He is also given express, but discretionary, powers "to conduct tests and surveys to determine the extent of pollution of water, land, or air;" and "to examine into all existing or proposed means for disposal of sewage, waste materials, or contaminants ..."(ss.10[c],10[d]). Field branch engineers have the power to enter private lands or premises (s.11[b]), and, in practice, the branch has required its permittees to monitor their own effluents and the receiving environment continuously by appendices attached to permits.

These powers suggest a clear legislative recognition that the branch's role goes beyond mere legalistic administration of a permit system and encompasses both problem identification and the assessment of alternative disposal systems. However, the act places no duties upon the director to establish water quality standards, nor does it offer guidance concerning the factors that should be considered in deciding to issue or amend permits. The act does, however, contain assurances that other agencies of government will be consulted concerning the granting of permits by expressly requiring the director to forward copies of each application within ten days of its receipt[103] to the Comptroller of Water Rights, who has the responsibility for granting the right to make consumptive use of water, to the Deputy Minister of Health, the Deputy Minister of Agriculture, and the Deputy Minister of Recreation and Conservation (s.5[4]). Each of these officials is given thirty days within which to file recommendations, and the director is required to give consideration to the recommendations (s.5[5]). Although not required to, the director has adopted the practice of forwarding copies of applications to the federal Environmental Protection Service.

The potential the referral system has for broadening the scope of viewpoints considered during the decision-making process is apparent if the orientation and capabilities of the Fish and Wildlife Branch of the Department of Recreation and Conservation are considered. This Branch administers the Wildlife Act and the provincial Fisheries Act.[104] In addition, by an exchange of letters at the ministerial level in the 1930's, the federal government has delegated the management of fresh-water (excluding anadromous) fisheries, under the federal Fisheries Act, to the branch. The branch also plays a significant role, together with the Canadian Wildlife Service, in the management of non-resident wildfowl under the Migratory Birds Convention Act.[105]

Fisheries administration is rather complex in the Lower Fraser Valley.

The main stem fresh-water fishery to an arbitrary line drawn at Mission is administered by the federal government while the branch looks after all tributary streams. The federal Fisheries Service administers the tidal and anadromous fishery, especially salmon and steelhead wherever they occur.

Some overlap in jurisdiction is apparent in the fresh waters in which salmon spawn. The provincial Fish and Wildlife Branch has considerable responsibility in habitat protection in the Fraser delta because of its responsibilities relating to wildfowl. Generally the branch has responsibility for: fisheries and wildlife resource evaluation; habitat protection and improvement; fish culture; sport fishing and hunting regulation and enforcement; and public education.

Like other resource management departments, the branch has the dual function of measuring and conserving the resource and regulating the harvest. Unlike other departments, the branch has limited powers to control activities that affect the resource. It does have the power to object to water rights applications and pollution control permit applications, and it does have a field staff to enforce provisions of the federal Fisheries Act. Beyond this, however, it must rely on other departments, such as the Forest Service, for the implementation of its conservation policies and the protection of wildlife habitat. The branch staff themselves feel that they would be more effective if they were involved in the planning stage rather than merely assigned the function of ameliorating the effects of decisions over which they have little or no control. [106]

The value of the referral system, as actually practised is in some doubt. As a means of facilitating the exchange of information between departments it is laudable because it requires consistency. The opportunity given to other government departments to comment on applications should also, theoretically, expand both the consideration given to the effects of the effluent on the receiving water and the perspectives of water users. However, some deficiencies are evident. The referral to the federal agency is not statutorily required and has been discontinued for periods of time owing to disputes between the agencies. In addition, the application itself contains very little information of a background nature, merely specifying the amount of the discharge and its composition. Furthermore, the amount of time given for comment on the application precludes any comprehensive assessment by agencies other than the Pollution Control Branch. Although branch officials indicate that additional time would be allowed for any government department to comment in any case where it is shown that the proposed effluent presented a clear risk, [107] personnel of the Fish and Wildlife Branch have pointed out that not enough time was available in many cases. They also complained that the Pollution Control Branch does not reply to their comments and objections. Of seventy-four applications on which the Fish and Wildlife Branch made comment, they were notified of the final outcome in only five cases, and even in these cases they had to make specific inquiries.[108]

Since we interviewed only a few persons from each branch, we would be unwarranted in drawing any firm conclusions from these data. In addition, with the change in government in 1972, the policies of the branch were undergoing change during the time when our interviews were being conducted. Nonetheless, the criticisms made of the referral system by the Fish and Wildlife personnel do raise serious questions about the system and suggest the need for a thorough evaluation of existing practices.

The Federal Fisheries Act

When combined with other statutory provisions, the Fisheries Act also confers adequate powers for the acquisition of information. The act itself contains three sections of relevance, one which empowers the Minister of the Environment to require production of plans and specifications of works which will or are likely to result in the deposit of deleterious substances (s.33.1[1]) and another which permits fisheries officers or an agent to enter private property (s.39). A third requires persons who are believed to be depositing deleterious substances in the waters to produce such information, including samples, as would enable the minister to analyze "the nature, quantity, and quality of any effluent"(s.33.1[3]). Furthermore, it is an offence under the act to fail to provide samples or information pursuant to the latter section within a reasonable time (s.33.4[1][c]).

Prior to the introduction of the latter section of the Fisheries Act, the Fisheries Service (then entrusted with the federal pollution control responsiblity) relied upon the Fisheries Research Board Act,[109] which allowed "the conduct and control of investigations of practical and economic problems connected with marine and fresh-water fisheries, flora and fauna ..."(s.6). These powers were enhanced by the Government Organization Act, 1970,[110] which authorizes the Minister of the Environment to initiate and co-ordinate programmes designed to facilitate the adoption of standards and pollution control (s.6). Interestingly, the duty is mandatory, in the sense that Parliament has chosen to say the minister *shall* initiate such programmes, but the rest of the section is too vague to provide any basis for private citizens to force him to exercise these powers.

POLICY DEVELOPMENT AND PUBLIC PARTICIPATION

Although most of the legislation covered in this study concerns the means of implementing policy, it fails to articulate any clear policy and provides very little guidance concerning how policy should be developed.

For example, the Pollution Control Act establishes a permit system for controlling effluent discharge, but it does not establish any goals for the desired quality of the waters of the province. Rather than debate the objectives to be achieved, the legislature has delegated the task of problem identification and standard setting to a Pollution Control Board and to the Director of Pollution Control. The federal Fisheries Act does specify a kind of standard by stating that deleterious substances shall not be placed in waters frequented by fish. However, the term "deleterious" is so vague that the practical effect of the enactment is to delegate the definition of the standard to the courts and enforcing agencies.

In a democracy such as ours, individuals should have an opportunity to influence major policy decisions. Our system of government allows the individual to participate through his Member of Parliament. In theory, the values and preferences of the society are accurately reflected by the composition of the legislature. But this does not guarantee that societal preferences will be reflected accurately in policy decisions when the legislature leaves the task of policy formulation to administrative boards and tribunals, as it has done in the field of water quality management.

What assures that societal values will be represented in decisions that are made by administrative agencies? One possible mechanism for making administrators aware of individual preferences is to allow individuals to express their views through public hearings or similar forums. Moreover, public hearings can play other important roles. First, they may provide useful information that has not come to light through other means. Second, and perhaps most important, they can help to keep scientists, consultants, government officials, and all the other participants honest by providing a forum where independent individuals may ask embarrassing questions. All too often scientific data is interpreted by consultants in favour of their client and government officials are afraid to speak up because of the secrecy currently required of public servants and the risk of offending a Minister who may favour the scheme under review.[111] During our study we made an effort to determine the degree to which this means of participation is available to a resident of British Columbia interested in water quality management.

At the provincial level two separate decision-making tasks need to be considered. The first relates to the granting of pollution control permits by the Pollution Control Board. The Pollution Control Act allows those whose interests may be affected by the granting of a permit to file an objection with the director (s.13), and, according to court decisions, the director is required to give the objection fair and judicial consideration.[112] Members of the public are also allowed to file objections, but these must be filed with the Pollution Control Board, and the director is not required to give them any consideration unless the board certifies that the public interest requires the director to consider them (s.13[6]).

The director is empowered to hold a hearing concerning any objection, but whether he does or not is within his own discretion (s.13[4]). The only occasion in the past when a hearing took place was when a serious confrontation developed between the government and a leading citizens' environmental organization over the application of Utah Construction and Mining Company to discharge mill effluent in Rupert Inlet. In fact, the hearing took place too late in the planning and development process to allow serious consideration of the points of view and new information presented. At the conclusion of the hearings on this application the responsible minister was forced to admit publicly that the plant had to be allowed to discharge its wastes in Rupert Inlet because such a large amount of money had already been spent in development of the site.[113]

The second area of provincial decision making that must be considered is the formulation of effluent objectives by the Pollution Control Board. Unfortunately, the legislature has not provided much guidance concerning how the board should develop water quality objectives. Section 4 of the Pollution Control Act merely gives the Pollution Control Board the following powers and duties:

(a) To determine what qualities and properties of water, land, or air shall constitute a polluted condition;

(b) To prescribe standards regarding the quality and character of the effluent or contaminant which may be discharged into any waters, land, or air;

(c) To appoint such advisory or technical committees from time to time as may be deemed necessary to inform the Board with regard to whatever matters may be referred by the Board;

The board is empowered, but not required, to hold hearings. Neither the procedures to be followed in such hearings nor even the factors to be considered are specified in the act. They are instead matters for the board itself to determine (s.3[4]). The board has been proceeding, on an industry by industry basis, to establish effluent standards and has, at this writing, held hearings with respect to five specific industry groups (see p.000 above). In a number of cases, the Director of Pollution Control adopted the view that the hearings were to deal only with "technical" matters. The briefs submitted by participants were edited by unidentified people either within the Pollution Control Board or the hearing panel itself, and all references to economic or aesthetic considerations were deleted. Participants were not allowed to address these points in the hearings.[114]

The hearings themselves were highly formal. An advisory panel was appointed comprised of experts drawn from the public service and private life. Each participant was asked to prepare a brief on the subject of the inquiry. No background information was supplied by the Pollution Control Board or Branch. At the time of the hearing each participant designated one spokesman who was required to carry the entire burden of presenting his organization's brief and cross-examining the spokesmen for other participants. No substitutions were allowed in spokesmen, placing an intolerable burden on volunteer organizations whose spokesmen might have to take up to a week off from work to participate.

The order of presentation was determined by the hearing chairman (usually the Director of Pollution Control). Each spokesman in turn presented his organization's brief and was then cross-examined by each of the other spokesmen. Next, the members of the advisory panel were allowed to ask questions. Finally, the spokesman presenting the brief was allowed to sum up.

The procedures used had the advantage of allowing participants the privilege of full cross-examination, but many of those participating on behalf of citizen organizations felt that hearings were too formidable and that the terms of reference were too narrow.[115] Another complaint was that the technical advisers were not allowed to do the cross-examination on technical subjects, contributing to the understandable confusion when a layman attempted to ask questions that had been handed to him in writing by his advisers. Despite these criticisms, British Columbia pollution control officials deserve to be complimented for holding hearings concerning the development of effluent standards. It remains one of the few examples of public participation in agency decision making in Canada.[116]

The federal Fisheries Act is completely silent on whether and by what means public participation should be achieved. Although it seems clear that the minister could hold hearings or informal consultations with wide elements of the public, it is equally clear that it is not federal government policy to do so. When regulations were issued under the Fisheries Act and the Canada Water Act, the government consulted informally with the industries most intimately affected and with some of the provincial governments, but it did not afford the same opportunity to private, public, and other corporate interests.[117]

Finally mention must be made of statutory guarantees in the relatively unused Canada Water Act. Public participation in the formulation of water management plans is encouraged by the requirement that such plans be "based upon an examination of the full range of reasonable alternatives and taking into account views expressed at public hearings and otherwise by persons likely to be affected by implementation of the plans" (s.4). A parallel provision exists relating to water quality management agencies (s.13[1]). Water management studies performed under this act included some elaborate attempts to involve the public.[118]

CONCLUSION

The objective of this study was to identify the approach taken to water quality management by the provincial, federal, and local governments. Our survey covered over twenty-five separate statutes and regulations having some relevance to pollution control and included interviews with twenty-seven of the officials responsible for enforcement of these statutes.

Aside from the familiar collection and treatment of sewage undertaken by most municipalities, the emphasis of government efforts to manage water quality has been on regulatory measures that specify norms of acceptable conduct and prohibit non-compliance, with enforcement usually by criminal actions. No less than thirteen separate federal and provincial offences exist for creating water pollution. Many of these measures are either sporadically enforced or not enforced at all.

The principal measures are the B.C. Pollution Control Act and section 33 of the federal Fisheries Act. The reason often given for non-enforcement of other regulatory measures was that the Pollution Control Branch and Environment Canada looked after water quality enforcement. Some regulatory measures were found that seek to reduce water pollution by controlling the manufacture and use of products that might cause pollution, but these measures deal with a very small number of contaminants compared with the volume of new products introduced annually (estimates of these range between five and ten thousand).

A number of other patterns emerged. In the first place, decision making appears to be highly compartmentalized, with the result that important decisions are currently being made by small groups of people, often without the benefit of much input from either other governmental organizations or the public. Public participation has rarely been used by the principal regulatory bodies as a vehicle for gathering information and identifying individual preferences. Hearings held by the Pollution Control Board for the purpose of setting effluent objectives are notable exceptions. However, participants in many of these hearings have felt that they did not receive a fair opportunity to express their views because of the rigidity of the particular procedures adopted for those hearings. Unfortunately, a survey of literature with respect to public participation failed to yield any significant data concerning the relative merits of different procedural mechanisms that might be used.

Consideration of pollution control often arises too late, if at all, in the planning and development process to allow significant modification of the plans. Moreover, communication between the agencies responsible for different aspects of water management seems to be lacking. For example, the regional districts could have an enormous impact on water quality through control over the developments they allow to take place in the valley, but they do not seem to recognize this aspect of their work or receive significant input from the concerned provincial and federal agencies. Agencies that might present a broader view of the alternatives, such as the Fish and Wildlife Branch, seem to be consulted too late in the planning process to have any real impact and are often hamstrung by a lack of resources.

Many of these defects appear to result from the failure of the legislature to give adequate guidance to the agencies it has trusted with the responsibility of water quality management. Most statutes do not express the purpose or goal sought, but instead merely delegate the responsibility to existing or newly created administrative agencies. They provide little more than the framework within which the agencies are to operate, leaving the tasks of developing policies and programmes to implement them to the agencies themselves and to the cabinet ministers who are responsible for their activities. Moreover, with the exception of the Canada Water Act, which remains relatively unused, none of the acts studied impose any clear duty on the public officials charged with implementation to conduct studies, collect information, or formulate policy statements concerning water quality. The mandate given to the agency usually fails to specify the procedures within which the agency should operate. Matters such as whether hearings should be held, what information should be considered relevant to the task delegated to the agency, and how that information should be acquired are left entirely to the discretion of the agency.

We have noted some patterns that disturb us. Among them:

1. Our legislatures have delegated broad responsibilities to agencies without telling them what is expected of them;

2. Decision making is highly compartmentalized, and small groups of officials make significant decisions without much input from anyone else;

3. Direct public participation in decisions through hearings, or otherwise, is rare;

4. Existing hearing procedures seem deficient; yet, the literature does not indicate how effective they are, or how they might be improved; and

5. Considerations of water quality management tend to arise too late in the decision-making process to allow modification of plans.

It is a measure of our collective ignorance that we must conclude this paper with two questions: First, *how significant are these patterns?* And second, if they are significant, as we suspect, *what should be done about them?*

Appendix A

The proposed calendar of national effluent regulation has been indicated and is as follows:

Regulations and/or Guidelines	Anticipated schedule (To completion of Technical Aspects)
Petroleum Refinery Effluent Regulations	Feb. 1973 (Phase 1)
Fish Processing Plant Effluent Guidelines	Feb. 1973
Potato Processing Effluent Regulations	Sept. 1973
De-Inking (Pulp and Paper) Operations Effluent Guidelines	Mar. 1974
Chlor-alkali (Mercury) Regulations (Phase II)	Mar. 1974
Oil and Gas Storage Regulations	Mar. 1974
Mining Industry Effluent Regulations	
Base Metals, Guidelines	Feb. 1974
Fuels, Guidelines	July, 1974
Industrial Minerals, Guidelines	Mar. 1975
Precious Metals, Guidelines	Sept. 1975
Iron, Guidelines	Dec. 1974
Pyro and Hydrometallurgy	July 1975
Dredging Guidelines	April 1974
Recycling of Crank Case Oil, Regulations	June 1974
Animal Feedlot Guidelines	July 1974
Municipal Wastewater Effluent Guidelines	July 1974
Plastics Industry Effluent Regulations	Nov. 1974
Metal Plating Industry Effluent Regulations	Dec. 1974
Steel Industry Effluent Regulations	
Coke ovens	Sept. 1975
Rolling Mills	Sept. 1975
Petrochemical Industry Effluent Regulations	March 1975

Cadmium Using Industries, Effluent
    Guidelines   Nov. 1974
Textile Industry, Effluent Regulations   March 1975
Inorganic Chemical Industry Effluent
    Regulations (Phase I)   June 1975
Cement Manufacturing Industry Effluent
    Guidelines   July 1975
Glass Manufacturing Industry, Effluent
    Guidelines   Oct. 1975
Effluent Regulations for Selected
    Toxicants   Various

Notes

1. For an excellent description of the Fraser and its history see B. Hutchinson, *The Fraser* (Toronto: Clarke, Irwin, 1965).

2. Westwater Research Centre, University of B.C., *Water Quality In the Lower Fraser: What We Are Learning,* Westwater Notes on Water Research in Western Canada, No. 9 (January 1975).

3. Selective field investigations consisted of a total of 27 interviews conducted by the authors primarily over the period May to August 1972. One or two interviews were conducted with each of the various agencies either directly concerned with water quality management or affecting water quality conditions.

4. See, for example, B. Laskin, "Jurisdictional Framework for Water Management" in *Resources for Tomorrow Conference,* (Ottawa: Queen's Printer, 1961), 1:211-25; B.A. Stamp, "The Constitutional Aspects of Water Pollution and the Need for Governmental Cooperation" in *Constitutional Aspects of Water Management,* Agassiz Centre, Research Report no. 2 (University of Manitoba, 1968), notes 14-18; R.J. Harrison, "Constitutional Jurisdiction for Water Legislation in Canada", in *Proceedings of the Peace-Athabasca Delta Symposium* (Water Resources Centre, the University of Alberta, 1971), p. 255; Leo McGrady, "Jurisdiction for Water Resource Develop-

ment," *Manitoba Law Journal* 2(1967): 219; Dale Gibson, "The Constitutional Context of Canadian Water Planning," *Alberta Law Review* 7(1968-69): 71; and, Dale Gibson, "Constitutional Jurisdiction over Environmental Management in Canada," *University of Toronto Law Journal* 23 (1973): 79-85.

5. (1867) 30 & 31 Victoria, s.3, as amended (U.K.), hereinafter cited as the B.N.A. Act.

6. Laskin, "Jurisdictional Framework," p. 218; Gibson, "Constitutional Jurisdiction," p. 73.

7. *The Queen* v. *Robertson* (1882) 6 S.C.R. 52 at 120.

8. *A.-G. Ontario* v. *Hamilton Street Railway* [1903] A.C. 524 at 529.

9. *Reference Re: Section 5(A) of the Dairy Industry Act* [1949] S.C.R. 1 at 50.

10. For a review of the literature on this subject see B. McDonald, "Constitutional Aspects of Canadian Anti-Combines Law Enforcement" *Canadian Bar Review* 47 (1969): 186. Professor McDonald does not believe the power is limited in this way. The provinces, by s.92(15) of the B.N.A. Act, have the express power to impose penalties for breaches of provincial statutes. This authority differs from the federal power over criminal law in that it is not a head of power which can, of itself, support legislation. See also, Gibson, "Constitutional Jurisdiction," p. 83.

11. [1957] S.C.R. 198.

12. B. Laskin, *Canadian Constitutional Law,* 4th ed. (Toronto: Carswell, 1973), p. 507.

13. R.S.C. 1970, c.N-10. A discussion of the spending power appears in Gibson, "Constitutional Jurisdiction," pp. 63-64.

14. *Munro* v. *National Capital Commission* [1966] S.C.R. 663.

15. (1973)35 D.L.R. (3d)109, a decision upholding provincial environmental legislation by Ontario Supreme Court Judge O'Driscoll, March 1973, on appeal from (1973) 10 C.C.C. (2d) 141, Provincial Court Judge Clendenning, Prince Edward County, Ontario, who had held the Ontario legislation *ultra vires*.

16. See Gibson, "Constitutional Jurisdiction," p. 83. The power to implement (as opposed to concluding) treaties contained in s.132 of the B.N.A. Act is sometimes mentioned as a source of federal power;

however, the better view is that the power to implement treaties is limited to "Empire Treaties" made before Canada became an independent nation and to treaties on subject matters over which the federal government has legislative jurisdiction. See Gibson, "Constitutional Jurisdiction," p. 65, and Gerald Morris, "The Treaty-Making Power: A Canadian Dilemma," *Canadian Bar Review* 45(1967): 486. *Note:* New light has been shed on this issue by a recent Supreme Court of Canada decision, *Interprovincial Co-operatives Ltd. and Dryden Chemicals Ltd.* v. *The Queen in Right of Manitoba* (1975), still unreported at press time, suggesting that the federal government has exclusive jurisdiction over water quality in interprovincial rivers.

17. By the terms of admission of British Columbia to the Union on 16 May 1871, Order-in-Council under s.146 of the B.N.A. Act, R.S.C. 1970, Appendix S, part. 10, whence s.109 of the B.N.A. Act was made applicable to British Columbia.

18. See Blair T. Bower and Walter O. Spofford Jr., "Environmental Quality Management" *Natural Resources Journal* 10 (October 1970): 655; and John Dales, *Pollution, Property and Prices* (Toronto: University of Toronto Press, 1969), chapter 6.

19. S.B.C. 1967, c.34, as amended; S.B.C. 1968, c.38; 1970, c.36; 1972, c.45, s.5(1), hereinafter cited as the Pollution Control Act.

20. A more complete discussion of the Pollution Control Act will be found in A.R. Lucas, "Water Pollution Control Law in British Columbia," *U.B.C. Law Review* 4 (1969): 56. See also A.R. Lucas, "Legal Techniques for Pollution Control: The Role of the Public," *U.B.C. Law Review* 6 (1971): 178-80; P. Good, "Anti-Pollution Legislation and its Enforcement: An Empirical Study," ibid pp. 274-75. In 1972 there were 202 registered dischargers who were ordered to apply for permits.

21. B.C., Water Resources Service, *Annual Report, 1972*, p. Y-118.

22. R.S.B.C. 1960, c.405, as amended. For a discussion of the Water Act see R.S. Campbell, P. Pearse, and A.D. Scott, "Water Allocation in B.C.: An Economic assessment of Public Policy," *U.B.C. Law Review,* 7(1972): 247.

23. M. Holden, "Pollution Control as a Bargaining Process," Cornell University Water Resources Centre, Report no. 9, 1966.

24. "Polluters Heed Warning," *The Province*, (Vancouver), 30 October 1970, p. 6.

25. B.C., Water Resources Service, *Annual Report, 1971,* p. 104. No explanation of the discrepancy between the estimates was found.

26. S.B.C. 1972, c.45.

27. B.C., Water Resources Service, *Annual Report, 1972,* p. Y-118.

28. *Re Hogan and the Director of Pollution Control* (1972) 24 D.L.R. (3d) 363 (B.C.S.C.).

29. Interview with R.H. Ferguson, Assistant Director, Pollution Control Branch, 3 October 1973.

30. R.S.C. 1970, c.F-14, as amended, S.C. 1969-70, c.63, hereinafter cited as the Fisheries Act. The federal government has also passed the Canada Water Act, discussed below, but it is not often used.

31. Pulp and Paper Effluent Regulations, SOR/71-578, 2 November 1971, *Canada Gazette,* vol. 105, no. 22, p.1886.

32. Chlor-Alkali Mercury Regulations, SOR/72-92, March 28, 1972, *Canada Gazette,* vol. 106, no. 7, p.436.

33. C.G. Morley, "Pollution as a Crime: The Federal Response" (Unpublished manuscript presented to the Law Society of Upper Canada, 11 May 1972).

34. The Government Organization Act,, S.C. 1970-71, c.42, gave this department the jurisdiction over *inter alia* sea coast and inland fisheries, renewable resources, and the protection and enhancement of the quality of the natural environment.

35. See Appendix A.

36. See Good, "Anti-Pollution Legislation," pp. 282-85.

37. A number of factors can be mentioned. For example, on numerous occasions the commercial fishermen who form the clientele of the Fisheries Service publicly demanded prosecution of particular offences against the salmon resource. On the other hand, the Pollution Control Branch did not have an identifiable clientele group when it was created. Most of its contacts were with the industries it regulated, and a certain amount of co-option should be expected to have occurred. In addition, the branch forms a part of a small provincial bureaucracy that may be more responsive to the government in power, which, before the last election, was very development oriented.

38. R.S.C. 1970, c.S-9, as amended, S.C. 1970-71, c.27, hereinafter cited as the Canada Shipping Act.

39. Oil Pollution Prevention Regulations, SOR/71-495, 21 September 1971, *Canada Gazette,* vol. 105, no. 19, p. 1723; Garbage Pollution Prevention Regulations, SOR/71-654, 14 December 1971, *Canada Gazette,* vol. 105, no. 24, p. 2134.

40. R.S.C. 1970, c.N-19.

41. R.S.C. 1970, c.M-12. This statute has been constitutionally upheld by the Supreme Court of Canada in *Daniels* v. *The Queen* (1969) 2 D.L.R. (3d) 1, where it was decided the act was not overruled by the British North America Act, 1930.

42. SOR/71-376, 20 July 1971, *Canada Gazette,* vol. 105, no. 15, p. 1284, as amended, s.35.

43. Migratory Birds Convention Act, R.S.C. 1970, c.M-12, ss.12(1), 12(2).

44. SOR/70-440, 6 October 1970, *Canada Gazette,* vol. 104, no. 20, p. 1099, s.27.

45. SOR/55-49, 23 February 1955, *Canada Gazette,* vol. 89, no. 3, p. 1012, as amended, s.24.

46. R.S.B.C. 1960, c.284, as amended.

47. S.B.C. 1965, c.33, ss.124A, 124B.

48. S.B.C. 1965, c.31.

49. S.B.C. 1967, c.25.

50. S.B.C. 1970, c.17.

51. S.B.C. 1970, c.22, as amended.

52. B.C. Regulations 142-59, as amended.

53. R.S.B.C. 1960, c.170, as amended.

54. R.S.B.C. 1960, c.255, as amended, hereinafter cited as the Municipal act, s.519.

55. In the period February 1969 to February 1971 there were a total of forty-six prosecutions in British columbia under the Fisheries Act compared to a total of fifty-seven for Canada, exclusive of Quebec in the same period: *Canadian Environmental Law News,* vol.1, no. 3 (1972).

56. For example, interview with Ron Thomas, Assistant Chief, Fisheries Management, Department of Recreation and Conservation, 22 August 1972.

57. For example, interview with Captain J.W. Kavanaugh, Port Manager, Fraser River Harbour commission, 20 July 1972, and George McIndoe, Fisheries Service, 24 July 1973. The latter official indicated that a distinction ought to be made between populated areas, in which this statement holds true, and remote areas where, understandably, enforcement personnel do not often receive complaints.

58. R.S.C. 1970, c.P-10.

59. Pest control Products Regulations, SOR/72-451, 9 November 1972, *Canada Gazette,* vol. 106, no. 22, p. 1993, s.6.

60. R.S.C. 1970, c.H-3.

61. R.S.B.C. 1960, c.282, as amended, S.B.C. 1965, c.34, s.45B.

62. R.S.C. 1970, c.52 (1st Supp.), ss.17-19, hereinafter cited as the Canada Water Act.

63. Phosphorus Concentration Control Regulations, SOR/70-354, 29 July 1970, *Canada Gazette,* vol. 104, no. 16, p.863.

64. SOR/72-416, 5 October 1972, *Canada Gazette,* vol. 106, no. 20, p. 1820. For a discussion of the legislative history of these provisions and the regulations, see Morley, "Pollution as a Crime."

65. It should be noted that Vancouver operates under a separate charter.

66. These representatives were appointed by the member municipalities, but recent amendments to the Municipal Act have provided for their election, S.B.C. 1973, c.59, s.21, amending s.769 of the Municipal Act.

67. Incorporated under a provincial statute of the same name, S.B.C. 1956, c.59, as amended.

69. *Health Act,* R.S.B.C. 1960, c.170, as amended, s.25.

68. B.C., Department of Municipal Affairs, *Annual Report, 1970.* However this did not occur in 1971 or 1972. See ibid., 1971, 1972 *Annual Reports.*

70. R.S.C. 1970, c.N-10.

71. Municipal Finance Authority Act, S.B.C. 1970, c.30, s.4.

72. S.B.C. 1973, c.60, s.3.

73. S.B.C. 1969, c.25.

74. Correspondence from G.S. Bryson, Deputy Minister of Finance, 15 October 1973.

75. S.C. 1970-71-71, c.63, as amended, s.20(1)(a). Income Tax Regulations, s.1100 (1)(f), sch. B, 24, 27.

76. R.S.C. 1970, c.E-13, s.21 and sch. III, Pt. XII, as amended.

78. Municipal Act, s.327(1)(p).

77. *Canadian Current Tax,* vol. 13, no. 22, 2 June 1972.

79. Taxation Act, R.S.B.C. 1960, c.376, s.24(x).

80. Interview with R.H. Ferguson, 5 October 1973. A notable exception occurred when the branch was consulted on a proposed copper smelter at Clinton.

81. By Declaration of the Minister of Municipal Affairs under the Town Planning Act, *B.C. Gazette,* 23 June 1949.

82. Municipalities Enabling and Validating Act, R.S.B.C. 1960, c.261, ss.131(1), 146. The same responsibility has now been placed on all regional districts. Municipal Act, ss. 794, 795, as amended, S.B.C. 1970, c.39, s.32.

83. S.B.C. 1971, c.17.

84. *British Columbia's Environmental and Land Use committee* (Victoria: Queen's Printer, 1972).

85. It is not clear what is meant by the word *prescribed* in this clause. It certainly includes the power of the cabinet to issue regulations specifying the classes of substances that are deemed to be wastes (see ss.16, 2[2]). However, it is unclear whether the term also includes any standards that might be contained in a water quality management plan that has been developed by a water quality management agency and has received the necessary ministerial approvals. Further criticism of the s.8 approach is found in C.G. Morley, "Legal Developments in Canadian Water Management," *Western Ontario Law Review* 12(1972): 139.

86. Saskatchewan-Nelson Basin Agreement, October 16, 1967; Okanagan Basin Agreement, October 29, 1969; St. John Basin Agreement, June 30, 1970; Qu'Appelle Basin Agreement, August, 1970; Souris Basin Agreement, November 19, 1970. While some predate passage of the act, federal officials indicate that these agreements are being administered as though they had been entered into under the act.

87. A.R. Lucas, "Environmental Impact Assessment, A Legal Perspective," 1973, to be published in Agassiz Research Centre, Universsty of Manitoba, Proceedings, National Conference on Environmental Impact, See "Environment Project Reviews Near," *Vancouver Sun,* 14 March 1974, p. 40.

88. R.S.C. 1970, c.F-24.

89. *Spooner Oils* v. *Turner Valley Gas Conservation Board* [1933] S.C.R. 629 (S.C.C.).

90. Laskin, *Canadian Constitutional Law,* p.529.

91. Interpretation Act, R.S.B.C. 1960, c.199, s.35; and Interpretation Act, R.S.C. 1970, c.I-23, s.16.

92. *Re Wheatley, Re Kodak and Marsh* (1958) 24 W.W.R. 323 (B.C.S.C.).

93. *Ottawa* v. *Shore & Horowitz Construction* (1960) 22 D.L.R. (2d) 247 (O.H.C.).

94. *R.* v. *Karchaba* (1965) 51 W.W.R. 314 (B.C.C.A.).

95. Under the authority of the National Harbours Board Act, R.S.C. 1970, c.N-8, as amended, the first administers the port of Vancouver and Roberts and Sturgeon Banks. The second operates under authority of the N.F.R.H.C. Act, S.C. 1913, c.162, as amended. And the third was established under authority of the Harbour Commissions Act, R.S.C. 1970, c.H-1 by S.O.R./65-157, 28 April 1965, *Canada Gazette,* vol. 99, no. 8, p. 546.

96. R.S.C. 1970 c.H-1.

97. Harbour limits are defined to extend to the average high water mark. SOR/67-468, 27 September 1967, *Canada Gazette,* vol. 101, no. 18, p. 1515.

98. C.N. Forward, cited in N. Pearson, *Fraser River Harbour Development Study* (Vancouver: Fraser River Harbour Commission, 1972)

99. There are nine such municipalities involved in these appointments—Delta, Richmond, Pitt Meadows, New Westminster, Coquitlam, Port Coquitlam, Surrey, Maple Ridge, and Langley.

100. J.W. Pickersgill, Canada, Parliament, House of Commons, *Debates,* 26th Parl., 2d. sess., 10 November, 1964, p. 9981.

101. N. Pearson, *Fraser River Harbour Development Study,* p.2.

102. Interview with Captain Kavanaugh.

103. B.C. Regs. 96-67, Part 4.01.

104. Wildlife Act, S.B.C. 1966, c.66, as amended; Fisheries Act, R.S.B.C. 1960, c. 150.

105. R.S.C. 1970, c.M-12.

106. Interview with W. Glen Smith, Wildlife Management Division, Department of Recreation & Consevation, 22 August 1972.

107. Interview with R.H. Ferguson.

108. Interview with Ron Thomas.

109. R.S.C. 1970, c.F-24.

110. R.S.C. 1970, c.14 (2nd Suppl.).

111. See R.T. Franson, "Governmental Secrecy in Canada," *Nature Canada*, No. 2 (April/June 1973): 31.

112. See *Western Mines Ltd.* v. *Greater Campbell River Water Dist.* (1967) 58 W.W.R. 705 (B.C.C.A.); *Re Application of Hooker Chemicals (Nanaimo Ltd.)*, (1972), 75 W.W.R. 354 (B.C.S.C.); *Re Hogan and Director of Pollution Control* (1972) 24 D.L.R. (3d) 363 (B.C.S.C.).

113. A. Lucas and P. Moore, "The Utah Controversy: A Case Study of Public Participation in Pollution Control," *Natural Resources Journal*, 13 (1973): 67.

114. These remarks and the description of the hearing procedure that follows are based on the personal observations of R.T. Franson, who participated in the hearings relating to Mine and Mill Wastes and advised a citizens' organization with respect to other hearings. This policy may have been changed. At the recent appeal regarding Rayonier's Port Alice pulp mill, socio-economic factors were considered for the first time.

115. These remarks are based on interviews conducted by one of the authors, R.T. Franson, with representatives of citizen organizations that participated in the hearings; among them, Lois Boyce, A.R. Lucas, P. Moore, Colin Clark, G. Culhane, M.A.H. Franson.

116. At the regional district level public participation has been nonexistent, largely because most of the public is unaware of the powers, operation, or even existence of the districts. INTERMET, Ways of Improving Decision-Making in Metropolitan Areas—The Vancouver Region (1971), p. 15.

117. C.G. Morley, "Pollution as a Crime."

118. See, for example, Study Committee, Canada-British Columbia Okanagan Basin Agreement, *The Public Involvement Program*, Preliminary Study Data—Bulletin No. 8, (1972).

4

Reflections on a Planning Failure: Ontario Hydro's Proposed Nanticoke to Pickering Transmission Corridor

John Graham*

While [the democratic mind] acknowledges the need for authority in certain situations and on certain levels of social organization, yet the aim is still to minimize domination by new social inventions, to replace forms of organization based on domination by more humanized ones, and to bring power under the control of the community.

Karl Mannheim

INTRODUCTION

There is mounting evidence from such diverse fields as urban transportation, education, Indian affairs, and urban renewal that planning processes dominated by experts and politicians no longer work. The Spadina Expressway issue is perhaps the most dramatic example of such a failure. Whether or not the Ontario government's decision to stop the expressway was good or bad, it is difficult to imagine how a decision-making process could generate such an unappealing set of alternatives at the eleventh hour. By deciding not to complete the expressway, the government had wasted a huge capital investment, had not provided a solution to the transportation problems of citizens in the northwest quadrant of Metro Toronto, and had strained the relationship between Metro Toronto and the provincial government. However, had the decision been made to complete part or all of the expressway, the human and environmental costs as perceived by a significant number of citizens would have been enormous. Subsequent

* When this paper was written the author was on contract with the Ontario Government. The views expressed in it are those of the author, and do not necessarily reflect the views of the Ontario Government.

relationships between these citizens and both levels of government would have been severely damaged. In either event, the long delay in reaching a decision meant a substantial loss of potential interest from the initial capital investment.

Ontario Hydro's efforts to establish a transmission corridor from its Nanticoke Generating Station on Lake Erie to its new nuclear establishment at Pickering on Lake Ontario should also be added to the growing list of planning failures. Despite some five years of planning for this project, strong and persistent opposition from citizens' groups and environmentalists finally forced the Ontario government to shelve Hydro's proposals for the route in the summer of 1972 and to establish a commission of inquiry, headed by Dr. Omand Solandt, with a broad mandate to re-examine the whole issue.

Although the costs of this planning failure are not of the same magnitude as those of the Spadina situation, they have been significant. To those individuals who are beginning to place an increasing value on "moving toward harmonious and mutually enriching relationships,"[1] the anxiety, mistrust, and anger displayed by many at various times throughout this five year period can only be seen as extremely distressing. To these costs one must add those of the Solandt Commission as well as the costs associated with the time and effort of many individuals, both within and outside government, who took part in this planning "battle."

By using the routing of the Nanticoke to Pickering transmission corridor as my primary source for examples, I hope to accomplish two objectives. First, I shall try to enrich and sharpen our understanding of why planning processes like this one are failing. Secondly, I shall explore the implications of various alternative decision-making processes which might be applicable to similar situations in the future.

In dealing with these topics, I believe that the relevance of the ideas presented below goes well beyond Ontario Hydro. Many other government ministries and agencies are or will be wrestling with similar problems. As well, the similarities between Hydro and "private" corporations suggest that the problems extend into the non-government sector as well.

TOWARD AN UNDERSTANDING OF WHY PLANNING PROCESSES ARE FAILING

On reading the Hydro submission to the Solandt Commission and the speeches which introduced it, one would be hard pressed to find any succinct statement of how Hydro officials understood the planning malaise in which they found themselves. They acknowledged that they were operating in a "new environment" and that "Hydro like everyone else was feeling its way." If anything, in Hydro's view, could explain what was happening, it was the changing attitudes of people concerned about ecology and the environment and the resulting conflict in values. As Mr. D.J. Gordon, Hydro's general manager, stated, "there are no instant answers or tailormade formulas for resolving the conflict between opposing needs and wants."[2]

While a heightened environmental awareness is an important phenomenon of the past few years, it does not in itself explain why Hydro along with most other institutions—governments, corporations, universities, unions, and social agencies—have recently faced angry groups of people from a variety of backgrounds asking why such a decision was taken and why they were not consulted. Nor can environmental concerns fully explain the increasingly jaundiced attitude toward experts—an attitude that appears to be an important by-product of most planning failures, including the routing of the Nanticoke to Pickering Hydro transmission corridor.

Rather, what appears to be at the heart of these planning failures is the rejection of the *traditional problem solving mechanisms themselves*. Many people seem no longer content to tolerate unilateral decision making on the part of our institutions. They feel they must involve themselves first hand in the events of the day, trust their own perceptions, and make their own judgments. Seen in this light, planning failures represent an *authority crisis*—a questioning of the legitimacy of both the decision-makers themselves and the traditional processes of making decisions.

The routing of the Nanticoke to Pickering Hydro corridor illustrates this contention exceptionally well. In making representations to the provincial government prior to the establishment of the commission, what environmental groups and local citizen groups were after was *not* for Hydro to redo their planning by giving higher priority to environmental and human criteria. Instead, they requested the government *to change the decision-making mechanism itself* by taking away Hydro's authority for selecting the route and by establishing a commission of inquiry to whom they could present their case directly.

Increasing environmental concerns, therefore, can be viewed as only one of the several factors which taken together can help explain this authority crisis. Some of these other factors require further elaboration.

The Beginnings of a Major Cultural Shift

Whether or not we are into an era of fundamental economic and social change akin to that brought about by the industrial revolution in the eighteenth and nineteenth centuries is not known yet. But there is little doubt that at the very least our era has generated a process of questioning fundamental assumptions about how we live, how we think and perceive, and how we govern ourselves.[3] Indeed, it is difficult to pick up a current piece of thoughtful writing that does not raise the kind of questions posed by Bruce Hutchison in the September 1972 issue of *Maclean's:*

The question would still be inescapable even if the computers [of the Club of Rome] were wrong, even if the planet were in no danger, even if a foolproof political and economic system were devised overnight. Assuming these unlikely miracles, will anyone say that happiness for mankind at large can be found in our present course? Will anyone say, on the other hand, that we should be less happy if we demanded less immediate wealth in our purses and more in our minds, if life were simpler, safer and saner, if the Gross National Product shrank a little outwardly and men expanded more inwardly, if we knew for sure that our children would not inherit a civilization doomed to be poor, nasty, brutish, and short?[4]

This greater willingness to question, to criticize, and to confront has extended to all forms of institutional life. John Crispo observed before a gathering of public administrators that from an institutional perspective "people aren't as nice as they used to be."[5]

But how do we explain this phenomenon? Better education and increasing material satisfaction are partial answers but more significant than these appear to be the following.

The Narrow Rationality of Institutional Decision Making

Increasing numbers of people are beginning to perceive that government and other institutions base their decision making on a too narrowly defined understanding of what constitutes human well-being:

...most institutional decision-making is based on the assumption that scarcity is mankind's central problem. Society's progress is therefore defined in terms of output—more roads, more buildings, more jobs, higher incomes—to overcome scarcity.... Thus elements which many people consider of paramount importance—beauty, diversity, meaningful human relationships, self-development and growth, a pleasing environment—are often bypassed or given secondary consideration.[6]

The primacy of the growth ethic is well illustrated in the proposed siting of the Nanticoke to Pickering Hydro corridor. Ontario Hydro began its case by arguing tht the new facilities must be built to meet demand projections. As Mr. George C. Gathercole, chairman of Ontario Hydro, stated in his opening remarks: "The route of the line may be changed. Its course may be modified. Different towers may be employed. But if the electrical power needs of the people of this Province are to be met, the corridor is required.''[7] Having justified the need for the route, Hydro then proceeded to find the minimum "cost" corridor:

From our point of view, the best route is one which
*causes the least disruption to people and property,
*creates a minimal effect on the ecology and environment,
*meets technical requirements within a reasonable cost range.[8]

Nowhere, then, did Hydro raise the fundamental question: are the benefits to human well-being derived from meeting the power demands worth the human and environmental costs? By not raising this question, Hydro clearly affirmed the growth ethic, relegating human and environmental considerations to a secondary position. Even when the human element was considered in the comparison of routes, one can only shudder at the crudeness. Hydro simply counted the number of owners affected by each route and accorded a certain weight to the difference. In effect, the assumption was that all individuals have identical reactions to the Hydro route and that these reactions should be treated no differently from the effect of the corridor on woodlots, the Niagara Escarpment, or municipal plans.

The way in which Hydro has dealt with the human side of the corridor siting is good illustration of what Gail Stewart and Cathy Starrs perceive to be the different understandings of human and societal well-being that run within most of us as we operate in our private and public lives.[9] In our capacities as professionals and specialists, we tend to employ narrow understandings of what it means to be human (economists, for example, have long assumed that work is a disutility for which wages are paid in compensation), whereas in our home and family lives, the criteria against which we make decisions tend to be broader, more imaginative and flexible, and more open to changing perceptions. Consequently, our relationships with others and even our environment are often markedly different in our professional and private lives.

If the Hydro planners, then, were to treat their families and friends in a manner they have seen fit to employ in their public lives, the results would be predictable—fear, distrust, anger, disbelief. Is it little wonder that their planning process has elicited these emotional responses from the environmentalists and people living along the proposed corridors? And is it little wonder that these people have chosen to resist Hydro's impingement on their lives?

Change and "Conservative Drag"

Even if it is assumed that planners could give primary consideration to human and environmental concerns, there is still an argument that the potential for failure has not been removed. As Holtan Odegard contends, we have a 'conservative drag' in us all—that is, we have an inherent tendency to resist change imposed by others. He elaborates on this point:

A particular proposal for change (for example, a suggestion to change from hourly work to piece work, or to reorganize a filing system) meets positive opposition, to be sure, by those who would be hurt by the change. But it also, and more immediately, encounters conservative drag, an almost automatic resistance on the part of those concerned whose decision it was not. Opposition to federal aid to education comes first from those local individuals and groups who fear that future decisions will no longer be their own. This is not a struggle for "power" as usually interpreted, nor simply resistance to change per se. It is a direct derivative from a simple reaction against the fact or fancy of a (person or persons) unilaterally decreeing or proposing where (others) are involved.

What is making this "conservative drag" more apparent and visible is the remarkable impact that institutions now have on our lives. Thus, from this feeling of increasing helplessness may come a powerful urge to insert ourselves directly into the decision-making process and to resist unilateral decisions.

Questioning the Effectiveness of Voting and Representation

The notion that somehow government is "limited" has been an important tenet in our political theory for centuries and has kept many activities, especially economic and administrative ones, outside of politics. Thus, civil servants are seen to be "neutral," carrying out the policy directives made by politicians whose authority is derived from a legislative body. Planning processes, such as the siting of the Hydro corridor, put some of these assumptions in doubt. Here we have supposedly "neutral" public servants making judgments about the relative values of woodlots, people, and the Niagara Escarpment. As Mr. Gordon in his opening remarks to the Commission put it: "I concede that many of the decisions made in arriving at a final route selection are judgments—expert and conscientious—but judgments nonetheless."[11]

Questions, then, immediately arise as to the legitimacy of public servants making these judgments. The traditional mechanism for controlling and influencing those who govern us—voting—has little relevance for citizens facing private or government planners. They obviously cannot throw Hydro "out of office" at the next election, nor do they want to wait for the next election. The reality is a Hydro corridor about to go through their backyards, and it is this decision which is relevant, not the issues which will dominate an election several years away. In addition, the elected representatives from their area are seen to have little influence on the administrative machinery. Increasingly citizens are finding out that appeals directly to the cabinet minister involved or even the premier have a greater chance of influencing the administrative decision. An American political scientist sums up this argument, which applies equally to Canada, as follows:

> We live in the "administrative state"—that is to say, in a country where the preponderance of institutions is administrative. Yet we cling to a theory of republican government and democratic politics that matured while government was mostly made up of representative legislative institutions— the "legislative state." The vision and ideal of democracy still current after many years of de facto administrative government depicts the rule of the people through their elected delegates in a representative assembly. Can the people also rule in an administrative state in any meaningful sense?[12]

To sum up, then, a number of important factors lie behind the authority crisis outlined in this section. More individuals are becoming increasingly demanding and critical of institutions which stress scarcity as the primary societal problem and thus regard human and environmental considerations as being of secondary importance. Moreover, increasing numbers of people are reacting angrily to the narrow understanding of human and societal well-being that so many of us employ in our public lives. Then, as institutions become an increasingly pervasive part of our lives, the "conservative drag" in us all becomes more apparent as a strong resistance to unilateral change. And, finally, doubts are beginning to be raised about the effectiveness of the traditional mechanisms by which we have controlled those who govern us.

SOME OPTIONS FOR FUTURE PLANNING PROCESSES

The implications of examining alternative planning processes for siting Hydro corridors go well beyond Ontario Hydro. As I pointed out in the previous section, planning processes are failing in a number of policy areas, and therefore solutions posed here may have applicability in the planning of an urban transportation system, the establishment of an airport, or the design of local health and education facilities. Equally important, the alternatives below might well be extended to the private sector. Indeed, the legitimacy of corporations, universities, or other large institutions making unilateral decisions with major human and environmental ramifications is also becoming open to question. What, then, seem to be the options?

Option One: Variations on the Status Quo

From the Hydro submission to the commission, and from the brief introductory speeches introducing it, one can surmise Hydro's intentions for improving their future planning processes. These improvements would probably proceed along two lines:

1. obtaining better information from which to plan, by hiring more environmental experts and by increasing consultations with affected citizens;

2. massaging this information more effectively, primarily by developing "scientific" decision techniques, such as quantitative matrix arrangements or sophisticated overlay mapping methods.

Both these improvements are essentially variations on the status quo. Put succinctly, Hydro's response to the planning failures was to do what they were doing, only better. Thus, future planning as now would be done completely by Hydro's experts, with decision-making authority resting with Hydro, subject to cabinet approval on major questions at a time when the planning is all but completed and deadlines are pending.

While Hydro and similar agencies should be encouraged to introduce environmentalists into their management ranks and to consult more often with citizens, these improvements simply by themselves are not adequate for two reasons. The first is a pragmatic one—planning processes dominated by experts, no matter how skilled or from whatever disciplines, will continue to fail. What the analysis in the previous section points out is that the fundamental problem in planning failures is one of legitimacy. Increasing numbers of individuals want to involve themselves in some of the major decisions affecting their lives.

But even more important, the option of "more of the same, only better" should be rejected on ethical grounds. First, these decision processes are inherently undemocratic. They place immense power in the administrative side of government over which the legislature and the ordinary citizen have little formal control save a question in the House or a direct plea to the individual minister involved. Even a cabinet minister's ability to influence the administrative machinery is sharply constrained by the immensity of the time pressures on him[13] and the fact that the problems and "viable" alternatives have already been defined by his planning staff. Where the emphasis must be placed in future, then, is not on making our administrative processes more efficient or even more responsive, but rather on making them more democratic.

A second ethical reason for rejecting variations on the status quo has to do with the negative effects on human beings and their relations with others. In a society where enterprise and individual initiative are supposedly prized, prime value seems to be placed on maintaining a citizenry which is essentially passive. In contrast, there is a long tradition of political thought which has defended democracy in terms of its salutary effects on the individual.[14] John Stuart Mill's view of effective government is worth quoting:

> ...the most important point of excellence which any form of government can possess is to promote the virtue and intelligence of the people themselves. The first question in respect to any political institution is how far they tend to foster in the members of the community the various desirable qualities, moral and intellectual.[15]

Moreover, when individuals "outside" the planning processes become active participants, the situation often degenerates into a confrontation, with mistrust and anger characterizing much of the human interaction. Therefore, on both pragmatic and ethical grounds, future variations on the present planning process which maintain decision-making authority within present institutions should be rejected.

Option Two: An Environmental Impact Agency Coupled with a Quasi-Judicial Board

An alternative favoured by many environmentalists (including the Sierra Club in Ontario) and certain public servants centres on adding two new structures to government:

1. a screening device, often referred to as an environmental impact agency, which would assess the environmental implications of proposed projects of both the governmental and private sectors; and

2. an adjudicative body or quasi-judicial board, patterned along the lines of the Ontario Municipal Board (OMB) to provide a forum for public input and to resolve potential conflicts among the contending interests. Such a board might be closely connected with or even part of the screening mechanism described above.

This option, unlike the preceding one, cannot be easily dismissed on the pragmatic grounds that it will not be acceptable to those demanding change. The key mechanism here is the adjudicative process. Not only are such proceedings widespread already (they extend throughout business, government, the courts, and other institutions), but also their further extension is characteristic of most current proposals for social change. Indeed, what seems to characterize the latter stages of many current planning processes which meet citizen opposition is a call for the establishment of a quasi-judicial hearing so that final decision making authority is removed from the "offending" agency. The Pickering Airport dispute is the most recent example of the use of this strategy by citizens affected by a proposed change.

While there appears to be little doubt about the short run acceptability of this option, the same questions about the legitimacy of the decision-makers may well begin to pop up as citizens begin to "lose" a few decisions in these quasi-judicial courts. The Ontario Municipal Board provides an illustration of this point. Recent decisions by this board to reverse decisions made by municipal politicians have brought howls of protest from the politicians, many of whom have called for the removal of the Ontario Municipal Board altogether. While the board has pleased "people power" advocates by many of its decisions, one need only contemplate a reversal of the present situation—that is, a municipal council, dominated by the new "reform" group, facing an OMB decision which is perceived as "reactionary." Under this situation, the favourite locale of demonstrations will shift a few blocks, from the municipal council chambers to the offices of the OMB.

What the OMB example illustrates is the increasing difficulty in our society of anyone "playing God"—be he/she civil servant, politician, or judge. The establishment of an adjudicative process will not solve the legitimacy question in the long run, but will only postpone thinking about a real solution.

Related to these questions of legitimacy is the concern about the practical ability of an adjudicative proceeding to handle issues like the siting of a transmission corridor. Lon Fuller, a law professor at Harvard, maintains that "there are certain kinds of social tasks that are not suitable raw materials for the adjudicative process."[16] He defines such tasks as those problems having no single issue on which the affected parties may focus their arguments and calls them "polycentric" or multi-centered problems. He adds in a later paragraph,

> ...the greatest failure in American administrative law has been with respect to those agencies that were assigned, or assumed for themselves polycentric tasks which they attempted to discharge through adjudicative forms.... It is as if the courts of common law, instead of laying down rules governing the making and interpretation of contacts, had from the beginning felt compelled to write contracts for the parties, and had attempted to hold a separate hearing for each clause as the contract was being written.[17]

Questions like the location of airports or the routing of highways and hydro lines are, I would submit, examples of Fuller's polycentric problems. The large number of possible locations, the wide variety of interrelated social, economic, and environmental factors associated with each location, and the lack of agreement on the relative importance of any of these factors, all combine to produce a problem that has no single issue on which the affected parties can focus. Indeed, any adjudicative process dealing with such problems would be in the realm of politics—in the writing of contracts to use Fuller's analogy, not in their mere interpretation.[18]

Whether or not in the longer run adjudicative processes appear legitimate and workable, this second option should be rejected on ethical grounds. First, the prospect of new battalions of civil servants manning an environmental protection agency is indeed disheartening to those of us concerned about the many dehumanizing aspects of organizational life, the inability of government to function properly even at its present size, and the increasingly regulatory nature of government. Moreover, the built-in growth potential of such an agency would be enormous as "environmental" impact becomes translated into "social" impact and as increasing numbers of decisions are sifted through the bureaucratic screen.

But even more disheartening is the prospect of widespread use of adjudicative processes for dealing with social issues. They are costly, time-consuming, cumbersome, and often discriminate against many interests which cannot afford the time or money to participate. In addition, the use of experts and reliance on procedures inhibits many people. Moreover, the adversary nature of the process encourages the participant to assume the role of the tough-minded lawyer probing the weaknesses in his opponent's argument rather than that of a responsible individual who can recognize and be sensitive and sympathetic to the values and perceptions of others. The inevitable result of such role playing is to create tensions and anxieties not only between us but within us as well.

A final argument that can be levelled at adjudicative processes is that they structure our problem-solving exercises into win/lose situations (game theorists call these situations zero-sum games), where the primary perception is "more for you means less for me." But such a perception may indeed be inappropriate and even harmful. If the present environmental crises have revealed anything of importance thus far, it is that "we are all in this together." To survive, we must no longer perceive ourselves as separate, competing individuals out to "make it" in Horatio Alger fashion. Cooperation must be the dominant theme where "more for me means more for you too."

To summarize, this second option, which combines an environmental impact agency with an adjudicative process, must be rejected on several grounds. Neither of these mechanisms gets at the root of the present planning malaise—that is, the questioning of the legitimacy of the mechanisms themselves. But more important, they should be rejected on ethical grounds. Their continued use would discriminate against the poor, encourage role playing, heighten social conflict, and promote values that seem inimical to our chances of survival. So a search for a new method of planning and decision making seems called for—a method that will be truly democratic and humane and one that will more adequately deal with social conflict.

Option Three: Planning Based on Participation

Planning processes based on the direct and genuine involvement of individuals affected by the planning decisions have the potential of overcoming the objections levelled at options one and two. By refusing to exclude any group or interest from participating in the decisions emanating from the planning exercise, participatory processes appear to answer the questions of legitimacy raised when public servants, judges, or even elected officials are left to be the final arbiters. In addition, such processes offer the potential of being truly humane in the sense of reducing the coercive aspects and resulting tensions of traditional planning decisions. Even more important, the participatory process itself might be designed in such a way as to contribute to individual growth and to the development of meaningful human relations.

Because practice is running well ahead of theory in this area, I shall begin by outlining three examples of participatory processes which appear to offer some promise. I shall then return to the theoretical side of the problem and outline some general principles on which to base further experimentation.

1. The Trefann Court Urban Renewal Scheme. The initial plan for the redevelopment of the Trefann Court area in Toronto followed traditional patterns—that is, planners working in isolation to produce a scheme which was eventually submitted for approval to city council. Faced with fierce criticism from local residents over the initial proposals, city council established a working committee composed of local politicians and citizens who were free to hire their own planner. This working committee, after months of meetings and negotiations involving all affected individuals within the five-block community, produced a plan which was quietly passed by the Toronto City Council in March 1972. The first phase of this plan called for expenditures totalling $2 million.[19]

2. Kensington Community School. In May 1971, the property committee of the Toronto Board of Education approved a plan submitted by a group of ratepayers for a Kensington Community School which would cost over $1.8 million. The plans were the product of numerous meetings between residents and local community service organizations. Speaking to the Ontario Education Association, Ronald E. Jones, Director of Education for Toronto, commented that the linkages between Kensington residents and the school board were a pacesetter for the city as a whole and added: "It is my prediction that never again will the Toronto Board of Education build a neighbourhood school without the active involvement and participation of the neighbourhood residents."[20]

3. Northern States Power Company — Minnesota. At the end of 1969, the Northern States Power Company, battle scarred and weary from a protracted conflict with environmentalist groups over radiation standards for a nuclear power plant, faced the prospect of siting yet another thermal facility. The company decided that direct involvement of citizens was a way of avoiding another confrontation situation, and therefore established a citizens' task force, composed of some thirty environmentalist and citizen groups who were thought to have an interest in the problem. Additional groups were added when they asked to participate. After several months of deliberations, the task force produced a preferential ranking of the available sites owned by the company and a rationale for their choice. Subsequently, the group also produced recommendations on emission control standards in general and on the company's marketing policies. The company accepted the task force's recommendations on the site despite the fact that their own preference had been endorsed by the state governor's environmental cabinet. It is interesting to note that a new citizens' task force has been established by the state government to look at the *need* for a plant in 1979 as well as the question of site selection.

What emerges from these examples and from what we know about administrative practice and theory are the following general principles about future participatory processes[21]:

1. Many of the issues of the deepest concern to individuals are those closest to home—the design and operation of the local health centre or school, the location of a nearby highway or hydro facility, or the design of public housing units. Therefore, the place to begin experimentation with participatory planning processes is with these kinds of issues and not with those with a national or province-wide scope like tax reform or environmental policy.[22]

2. The fundamental unit or organization should be a temporary, collegial, problem-solving group consisting of five to twelve people. It should be large enough to include individuals with the perspectives and expertise to deal with the problem at hand but small enough to ensure that each participant's contribution is substantial and meaningful. If too many individuals are involved for this type of effective, small-group decision making, a number of small sub-groups could be established, linked to one another through common membership. In graphical terms, it is important to think of the planning organization not as the usual pyramid, which is representative of most hierarchical organizations, but rather as a series of overlapping circles (commit-

tees) which are constantly changing and being redefined.

3. Membership in these linked small groups should include civil servants and local politicians from various levels of governments and representatives from concerned citizen groups. Provision should be made to expand the membership as additional groups become interested in the course of the planning exercise. It must be stressed that all perspectives within a community wanting to be heard must be included on these committees. A decision process closed[23] to any group affected by the decision is not a positive form of participation and should be discouraged.

4. Individuals cannot and will not choose to participate in every decision affecting their lives. However, when they do choose to participate, their involvement will be extensive and time-consuming.

5. As in the Trefann Court example, the problem-solving groups should be given enough resources to hire their own experts and to administer themselves.

6. Conflict resolution should be the responsibility of the members within these groups, not of some final arbiter above the process. New sub-groups, responsible for working out any conflicts which might arise, could be formed as discussions proceed. The ultimate aim (as realized in the Trefann Court example[24]) is to forge a consensus among all participants involved.

7. The results of the planning process would be submitted as recommendations to an elected body (or bodies) for final approval. Assuming a consensus is reached and assuming the active participation by concerned government officials throughout the planning stage, this final step may well be a formality. (Again the Trefann Court urban renewal scheme is a good example.)

Briefly applying these principles to the siting of an Ontario Hydro installation, the first step would be the establishment of an advisory committee to a minister, perhaps the Provincial Secretary for Resources Development. The committee would be composed of Hydro officials, officials from other government ministries such as Treasury, Economics and Intergovernmental Affairs, and Environment Ontario, local politicians (municipal, provincial, and perhaps federal), representatives from interested environmental groups such as the Sierra Club, and representatives from local citizen groups who are visible and concerned. More important than this initial selection of members, however, is the willingness to add new members from groups who "surface" as the committee's work proceeds.

The chairman of the committee might be appointed or might be chosen by the committee itself. His or her role would not be one of providing directive leadership. Rather, what is required is a facilitator or an enabler, who is recognized by others as a "neutral" attempting to identify and resolve conflict among them and to keep people informed of what is going on.

The first issue on the committee's agenda would be the need for the facility. After Hydro had presented its case, the committee might wish to "spin off" sub-groups who would concentrate on particular aspects of the problem (for example, one group might examine the possibilities of the underground transmission of power). Additonal expertise from Hydro or government might be incorporated into these new sub-groups or, alternatively, expertise from outside the government could be hired. Other sub-groups could be formed to deal with conflicts arising from these initial discussions.

Assuming agreement could be achieved on the size and type of the facility, location would be the next problem. Additional sub-groups linked through common members might be established, perhaps on a geographic basis, adding along the way new members from other local councils and citizen groups. Other sub-groups could be formed to examine more general issues like compensation policy for those people affected by the facility. The process outlined above would take considerable time—one to two years at a minimum, judging from the examples in this section. But the potential for involving a significant number of people using the linked small-group technique is high. Indeed, one can envision several hundred people participating directly in at least one aspect of the problem. Hundreds more would be indirectly involved.

Holtan Odegard in *The Politics of Truth* points out the kind of distinguishable processes that should arise from a participatory planning exercise as outlined above:

1) getting a sharply defined perception of the essential aspects of the conflict,

2) developing a disturbing concern for the satisfaction of interests opposed to each other,

3) hitting upon new possible aims in which conflicting ones can be absorbed to the larger advantage of all that is at stake,

4) embodying the new aims in a practical program,[25]

5) formulating the ideas employed throughout the procedure in a way which will provide for the identification of their deficiencies as they are employed.[26]

Arguments can be made that in a confusing and fractured society like ours anyone believing that Odegard's third step can be achieved is guilty of "Utopian thinking." Indeed, as Alderman Karl Jaffary states:

One of the greatest inhibitions to the exercise of power is the liberal notion that reasonable men will finally agree on the best solution, and that the obligation of the reasonable man is to advance the position he thinks best, but with a tacit agreement to finally abide by the will of the majority. If you are interested in social change and believe it comes through struggle and power, you don't do that.... I sometimes think that the real enemy must be the liberal, because why else would he advance such arrant nonsense?[27]

Jaffary may well be right, but even if we reach only step two in Odegard's list, the benefits of the participatory exercise may well be worth the effort. Perhaps all we can hope for in the initial steps at formulating a new societal consensus is for individuals with widely varying perspectives to begin to understand and trust each other. Without such a base, it is difficult to imagine how we can evolve peacefully toward a more humane and democratic society.

But what is needed to begin? Clearly it is not new legislation or the establishment of new structures within government. Rather, what is required is a willingness of people within and outside government to assume new roles and to experiment with new ideas. For politicians and civil servants this may mean placing greater stress on facilitating and enabling roles than on those emphasizing directive leadership. It implies a willingness to accept situations which seem unstructured and ambiguous, to place less emphasis on uniformity and more on diversity, and to try out ideas which run counter to existing theories of administration.

However, the onus for trying out new ideas does not rest solely with politicians and civil servants. As Frederick Thayer states in a paper prepared for the Committee on Government Productivity,

Many advocates [of participation] seemed trapped within the boundaries of some of the oldest theories imaginable. They seem to argue that they should replace the existing "establishment" and exercise the same power themselves, or that they should have a unilateral veto power over all decisions, or that every individual should participate extensively in every aspect of every decision that has any actual or potential effect upon his or her life. There is no shortage of proposals for "open hearings" in huge auditoriums, for neoclassical forms of "Athenian democracy," and for sophisticated and instantaneous referenda on all public issues, as in the oft-repeated suggestion that electronic home-voting consoles, attached perhaps to television sets, could enable everyone to record his or her vote on the 'issue of the day.'[28]

What is required, then, is an "attitudinal revolution"—a revolution that can come about quietly, through participants, both within and outside government, being part of and learning from a continuous series of experiments in participatory planning. There appears to be no better place for this experimentation to begin than with agencies like Ontario Hydro.

Notes

1. Gail Stewart and Cathy Starrs, *Gone To-Day and Here Tomorrow,* A Working Paper prepared for the Committee on Government Productivity (Toronto: Queen's Printer, 1972), p. 24.

2. D.J. Gordon, "Social and Environmental Criteria," Opening Remarks to the Solandt Commission, 31 July 1972.

3. See, for example, George Leonard's *The Transformation* (New York: Delacorte Press, 1972); and Theodore Roszak's, *Where The Wasteland Ends* (Garden City, N.Y.: Doubleday, 1972).

4. Bruce Hutchison, "The Storming of the World," *Maclean's,* September 1972, pp. 27-31, 47.

5. John Crispo in a speech to the Annual Meeting of the Institute of Public Administration of Canda, Fredericton, New Brunswick, 6 September 1972.

6. *Citizen Involvement,* A Working Paper prepared for the Committee on Government Productivity (Toronto: Queen's Printer, 1972), p. 12.

7. G.E. Gathercole, Opening Remarks to the Solandt Commission, 31 July 1972.

8. Gordon, "Social and Environmental Criteria."

9. Stewart and Starrs, *Gone To-Day and Here Tomorrow,* p. 27.

10. Holtan Odegard, *The Politics of Truth* (University, Ala.: University of Alabama Press, 1971),p. 163.

11. Gordon, "Social and Environmental Criteria."

12. Odegard, *The Politics of Truth,* p. 8.

13. These pressures are well documented in the Committee on Government Productivity's *2nd Interim Report* (Toronto: Queen's Printer, 1971), p.4.

14. The theories of Mill, Rousseau, and Cole are examined from this viewpoint by Carole Pateman in her book *Participation and Democratic Theory* (London: Cambridge University Press, 1970).

15. J.S. Mill, *On Representative Government* (London: Everyman Edition, 1862), p. 193.

16. Lon L. Fuller, "Adjudication and the Rule of Law," *Proceedings of the American Society of International Law* 54 (1960): 1-8.

17. Ibid.

18. It is interesting to note the experiment being conducted by the Canadian Law Reform Commission in East York. In co-operation with Metro Police, a small group of lawyers and law students are attempting to deal with some petty crimes through means other than the courts. The hypothesis being tested is that even petty crimes are "polycentric" in nature and therefore should not be resolved by adjudicative processes.

19. For an excellent description and analysis of the planning process which developed the urban renewal scheme for Trefann Court, see Graham Fraser's *Fighting Back, Urban Renewal in Trefann Court* (Toronto: Hakkert, 1972).

20. Ronald E. Jones in an address to the opening session of the Ontario Educational Association on 21 March 1971.

21. Most of these principles are outlined in Frederick Thayer's *Participation and Liberal Democratic Government*, A Working Paper produced for the Committee on Government Productivity (Toronto: Queen's Printer, 1972).

22. Conventional administrative wisdom argues that we should be attempting to establish specific national or provincial goals in every field of public policy. (See, for example, the Economic Council's *8th Annual Review*, September 1971.) Few such specific goals exist now, and if participation is held as an important societal value, then we should be moving in just the opposite direction, that is, developing national and provincial policies which have no specific goals and which call for as much flexibility and diversity as possible at the regional and local level.

23. I disagree with Holtan Odegard, who in the *Politics of Truth* distinguishes one justifiable reason for excluding groups—that is, a refusal on the part of immature and irresponsible people to understand the viewpoints of others and to work towards a mutually satisfying solution. Industrial relations is governed by a similar requirement of

"bargaining in good faith." In my view, there is no legitimate reason for excluding any person or group from a participatory decision-making process.

24. See Fraser, *Fighting Back, Urban Renewal in Trefann Court*, chapter 12.

25. Odegard, *The Politics of Truth*, p. 197.

26. Ibid., p. 217.

27. Karl D. Jaffary, Notes for a Presentation to the Couchiching Conference on the Question of whether the Development of Land should be entirely controlled by the State, 18 August 1972.

28. Thayer, *Participation and Liberal Democratic Government*, pp. 2-3.

5

Representative Government and Environmental Management

Edwin T. Haefele

The following drama was played throughout the land in one form or another during the 1960's. An announcement is made in local papers that a dam has been proposed upstream from central city which will (1) control floods, (2) ensure an adequate water supply to city residents, (3) provide recreation on the lake created by the dam, and (4) improve water quality in the river downstream. Mr. Average Citizen may read the announcement with only casual interest, comforted, perhaps, that the public officials are doing something worthwhile for a change.

As time goes on, he is puzzled, even bewildered or angered, by a mounting controversy over the dam. The dam is attacked by the people who live on what is to be the bottom of the lake created by the dam. It is attacked by some people who sneer at "flatwater" recreation and speak rapturously of the existing "white" water where the dam is to be placed. It is attacked by fishermen who talk about spawning grounds, by biologists who decry artificial lakes and predict silting, by economists who talk about flood plain restrictions, and by engineers who mention re-aeration of water as a cheaper method of improving water quality.

Mr. Average Citizen, if he does not screen out all this "noise" in his information channels, may well think, "they must have thought of all that." Mr. Bureaucrat, who did not think of all that, is even more bewildered by the clamour than is Mr. Average Citizen. But Mr. Bureaucrat is resourceful. Nobody is going to finger *him* with the blame; he is, after all, only following the law, and, besides, if other people want to get into the act, elementary strategy suggests that one should open the stage door and let them in. Once they are on the stage, they are as committed as anyone to making the act succeed. So, with one hand Mr. Bureaucrat hands the hot potato to the politician, and with the other he opens the door to additional interest groups that want in on the action.

Mr. Politician, who was born with infra-red vision, can spot a hot potato before it begins to glow. He swiftly fields the hand-off from the bureaucracy, writes some resounding phrases about the "need for public participation," "multiple use," "balanced programmes," and lobs the potato (now radio-active) back through the bureaucratic transom. For good measure, he creates an environmental agency co-equal to the agency proposing the dam in the first place, gives no one final authority, and wishes the judges good health.

My paper attempts to address the resulting problem, which can, perhaps, be categorized by the following three quesions: How do we achieve technical efficiency in water quality management? How do we choose the goals for water quality management? Who do we involve in the process of water quality management? It will be useful to start in the area of greatest knowledge and move from it gradually out into *terra incognito*. I have thus arranged the order of the questions and will so address them.

TECHNICAL EFFICIENCY

While there is still substantial argument over the means of accomplishing some of the objectives, it remains true that we recognize the necessary conditions for technical efficiency to be:

1. a geographical area which will allow for control, that is, a watershed, a tributary, or a reach on which boundary conditions can be specified and met.

2. a criterion for choosing among mutually exclusive projects, for example, benefit-cost in some form.

3. the absence of any bar *against* certain technical options, and, conversely, the absence of any external fiscal incentives which bias the technical choice *toward* certain technical options.

These conditions may be thought of as our geographical handle on the problem, our economic handle, and our functional handle. If any of them are defective, to the degree they are defective we will fail to achieve technical efficiency in similar measure. Unfortunately, as we all know, all three are defective to some degree.

We have just begun to understand how limited the hydrologic definition of the management area is. Not only is it apt to range so widely that it brings in problems (and people) of minimal interest to the management agency, but it is also at odds with the geography of two other interrelated problems—the management of gaseous and solid wastes. These problem sheds will rarely fit the geography of the watershed, yet there may be efficiency gains to be made by considering all three residuals in one management system. The efficiency gains may be significant in an area like

Washington, D.C., and the Lower Potomac, whereas tying the whole Potomac basin into such a management scheme may make little sense at present, the demands on the river above Washington being minimal.

Our economic criterion, usually some form of benefit-cost analysis, suffers from well-known vicissitudes on efficiency grounds, for example, choice of discount rates, but it is attacked with even heavier artillery when we get into distributional questions. The criterion remains, however, a potent tool by which to make aggregate, economic evaluations of mutually exclusive alternatives. That is a large enough benefit to confer on us, and we should not, as the large federal bureaucracies in Washington are trying to do, put more burden on the tool than it can accept. It will not tell anyone which distribution of costs and benefits are "best," nor does it provide a framework to evaluate non-economic costs or benefits.

It is notoriously well-known that management agencies are rarely allowed to look at technical options in an unbiased way. Governmental programmes typically give grants-in-aid for specific technologies, be they sewage treatment plants, dams, or whatever. Rarely, perhaps never, has an agency been able to review all technical options with a clear eye. The fiscal calculation of matching grants blurs every vision, even the strongest. Leading the solution toward a particular technology would, of course, be forgivable were there any rationality or larger optimization being served. None comes to mind.

Yet the lack of perfection in our ability to choose efficiently should not be taken too seriously. It remains true, as Kneese, Davis, and others have demonstrated, that we know how to manage river basins so as to make everybody better off. In practice we are still below, probably well below, the kind of efficient management we know how to achieve. Why do we not achieve it? In short, we do not because water quality management is imbedded in a legal and cultural heritage that values technical efficiency less than some other things. Moreover, technical efficiency would displace some people and some areas from a power and influence position they value very highly. Finally, consider the possibility that the legal and cultural context within which these matters rest is itself in a pathological state at the moment. The broader institutional structure of governance, particularly in the United States, is inadequate to the tasks that water quality management, or more generally environmental management, has placed upon it. How that came about leads us into an examination of the goal-choosing mechanisms available to us.

CHOOSING GOALS FOR MANAGEMENT

The common heritage of Canada and the United States consists of what is termed by the present generation of English historians as "the myth of the Anglo-Saxon Constitution." What was a myth in England became a reality on this side of the Atlantic as both countries established legislative supremacy (limited in the United States case explicitly by a written constitution with a bill of rights patterned closely after the English instrument adopted in 1689) and governments which consciously strove to determine social choices from individual voter preferences. The effort was in both cases built from the ground up, that is, from self-governing colonies and territories. While there are differences, there are greater similarities. One of the similarities is that there is a great deal of power lying dormant in legislative halls. In the United States, the power has, in many cases, been curbed by state constitutional amendment (following the legislative scandals of the early 1800's) but the potential to restore it is still there.

Gradually, however, during the nineteenth and twentieth centuries the remaining power of the state legislatures has seeped away, away to other parts of the state government under a well-motivated attempt to get efficient management, and been dispersed to other levels of government. The fiscal power went to the national government as a result of the passage of the sixteenth amendment, which authorized the personal income tax. The management power went to special districts, single-purpose authorities, appointed boards and commissions, and to bureaucrats charged with administering laws often vague and unfocused.

In Canada, it is my impression that less power has been absorbed nationally; certainly in fiscal terms this is so. It may be only slightly overdrawn to say that the Canadian province is a state, but that the American state has become a province.

The reason that I have taken you on this detour into governmental history is this: to the extent that state legislative power has been absorbed or diffused, the ability of government to choose, to set priorities, has been weakened. The pathology stems from that fact. As one agency gets control of transportation, another control of education; as one appointed board issues sewer permits, another reviews zoning plans and a third promotes economic development, the whole question of choosing social priorities becomes irrelevant, and we move ahead by chance. Establishing comprehensive planning arrangements and co-ordinating committees, while of interest to a growing bureaucracy, simply compounds the problem of choosing by burying the process from traditional public pressures. (Indeed, the rise of court suits, civil disobedience, and advocacy planning, about which I will speak later, are direct results of the traditional streams of advocacy—the party and the parliament—drying up.) If the game is really played in the offices of the bureaucrats or in the hearing rooms of the commission, why bother with parties and legislatures? And, since the bureaucrat and the commissioner are insulated, deliberately, from party pressures, perhaps the court suit was the only way to get into the game at all. Thus have many in the United States reasoned. If the special interest lobby could sit in the bureaucrat's office and help write the regulations, then perhaps the only recourse for the opposing special interest was to get into the room also. This method of influencing choices is now so common in the United States that sections requiring "citizen" participation in agency decision making at "every stage" are in several of the new environmental acts at the federal level.

Indeed, we may have gone through a whole revolution of decision making without the slightest attention being paid to it outside the quarters of the interested parties. It has attractions. The new method allows the politician to get off the hook by passing the decision making over to an appointed board or commission. He can then exist on platitudes and good feelings toward all. The political heat is drained off into a kind of infinite sink—a bureaucracy where no one is responsible but all have authority. The interest groups, to the extent they are organized, (and Olson has shown us which ones will be) can take their chances on the inside, helping to carve the turkey through informal deals and bargains. The bureaucrat cannot lose, as he becomes the indispensable middleman. And, of course, the outsiders and losers always have the courts.

Again, I must confine my judgment to the United States, but the process that I have just described is going on. It is not working. It will not work. It cannot work. Why not? It conforms to many textbook descriptions of the informal power structure of democracies. Moreover, it is consonant with both "pluralist" and "elitist" descriptions of group politics.

It does not, however conform, nor is it consonant with, the structure that some very hard-headed politicians put together in Philadelphia in 1787. One of the prime motivations of those men was to prevent a kind of "courtier" (we would say "bureaucratic") government by men not responsive to, or responsible to, the public will. They built well, exceedingly well, out of fire-hardened materials. Hence, today, when management agencies begin to get into important areas, such as influencing or controlling land use and making life and death decisions for communities and areas, they find themselves besieged in the courts. Politicians who practise consensus politics find it impossible to please everyone, and if the legislature does not decide the issue at stake, the one displeased can often bring the whole administrative process to a standstill in the courts.

Perhaps I belabour the obvious, but the point, no matter how obvious, must be driven home. Decisions made by general purpose legislatures, whose members are elected, can be overturned in the courts only on the most fundamental grounds of constitutional probity. Decisions made by any other governmental bodies, no matter how carefully designed, can be upset on innumerable procedural and technical grounds by anyone with "standing" in a court of law. Granting of "standing" to a broader and broader spectrum of interests, for example, class action suits, is going forward rapidly in the United States court system.

We in the United States are being estopped from doing more and more things. Highways are not being built, dams are not being constructed, buildings are not being put up, industries are not being located. Electrical generation capacity is not being expanded. The blockages are not happening everywhere, of course, but they happen in many and in an ever increasing number of places.

Two reactions are possible in such a period of impasse. One is to recognize why the original system does not allow decision making through bureaucracies and to solve the impasse by returning to the original system. The second, and the one we are lamentably following, is to attempt to tear down that part of the original system blocking action by bureaucracy and blast through solutions to the immediate problem. Attempts in the United States to draw these issues up to the presidency and to use presidential power (still after two hundred years only vaguely defined) will, if successful, fundamentally alter American government in a way precisely analogous to the efforts of the Stuart kings. The attempt will meet, indeed is now being met by, precisely the same response. Myth or no, in the final analysis, we will either govern ourselves or be ungovernable. My impression is that Canadians are still hesitating about putting their feet on this path that we have already travelled too far along.

My purpose here is not so much to dramatize these larger issues as to use them to provide the framework for more specific examination of mechanisms for choosing goals. Within the framework one can see the limited role that many sophisticated tools of decision making, for example, systems analytical tools with multi-objective functions, can play. If the fight is over the weights to put on each part of the objective function, whether to allow this or that constraint, when there are many decision-makers to contend with and consensus is impossible, these tools do not suffice.

A RESIDUALS MANAGEMENT APPROACH

Let me add quickly that while these tools may not suffice, neither are they useless. We are now, at Resources for the Future, in Washington, D.C., developing management models of just such form, that is, optimizing models with multi-objective function capacity. We are using them, however, in a legislative setting. Let me describe the effort briefly.

Our method has been to construct and experiment with a hypothetical region, modelling its residuals discharge activities and the natural systems which translate those discharges into ambient quality levels. This regional model has been linked to a model which simulates the vote-trading activities of a legislature assumed to be responsible for making the decisions about quality in that region. The regional model has been structured to give a great deal of information in physical as well as economic terms to each legislator. We hope to show that information in this form can be used in a systematic way by real legislatures to assist them in arriving at regional policy. Our legislative model is emphatically *not* an attempt to put real legislatures out of business but is simply a device for allowing us to accomplish two things: first, to design the regional model for use in a legislative setting; and, second, to compare the policies adopted by legislatures put together along different lines. The basic function of the simulation programme is to identify and accomplish the vote trades which would take place in a real legislature.

In an attempt to capture some of the complexity in the environmental issue, we introduce the idea of a preference vector which combines an ordinal ranking and a yes-no vote on a given set of issues. In the legislative model the issues consist of four quality measures of the natural environment[1] and the four measures of increased cost resulting from improvements in environmental quality.

Arbitrary preference vectors (reflecting differences of tastes, incomes, and so forth, were specified for each area. These are based on arbitrary upper limits on each of the eight measures. Thus, one area's upper limits vector is:

Area One

DOD	3.0	parts per million in reach 4
ΔT	5.0	degrees F in reach 4
SP	50.0	μ g/m^3 in area 1
SO$_2$	20.0	μ g/m^3 in area 1
Taxes	1%	increase of one per cent in the area
Unemp.	10%	increase of ten per cent
Elec.	50%	increase of fifty per cent to each household in every area
Heat	20	increase in dollars per year to each household in the area

If we allowed area one to be our decision-maker, these upper limits would be the constraints area one would put on the solution of the regional model. Since area one is only one of twenty-five areas, we wish to construct a social choice process to allow the upper limits vectors of all twenty-five areas to be expressed. Our preference vectors, one for each area, are designed to do that. For example, we may display area one's preference vector in response to a current situation as follows:

TABLE I
Area One — Preference Vector

	Area One Upper Limits	Present Situation	Area One Preference Vector
DOD	3.0	5.52	N
ΔT	5.0	9.89	N_1
SP	50.0	17.19	Y
SO₂	20.0	32.69	N_2
Tax	1%	0.0	Y
Unemp.	10%	0.0	Y_3
Elec.	50%	0.0	Y
Heat	$20	0.0	Y

The numerical subscripts in the preference vector indicate the ordinal ranking of three (in this case) measures. Thus we are ranking, by assumption, an upper limit of 5°F heat rise in reach 4 of the river of first importance in area one, an upper limit on SO₂ of μ g/m³ in area one as second in importance, and an upper limit of 10 per cent on unemployment as third most importance to area one.[2] (For ease of computation we do not rank all measures. Elements without subscripts are all assumed to be of equal importance but less important than any subscripted element.)

Area one's preferences may be summarized by saying that the citizens of area one are dissatisfied with the present situation in three out of four quality measures, while they are satisfied with the present tax and utility burdens. Since area one ranks the environmental measures above the financial ones, however, some additional financial burden would be accepted if necessary to achieve acceptable levels of water and air quality.

All other areas were assigned upper limits vectors and ordinal ranks to three or more measures. Using those vectors we can display all twenty-five preference vectors in response to the present situation (Table 2). The Y votes on each row are tallied in the far right column. We see a unanimous approval of all financial measures but much disapproval of the present quality of the air and water. The stage is set, assuming our preference vectors are such that not all can be met simultaneously, for some sort of social choice process to be invoked. Since the number of possible "solutions," that is, technically feasible alternatives, may be said to be almost infinite, the social choice process cannot be simply a blind groping for a solution acceptable to some given percentage of areas, for the process would prove to be inefficient and the "solution" ambiguous at best. Neither can we, without throwing away the concept of social choice, simply stand with arbitrary "solutions" that do not reflect the preference

TABLE 2
Vote Matrix, Present Situation

Area Issue	DOD	ΔT	SP	SO$_2$	Tax	Unemp.	Elec.	Heat
1.	N	N$_1$	Y	N$_2$	Y	Y$_3$	Y	Y
2.	N	N	Y	N$_1$	Y	Y$_2$	Y	Y$_3$
3.	Y	N	Y	N	Y$_1$	Y$_2$	Y	Y$_3$
4.	Y	N	Y	Y	Y$_2$	Y$_1$	Y	Y
5.	Y	Y	Y	N	Y	Y$_1$	Y$_2$	Y$_3$
6.	N	N$_3$	Y$_2$	N$_1$	Y	Y	Y	Y
7.	N	N	Y$_2$	N$_1$	Y$_3$	Y$_4$	Y	Y
8.	Y	N	Y	N	Y$_1$	Y	Y$_2$	Y
9.	Y	N	Y	N	Y$_2$	Y$_1$	Y$_3$	Y
10.	Y	Y	Y$_2$	N	Y	Y$_1$	Y$_3$	Y
11.	N	N$_3$	Y$_1$	N$_2$	Y	Y	Y	Y
12.	N$_5$	N$_4$	Y$_2$	N$_1$	Y$_3$	Y	Y	Y
13.	Y	N	Y$_1$	N$_3$	Y$_2$	Y	Y	Y
14.	N	N	Y	Y	Y	Y$_1$	Y$_2$	Y
15.	Y$_3$	Y	Y$_2$	Y$_1$	Y	Y$_4$	Y	Y
16.	N	N$_3$	Y$_2$	N$_1$	Y	Y	Y	Y
17.	N	N	Y$_2$	N$_1$	Y$_3$	Y	Y	Y
18.	N$_1$	N	Y	N	Y$_2$	Y	Y$_3$	Y
19.	N	N	Y	Y	Y$_2$	Y$_1$	Y$_3$	Y
20.	N	N	Y$_1$	N	Y$_2$	Y$_3$	Y	Y
21.	N	N$_2$	Y$_3$	N$_1$	Y	Y	Y	Y
22.	Y$_1$	N$_2$	Y	N$_4$	Y$_3$	Y	Y	Y
23.	Y$_1$	N	Y	N	Y$_2$	Y$_3$	Y	Y
24.	N$_2$	N$_4$	Y	Y	Y$_3$	Y$_1$	Y	Y
25.	Y	N	Y	Y$_1$	Y	Y	Y	Y$_2$
Tally of Y Votes	*11*	*3*	*25*	*6*	*25*	*25*	*25*	*25*

vectors, in the hope that the "objectivity" of any one of these solutions will cow the residents of our region into acceptance.

In a real world situation, whatever official has charge of the model (and a computation budget) might be tempted simply to meet the first and second ranked upper limits of enough areas to insure a majority (assuming there existed some political body through which these votes could be registered). Lacking any such political body, he might "play around" with meeting a few more high-ranked upper limits (chosen on the basis of judicious knowledge of which areas could be most difficult if their limits were not met) and balance the additional limits against protests from special interest groups, industrial and environmental.

It may be useful to explore in some detail what procedures could be used to find a solution based on the preferences of the twenty-five areas. The first method might be to see if all preferences (upper limits) of all the areas might be met simultaneously. If so, clearly it is Pareto-optimal to meet them. Since such a happy state is unlikely in the real world, we have set the upper limits vector so that it is not attainable in the regional model either. If all preferences cannot be met, then whose should be met and in what order?

A second method is to meet each area's upper limits by using each set separately as constraints on the regional model. This accomplishes two things: it allows us to make sure that each area's upper limits preferences are internally consistent,[3] that is, can be met simultaneously, and it allows us to see the kind of "overlap" or complementarity between one area's upper limits preferences and those of another area.

A third method is to pay more attention at the outset to the ordinal ranking of the different measures by each area. For example, we might try to meet the first- and second-ranked preferences of every area, or all first preferences, then all second preferences. Were we thinking about a strong party-oriented legislature or council, "all" might be replaced in the preceding sentence by "majority party." If "all" were possible, the "all" solution might have appeal over the "majority party" solution, but it would not necessarily be chosen by the majority party if meeting minority first- and second-ranked preferences meant giving up on majority party third- and fourth-ranked preferences. How the majority party acted would depend very much on what powers of retribution the minority party had when the next election was coming up and/or other political factors exogenous to our consideration here.

Any of the preceding methods could be employed in connection with the regional model presented in this paper, but they do not get us very far in terms of the reality of conflicting preferences and the loose party structure characteristic of most United States legislative councils. While replicating all of the complexities of United States legislative procedure and structure would be impossible, we can adopt a method which will replicate an important element in them, namely vote-trading. The essence of vote-trading is giving up on one issue to gain another issue valued more.

The basic idea of the vote-trading algorithm is to add constraints to the present situation such that N votes are converted to Y votes in some efficient, non-biased way. Vote-trading is efficient for this purpose because it focuses attention on high-ranked N votes (these are the upper limits violations of most concern to the area). They are the upper limits the areas want most to be put in as constraints on the regional model. However, with vote-trading such a constraint can be put in only if the area that wishes to put it in will accept (also allow to be added as a constraint) another upper limit on another issue that is desired by another area. Constraints are put into the solution, therefore, in pairs.[4]

Since vote-trading was explained as giving something up for something of higher value, what is it that each area gives up by this trade? To illustrate what is given up, let us pick out a vote-trade from Table 2 and see what happens.

	Area Thirteen Upper Limits →	Area Thirteen Present Situation →	Area Thirteen Preference Vector	Area Twenty-four Preference Vector	Area Twenty-four Present ← Situation	Area Twenty-four Upper ← Limits
DOD	3.5	3.4	Y	N_2	3.4	3.0
SO_2	80	103	N_3	Y	38	40

The result of the vote-trade shown is to put in, as constraints, area twenty-four's upper limit of DOD ≤ 3 on reach 2 of the river and area 13's upper limit of $SO_2 \leq 80$ in area thirteen. What area thirteen gives up is a 3.4 DOD outcome, an outcome it was happy with since it was below its own limit of 3.5. Area twenty-four gives up an SO_2 outcome of 38 in its area, an outcome it was happy with. The outcome of these trades, and further details on the model have been presented elsewhere.[5]

There is no reason to believe that any existing legislature or council would use the trading routine we have just outlined. There is no necessity for them to do so since the distributional information may be adapted to a variety of decision paths. Let us take some examples. In real councils there is often a desire, sometimes even a necessity, to let everybody win. A chairman might ask each member to write down one constraint that the member really wants, or needs, in his district or area. These constraints could be collected and used as the first set of constraints for the model. If the regional model can be solved with those constraints, the effects of the solution could again be examined and one additional constraint added by each member. This process could be continued until the regional model fails to solve. The last solution could be adopted or used as a starting solution to trades or bargains.

Bargaining could occur either after the process described in the preceding paragraph was completed or *ab initio*. In general terms, bargaining can occur whenever two or more council members perceive that some constraints are in direct conflict. In such instances, real council members may wish to bargain, that is, to agree to slack off their constraints slightly if the other side will do so also. In the process they may wish to use the regional model to help them find the most agreeable bargain—one with minimum change in both constraints, one with minimum variation in per cent rise between the two, or whatever other criterion is agreed upon by the pair of bargainers.

It will be seen quickly that such constraint slackening will probably come late in the game, since no one will be willing to change his upper limits until it is clear either that they cannot be met as they stand or that a majority favours a solution in which one's upper limits are greatly exceeded.

The actual use of the regional model, therefore, may vary considerably from one group to another. Some strictures on use are, however, apparent. For example, the distributional information has potentially explosive political content. That fact can be used to advantage for good or ill. Suppressing it may be politically expedient to some but can rarely, if ever, be either ethically or legally justified when taxpayers' monies are being used. It may not be desirable, however, to have all experimental runs made public so long as they are shared by all the council members. (The potential for mischief by a clique within the council or legislature, a committee for instance, would be very large. Such a group could construct a very biased solution.)

Another stricture on use relates to the choice of a method to follow once unanimity has broken down, as it inevitably will early on in any real situation. One can imagine, in a strong party legislature or council, that the majority party might well wish to give priority to meeting the constraints of its members, with minority preferences being met later, if at all. This method is not as bad as it might appear, so long as the distributional impact of their deliberations is known to all council members *and* the minority party has equal access to the regional model in order to design countersolutions. These latter solutions will, of course, attempt to meet minority preferences *plus* improving the lot of a sufficient number of the majority members to place the majority solution in jeopardy. That process will, in practice, turn out not too differently from our trading solution.

In more non-partisan situations the idea of coalition building may have appeal as an equalitarian procedure which may be able to reach a dominant solution in the absence of cycling.

In any event there will be some pressure on the operators of the model, who must be like Caesar's wife. Sometimes both majority and minority party staff will be needed to insure ease of access, shared results, and general trust. There will be opportunities for technicians to facilitate a solution or to obstruct one by purely technical means which go unnoticed by the members or their staffs. These opportunities and dangers are present in many public service posts and cannot be completely eliminated. Just as both sides in disputes have for centuries employed lawyers, they now must employ programmers, economists, and systems analysts if the technician's temptation to play God (always for the public good, of course) is to be minimized.

In the context of our discussion on choosing goals, a regional residuals management model is but a half-way house on the way to solving our problem. While it does treat residuals in an interrelated fashion and constructs a social choice from representative preference, it does not choose boundaries nor does it relate environmental issues and costs to other issues and their costs.

The latter issue is not too significant in the real world, *so long as the same people who sit in this legislature also decide the other issues.* A representative, in other words, can only rank issues if he has access to all the relevant games being played. If a man serves only on the school board, he does not have to judge between schools and environmental improvement..If he sits on both boards, he may have to choose between them, given the inevitable budget constraints faced by all governments.

Thus, since it is unlikely that we will soon put together the dismembered, general purpose legislature, (that is, abolish all special boards and commissions), it may be necessary to change our habits of selecting different people to serve on each of them. Such a course has salutary effects both on citizen participation and the boundary problem and is best discussed under our third and final question.

WHO PARTICIPATES?

I earlier outlined the growth, indeed the necessity of growth, of citizen participation in the bureaucratic governance process. Environmental groups, who feel they have previously been outside the decision process, have come inside with a vengeance. I have also suggested that this new emphasis on citizen participation, on widening the numbers of interests and groups, is doomed to failure. The bureaucrat's room simply is not big enough to accommodate all, and he has no criterion (nor can he have any) to select from competing claims for his attention.

This assertion may be given weight by calling attention to the present plight of the U.S. Corps of Engineers as they attempt to broaden their evaluation process to economic, social, and environmental effects of their projects.[6] These guidelines respond to Section 122 of Public Law 91-611 (River and Harbor and Flood Control Act of 1970) which asks, among other things, that the Corps evaluate "disruption of desirable community and regional growth." Attempts to comply would have their comic aspects were the issue not so serious. One example will have to suffice. In a small project, within one county, the Corps has several contending, legitimate representatives of portions of the citizenry saying different things. How is a bureaucrat to judge, assess, evaluate, or weigh these statements? What incentive, other than human compassion and professional pride, does he have for even making the effort? What recourse do those who lose because of his judgment have?

The immediate impact of this kind of dilemma has been to bring project evaluation to a halt while the Corps struggles in the flypaper of such evaluation. The longer run implication, however, is that questions of *quo warranto* and improper legislative delegation of authority will be raised. The courts have always held that legislative authority, being itself delegated from the people, cannot be delegated.[7] While we have not yet reached that stage, we are verging toward it when we give appointed officials powers to control land use, economic growth, and environmental quality by their actions in water management. Our present tendency, buttressed by whatever level of "citizen participation" the agency can muster, cannot stand against the ancient precepts of representative government. (It is amusing to reflect that we might go full circle, that is, political activists, in their search for ways for greater participation, may actually rediscover representative government.)

There is, I believe, no need to vex the Corps of Engineers and other agencies with tasks which they are, for good reason, constitutionally barred from doing. Let me suggest an alternative which has the advantage of dealing with the boundary problem as well. The suggestion is that instead of a citizen having many different men represent him—one on the school board, another in the sanitary district, a third in the city or suburban council, a fourth on the planning commission, and so on—the citizen should have one man, a general purpose representative, represent him in all those governmental bodies. The basic reason for focusing all citizen representation in one man (at the local level) instead of many is to enable the question of priorities, of goals and resolution of conflicting goals, to be managed.

If, for example, a general purpose representative (GPR) sits both on the school board and the sanitary commission, he can, indeed he must, decide whether to support a new school or a new sewer system if both cannot be funded. Citizens of his area, moreover, have one place to focus their attention on these questions, and they too must face the consequence that supporting the school means opposing the sewer.

There are two general points to be made about the suggestion before proceeding further. The first is to counter the perennial reaction that we ought to have "experts" representing us on the school board, the sanitary board, and so forth. This reaction is not so common now as it once was, but it still occurs regularly. The point is, of course, that we can hire, to suit, any number of experts of any persuasion. But if government involves the process of reflecting voter preferences, then representatives should be expert in winning elections, since that presumes some knowledge of voter preferences. The second point is more substantive. It is the criticism that I have merely shifted the boundary problem from that of creating the ideal general purpose local government to that of creating the ideal unit of local representation. The answer is to admit that I have, because the latter problem is solvable; in fact, has already been solved in many jurisdictions. Congressional districts, state senatorial districts, and state representative districts are constructed of equal population units for the purpose of electing a general purpose representative. The general purpose representative is, in point of history, the oldest form of representation. Political parties are well acquainted with all the problems and possibilities of drawing district lines. The channels of the judiciary are well worn with all the problems of achieving equitable solutions to disputes. In other words, a process is in place which is working, where reform has already occurred.

The use of GPRs could be of value in finessing the environmental boundary problem, by separating the question of the geographical reach of the management agency from the geographical area represented on the policy board(s) to which the management agency is responsible. While the details of this idea are elaborated elsewhere,[8] some discussion is necessary here. Think of a water control agency or environmental management agency as a public corporation created at the state level with power to operate anywhere (much as the Maryland State Environmental Services agency is set up) *subject to* policy direction and funding by councils composed of GPRs in all districts affected by the problem. Thus one council involves only the GPRs in the airshed, while another council (overlapping, no doubt) is composed of those GPRs in the watershed.

The idea may be difficult to think about at first, but the implementation involves nothing more complicated than taking two votes in the hall, one of brown-eyed people, the other of brown- and blue-eyed people. As the airshed expanded, as it will if the city grows, districts could be added automatically on technical evidence that new areas were being affected.

It will be obvious to many who are familiar with local government that what I am suggesting is in fact already happening in one form or another. Councils of government in the United States are generally composed of elected officials from local jurisdictions. Such men—mayors, councilmen, county commissioners, and the like—already serve as the voting members of transit boards and planning commissions. The GPR is essentially a rationalization and extension of that trend in an attempt to provide maximum chance for the elected official to control what happens in his area, and to receive the reward, or blame, for it happening.

The suggestion would have marked benefits for most professional staffs, for it gives them representatives to deal with who are real. Few things are more frustrating than trying to gauge community reaction through a board composed of appointees whose knowledge of, and interest in, community reaction is both limited and one-sided. If the GPR system has any merit it is that it provides incentive for the elected official to know what his constituents want and do not want. It also provides the constituents with an appropriate focus to register their feelings. In an era when the words "participatory" and "democracy" can be joined without any notion of redundancy arising, the incentive and the focus may be worth while.

CONCLUSION

We have taken a rather tortuous path through the thorny thicket. Perhaps some of it was unnecessary. If so, I apologize. One of my teachers, the late Louis Wirth, used to say, "the most important part of a man is what he takes for granted." Since we come to this conference from many different paths, it is likely we take different things for granted. Some of us are interested in the solution of immediate problems, others in asking why do we have such problems. My interest is in the latter, and I have contended at great length that we have them, in water management, because we are trying to go across the grain of our heritage.

My suggestions for changing direction are but sketchily drawn and will, undoubtedly, not work as presented. That they will not work does not distress me if they serve the purpose of pointing out a new direction—a direction that may appeal to you. Once we have agreed on a common direction, I have no doubt but what the means to move there can be found.

Appendix A

Guidelines for Assessment of Economic, Social and Environmental Effects of Civil Works Projects*

These guidelines are designed to ensure that all significant adverse and beneficial effects of proposed projects are fully considered.[1]

Effect (impact) assessment is an integral part of the planning process. It serves as one test of the adequacy of that process and of any positive or negative recommendations resulting therefrom. It is fully compatible with multi-objective planning.

Any alternative developed in the planning process may produce unintended effects which are not responsive to the planning objectives and which are not included in benefit-cost analysis. Such effects are the subject of these guidelines.

Effect assessment is an iterative process which consists of the following steps: identification of anticipated project-caused economic, social, and environmental effects; quantitative and qualitative description and display of the effects; evaluation of the effects, whether adverse or beneficial; and consideration of measures to be taken if a proposed project would cause adverse effects.

The sequence of steps in effect assesment is summarized below:

  1. Assemble a profile of existing conditions in the planning area;

  2. Extend the profile to make projections of "without project" conditions through the expected life of the project;

  3. Make "with project" projections, identifying causative factors and tracing their effects for each alternative;

  4. Identify significant effects;

  5. Describe and display each significant effect;

  6. Evaluate adverse and beneficial effects;

  7. Consider project modifications where adverse effects are significant;

  8. Seek assessment feedback from other sources;

* Department of the Army, Office of the Chief of Engineers, Washington, D.C., 28 September 1972.
[1] Pursuant to Section 122 of the River and Harbor and Flood Control Act of 1970, shown in Appendix A 1.

(Steps 1 through 8 are common to each iteration of the effect assessment process).
9. Use effect assessment in making recommendations;
10. Prepare a Statement of Findings;
11. Use effect assessment in preparing the Environmental Impact Statement.

This sequence is discussed in more detail in the paragraphs that follow.

EFFECT ASSESSMENT

1. *Assemble a profile.*
Portray existing conditions in a profile describing the relevant economic, social, and environmental characteristics of the affected area. Judgment is of critical importance in determining what information will be needed.

A tentative profile should be prepared early in the planning process. Subsequently, as alternatives are considered in greater detail, the profile should be made more precise and focused on identified significant effects.

The boundary areas of the profile will vary depending upon whether the focus of an effect is local or regional; whether the area is defined by political jurisdiction or by hydrologic unit; and by the nature of the project effects.

When completed, the profile should provide a clear understanding of the significant existing conditions, problems, and needs of the affected area and of the rationale for any action, if proposed.

2. *Make projections of "without project" conditions.*
Extend the profile of existing conditions to portray future conditions without any project action. Projections should cover the expected life of each alternative considered over a reasonable range of probable future conditions.

Utilize a range of values to compensate in part for the uncertainties of projecting the future.

Projection of existing economic, social and environmental conditions should yield pertinent information about the conditions, problems, and needs of the affected area in the future and provide a basis or baseline for a comparison of the effects of alternative plans. The projection may suggest issues to be addressed in designing alternative "with project" plans.

3. *Make "with project" projections, identifying causative factors and tracing their effects for each alternative.*
Make projections of the "with project" conditions for each alternative being considered, including pre-construction, construction and operation periods through its expected life.

Identify and list project-related causative factors (see Appendix B) and their likely economic, social, and environmental effects (see Appendix C) concurrently with the formulation of alternative plans.

The causative factors and effect elements should be set forth in sufficient detail for each alternative to ensure that all significant interactive relationships are considered. The inter-relatedness of economic, social, and environmental aspects cannot be overlooked and must be considered regardless of the category in which any given effect is placed.

Assessments initially should emphasize breadth rather than depth. Refinements should await later stages of plan formulation.

Effect assessment at any stage should be carried to a degree of detail commensurate with the alternative it addresses.

4. *Identify significant effects.*
Examine causative factors and the effects they produce for each alternative. Select those effects which appear significant in view of the conditions, problems and needs of the affected area as projected for the "with" and "without" project conditions.

A "significant" effect is one which would be likely to have a material bearing on the decision-making process.

A determination regarding significance should be made at the earliest stage possible in the assessment process. The determination should be reconsidered at each stage, particularly in the light of public input and reaction.

In the process of formulation, adjustments may be made in the alternative plans that avoid or reduce identified adverse effects. In such cases, only residual adverse effects should be identified for further analysis in the concurrent assessment process.

5. *Describe and display all significant effects.*
Describe the effects of the various alternative plans in quantitative terms to the extent possible. Where this cannot be done, effects should at a minimum be set forth in qualitative-descriptive terms.

The effects should be described objectively, and tentatively designated as adverse or beneficial.

Beneficial effects that are identified should be included, to the extent possible, in the benefit evaluation section of the survey report.

Beneficial effects of one kind cannot be considered to cancel out an adverse effect of another kind.

Display the effects of the alternative plans in a form that is easily understood, interpreted, and evaluated, and that clearly shows the differences among them. The display is to be used in consulting with State and Federal agencies and public groups with particular expertise. The display also provides one of the bases for assessing alternative plans, selecting a recommended plan, and assisting in public participation

6. *Evaluate effects.*
Place values on the significant adverse and beneficial effects in monetary terms where applicable, quantitatively where possible, and qualitatively in

any event.

The assumptions or criteria on which a judgment is based should be made explicit, since segments of the public may perceive any single effect quite differently.

Significant adverse effects must be sufficiently well displayed to facilitate the weighing of need and type of project modification, if any. No single method for determining relative value is generally accepted. Public policy, community preferences, and the magnitude and degree of severity of effect are factors to be considered.

The aggregate or systems interaction of combined economic, social, and environmental effects along with evaluation of individual effects. In addition, the possibility of individual effects being part of a larger cumulative process should be investigated.

Effects not significant, not relevant, or that can be adequately incorporated in benefit-cost evaluation should not be accommodated in the effect evaluation.

An evaluation cannot be validated without obtaining the review and reaction of other agencies and the public.

7. Consider project modifications where adverse effects are significant.
For each significant adverse effect, investigate the possibility of: (a) Eliminating the effect; (b) Mitigating the effect by minimizing or reducing it to an acceptable level of intensity; or by compensating for it by including a counter-balancing positive effect.

The costs of such measures, as well as any costs of reduced project performance, provide further bases for comparing alternatives and for deciding how or whether to modify them or to accept the adverse effects.

If effect assessment has not proceeded in step with the formulation of alternatives, the possibility always exists that an identified adverse effect may be of such magnitude or character that it cannot be accepted in the best overall public interest, or be corrected by project modifications. In such a case, one or more new alternatives must be formulated to avoid an unacceptable adverse consequence. "No action" is always one of the alternatives to be considered.

For each beneficial effect investigate the possibility of: (1.) Reflecting it in the benefit-cost analysis of the project formulation process; or (2.) Describing and displaying the effect for consideration by the public and in plan selection; or (3.) Considering it as an offset for a corresponding adverse effect.

8. Seek assessment feedback from other sources.
Effect assessment procedures require a variety of information sources and continuous feedback.

Informal exchanges with Federal, State, and private groups and with individuals should be sought at the beginning of any investigation and maintained throughout planning. More formal discussion occurs in the course of initial, formulation and late-stage public meetings.

Consultation with a wide range of interests tests the adequacy of identification of effects, validates their designation as beneficial or adverse, and provides commentary on measures considered for project modification.

Response should be solicited to ensure that effects have not been overlooked or that the significance of effects has not been misjudged.

Fully utilize all the public participation procedures of the planning process. For survey report investigations, known effects and the possibilities for project modification to overcome adverse effects of alternatives will be introduced at the initial public meeting, discussed in general terms in the formulation-stage public meeting, and detailed at the late-stage public meeting.

For continuing authority reports and Phase I General Design Memoranda, effect assessment will be tailored to the public participation requirements of existing regulations.

Steps 1-7 should be taken before each public meeting to complete a formal iteration of the effect assessment process.

9. *Use effect assessment in making recommendations.*

More detailed assessment will be applied to the alternatives, including the tentatively selected proposal, by the time they are presented in the late-stage public meeting. At this meeting, formal presentation of the alternatives and measures to overcome adverse effects will be made and the degree of public acceptance gauged.

The reporting officer should recommend the alternative that is in the best overall public interest considering the planning objectives, the benefits and costs, and the significant economic, social, and environmental effects, including costs of treating those that are adverse.

While assessment and appraisal from all sources influence the alternative recommended by the reporting officer, the burden of judgment and defense ultimately rests with him.

10. *Prepare a Statement of Findings.*

Include a summary of the completed effect assessment in the report immediately before the Statement of Findings.

The Statement of Findings presents the rationale of the reporting officer for his conclusions and recommendations in accordance with the "best overall public interest."

11. *Use effect assessment in the Environmental Impact Statement.*

The requirements of Section 122 supplement the requirements of P.L. 91-190 (NEPA). Consequently, the completed effect assessment for environmental effects should be used as input for the Environmental Impact Statement.

Appendix A 1

Section 122 - P.L. 91-611*

"Not later than July 1, 1972, the Secretary of the Army, acting through the Chief of Engineers, after consultation with appropriate Federal and State officials, shall submit to Congress, and not later than ninety days after submission, promulgate guidelines designed to assure that possible adverse economic, social, and environmental effects relating to any proposed project have been fully considered in developing such project, and that the final decisions on the project are made in the best overall public interest, taking into consideration the need for flood control, navigation, and associated purposes, and the cost of eliminating or minimizing such adverse effects and the following:

    1. Air, noise and water pollution;

    2. Destruction or disruption of man-made and natural resources, aesthetic values, community cohesion and the availability of public facilities and services;

    3. Adverse employment effects and tax and property value losses;

    4. Injurious displacement of people, businesses and farms; and,

    5. Disruption of desirable community and regional growth.

    Such guidelines shall apply to all projects authorized in this Act, and proposed projects after the issuance of such guidelines."

*Source: River and Harbor and Flood Control Act of 1970 (P.L. 91-611; 84 Stat. 1818).

Appendix A 2

Sample Causative Factors

In order to identify and evaluate the effects of a project, describe aspects of the project in terms of factors likely to produce significant effects. Evaluation of effects should not be carried out in greater detail than the project alternative being considered. THE LIST BELOW IS ILLUSTRATIVE. IT IS NOT TO BE CONSIDERED COMPLETE OR LIMITING.

INPUT FACTORS
  Natural Resources
    Water
    Land
    Resources Products
      Gravel
      Sand
      Coal
      Timber
      Crushed Rock
    Wildlife and Fish
    Aesthetics
    Flora (Plant life)
  Energy Resources
  Capital
  Labor

SYSTEMIC FACTORS
  Physical Alterations
    Channelization
    Excavation
    Dredging
    Draining
  Structures
    Dam/Lake
    Levee
    Jetty
    Channel
    Barrier
    Road and Utility Relocation

Institutional
Acquisition
Easements
Relocation

OPERATION AND MAINTENANCE FACTORS
Equipment Service
Resource Management
  Harvesting
  Planting
  Buffer Zone Maintenance
  Grazing
  Fencing
Maintenance
  Recreational areas
  Water Quality Protection
  Dredging Operations
  Navigation Controls
  Reservoir Controls and Procedures

OUTPUT FACTORS
Hydro-power
Flood Control
Navigation
Water Supply
Recreation
Irrigation
Fish and Wildlife
Water Quality
Shoreline Protection

(Example: A project alternative requiring a dam may need a great deal of sand for concrete. Sand, therefore, can be considered an Input Factor. The employment effects of hiring people to excavate and transport sand, the environmental effect of excavation, and the transportation effects of increased heavy traffic on roads leading to the project all need to be considered since they are all effects resulting from the one causative factor—sand. Similarly, the environmental, social, economic effects caused by construction of the dam should be identified and assessed, as should the effects caused by operation and maintenance of the dam and its post-construction outputs.)

Appendix A 3

Sample Project Effects

All significant effects of project should be identified and assessed. In some cases, a causative factor may result in only one significant effect. In other cases, the significant effects of a causative factor will be numerous and may require consideration in all three effect categories. (Example: a causative factor such as dredging may result in turbidity in the water for a brief period. This should be considered a predominantly environmental effect. Yet, because of the turbid water, a textile factory downstream may have to close down for a few days. This is an economic effect, and should be considered as a result of dredging even though it is a lesser effect than the environmental one. The increased turbidity may also have the effect of reducing water recreation temporarily. This is a social effect of dredging.) Judgment must be used as to the limits of tracing out effects. Generally, the degree of detail involved in assessment should be no greater than that of the plan it addresses. An asterisk denotes items specifically mentioned in Section 122. These must be identified and evaluated. If they are considered to be not significant, that should also be noted. Other effects should be identified and evaluated only if they are considered to be significant. THE LIST BELOW IS AN ILLUSTRATIVE ONE. IT IS NOT TO BE CONSIDERED COMPLETE OR LIMITING.

SOCIAL EFFECTS
*Noise
Population, e.g.
    Mobility
    Density
    *Displacement of people
*Esthetic values
Housing
Archeologic remains
Historic Structures
Transportation
Education opportunities
Leisure opportunities (recreation, active and passive)
Cultural opportunities
*Community cohesion

*(Desirable) community growth
Institutional relationships
Health

ECONOMIC EFFECTS
National Economic Development
Local government finance, e.g.
    *Tax revenues
    *Property values
Land use
*Public facilities
*Public services
Local/regional activity, e.g.
    *(Desirable) regional growth
    Relocation
Real income distribution
*Employment/labor force
*Business and industrial activity
Agricultural activity
    *Displacement of farms
    Food supply
National defense

ENVIRONMENTAL FACTORS
*Man-made resources
*Natural resources
Pollution aspects
    *Air
        CO
        Sulphur oxides
        Hydrocarbons
        Particulates
        Photochemicals
    *Water
        Pathogenic agents
        Nutrients N and P
        Pesticides, herbicides, rodenticides
        Organic materials
        Solids, dissolved and suspended
    Land
        Soils
Animal and plant
    Birds

Mammals
Amphibians
Fish, sport and commercial
Shellfish
Insects
Microfauna
Trees, shrubs and plants
Microflora
Ecosystems
  Habitats
  Food chains
  Productivity
  Diversity
  Stability
Physical and Hydrologic aspects
  Erosion
  Erosion and sedimentation effects
  Compaction and subsidence
  Slope stability
  Groundwater regime alteration
  Surface flow effects
  Micrometeorological effects
  Physiologic changes (e.g., wetlands destruction)

Notes

1. These include (1) the level of dissolved oxygen in each reach of the river (calculated in terms of a dissolved oxygen deficit): DOD; (2) increases in the temperature of each reach of the river: ΔT; (3) the level of suspended particulates in the air (measured in micrograms per cubic meter): SP; and (4) the level of sulphur dioxide in the air (measured in micrograms per cubic meter): SO_2. We realize these measures could probably not be used directly in a political process, although the experience in choosing levels of water quality in the Delaware shows a quick assimilation of technical information by

laymen, particularly if the technical measures are related to fish population, recreation potential, and health hazards.

2. The ordinal rankings by real actors would clearly change as one or more upper limits were met and/or other upper limits were greatly exceeded. We have not investigated how such ordinal shifts would affect the algorithm, although it is clear that convergence problems might well occur.

3. An area's preferences do not have to be consistent, since it could have "if not this, then that" preferences in it. Identifying these beforehand will be useful, however, in a real world situation.

4. There is nothing magical about "paired" constraints. Three or more areas could agree on a constraint before it was put in. Paired constraints are simply easier, computationally, to use in the vote-trading algorithm.

5. See C.R. Russell, W.O. Spofford, and E.T. Haefele, "Environmental Quality Management in Metropolitan Areas," *Conference on Urbanization and Environment, Lyngby, Denmark: Transport and the Urban Environment,* Proceedings of the International Economic Association, ed. J.G. Rothenberg and Ian G. Heggie (New York: Wiley, [1974]).

6. See "Guidelines for Assessment of Economic, Social and Environmental Effects of Civil Works Projects," Office of the Chief of Engineers, 28 September 1972. (Included as Appendix A to this paper.)

7. Locke's famous dictum *Delegate potestas non potest delegari* is but a re-statement of a much older tradition in parliamentary rules.

8. See A. Kneese and E.T. Haefele, "Environmental Quality and the Optimal Jurisdiction" (Paper presented at a conference on Comparative Urban and Grants Economics, University of Windsor, November 1972.)

6

Policy Perceptions and Management Mechanisms

John Dales

INTRODUCTION

This seminar has been convened to discuss different institutional arrangements for water quality management. As a social scientist I am very much aware that different institutional forms bias decision making and affect human behaviour in different ways—that the institutional framework clearly *matters*. I therefore welcome this topic. Our task is to find a set of institutional arrangements that will result in efficient and effective social control of water quality. In my opinion, however, we would be ill-advised simply to go shopping for institutional control systems and choose among them on the basis of the claims made by their purveyors about their suitability for solving our problems. If we are wise shoppers we will not go into the market until we have identified our needs as precisely and clearly as possible, for only then will we have a firm basis for picking and choosing among the many softwares and hardwares that politicians, lawyers, engineers, equipment manufacturers, economists, and ecological action groups press upon us. Impulse buying often leads to dissatisfaction and disillusionment, and perhaps this symposium is itself one reflection of a widespread feeling of dissatisfaction and disillusionment with the results of our present institutions for water quality management.

In this paper, then, I return to the drawing board. I work outward from the problems of water quality control toward the sorts of institutional arrangements that are needed to deal with them; once we know what we want, we should not have too much trouble finding it.

THE NATURE OF ENVIRONMENTAL PROBLEMS

What is the nature of environmental problems? I have noticed that engineers describe water quality problems in terms of nouns, such as mercury, phosphates, oxygen demand, or suspended solids; correspondingly their solutions run in terms of removing the offending substances either before or after these are discharged to natural waters. To judge by the hiring practices of governments and the decrees of governmental agencies, governments conceptualize the problem in much the same terms.

Ecologists perceive the environmental problem as the disruption of natural cycles and the consequent malfunctioning of natural ecosystems. The adjective "natural" is their operational word, and despite their protestations that man is a part of nature, they tend to see man and his activities as the villain in the piece. Their suggested solutions run in terms either of popular philosophy (replace the growth ethic with an environmental ethic) or of a crude appeal to the police power (ban this, curb that, prevent population growth, license technology, and keep corporations under close surveillance). The ecologists have won a wide following among the general public, have obtained support from the media and a section of the legal fraternity, and have received a good deal of lip-service from governments. They may take a large part of whatever credit is due for sundry laws and for the institutions of the ecological activist group and the environmental impact statement. (In Canada, the environmental impact statement tends to be used only after the event; in the United States it is required to be submitted before the event. In both countries it has increased the demand for paper, ecologists, and lawyers, but its significance, if any, for environmental control is not yet clear.)

While ecologists see environmental problems as disruptions in natural systems, economists see them as exceptions to market systems. A small but growing band of economists has set out to remedy this "market failure" and to protect the natural environment by bringing it under the shelter of Pareto-optimality. Economists have so far had no impact on institutional arrangements for controlling water quality, which is probably just as well, for in my opinion they have had an unfortunate effect on views that are widely held within professional and governmental circles about what optimal institutional arrangement for water quality control would look like. In particular, economists have made the problem seem so complex that elaborate simulation models processed by computers become necessary to calculate an optimum solution even for highly simplified models of actual pollution problems. I believe that this way of looking at water quality problems is socially dysfunctional, and I shall now turn to an extended discussion of why I think economists started down a blind alley when they first interested themselves in water quality problems.

THE ECONOMIST'S MODEL

Since markets and prices for the use of water for waste disposal purposes do not exist, economists set out to calculate shadow prices for them.

The prices were designed to reflect the damage done by so-called "technological externalities," which were thus to be internalized and, therefore, exorcised. The model most commonly employed was that of an upstream and a downstream user on a river. The solution was that the upstream user should be taxed, or charged an amount of money per ton of waste discharged that equalled both the marginal damage done by his discharge to the downstream user and the value to the downstream user of the marginal ton of abatement.

It is easy to see how this way of approaching the problem led immediately to awesome complexities. Instead of two users, assume two dozen. Then the damage done by each user to others depended on their relative positions on the river; moreover "damage" functions for parameters such as dissolved oxygen varied with space (or time) since water "purifies itself," and charges therefore depended on absolute distances between users as well as on their relative positions. Diffusion models became, in principle, necessary to allocate damages among dischargers. Then there arose the question of whether technological damage functions were proportional to dollar damage functions and whether linear technological functions were close enough approximations to the real situation to be useful. It was recognized that any change in location of the users (perhaps triggered by the charging system) or any entry or exit of users would necessitate calculating a whole new set of charges. As new parameters of water quality were added to the model, the complexity increased. Seasonal factors were added to take account of different flows in the river. Dozens of other complications could be visualized, but already, from the standpoint of actual water managers, the game was becoming of the same order of complexity as three-dimensional chess and was no longer of practical interest.

Despite the apparent reasonableness of the economist's model, it has, I think, serious conceptual flaws. An equilibrium price equates marginal cost and marginal value, which are therefore equal to each other when the market is in equilibrium. But it is, of course, impossible to calculate an equilibrium price from either the cost or demand function alone, except in a few special circumstances that are unlikely to be encountered in practice. In a frenzy to measure, however, economists pushed on. Benefits of cleaner water were considered unmeasurable because they included such things as the aesthetic values both of cleaner water itself and of ecological changes that would accompany cleaner water; it was therefore decided to measure the damages (or costs) done by pollution. Once the damage functions were sketched out on a discharger-by-discharger basis, the numbers that emerged became a set of "damage cost" charges that were to be levied on a discharger-by-discharger basis and that were implied to be optimum. In general they are not.

First, since damages are benefits foregone, one does not in general avoid unmeasurability problems by claiming to measure damages. It is clear that damage to aesthetic values cannot be measured and that in practice damage cost measurements are measurements only of measurable damage. Furthermore, in the absence of any knowledge about whether measurable damages are of the order of one per cent or of ninety-nine per cent of total damages or about the functional relationship between measurable and total damages, it becomes very difficult to maintain that some measurement is better than no measurement.

Second, the conclusion of damage cost analysis that charges ought to differ for every discharger strikes me as odd. I suspect it derives from some implicit assumption about space—and it should be noted that economics is notably weak where space relationships are involved. All I can do here is present an argument from analogy. Consider a market for potatoes in a town square. A single money price that "clears the market" is taken by economics to be a Pareto-optimum price. Yet it is clear that behind the observed money price lies a set of shadowy prices that differ for each marketer. The "utility price" that includes the time and trouble of getting to the town square and lugging the wretched potatoes home no doubt differs for each purchaser; similarly the "effort price" of growing and marketing the potatoes differs for each seller. There are of course some other "prices" that tend to even out these differences in the shadowy prices; rents that vary with land fertility and distance from the market and housing prices that decline with distance from the market are examples of spatial "eveners." In any event, markets do have a spatial dimension, or a zone of influence, and a single money price for a commodity within this zone has long been considered by economists as a sign of Pareto salvation. Imagine their horror if they were asked to recommend the following "damage cost" system of pricing potatoes. "Consumers do damage by buying potatoes. They use up soil fertility, human tissue, human time, machinery, oil, wood, and jute—not to mention the damage they do to other consumers by not letting *them* enjoy the potatoes. Consumers should pay different prices for potatoes grown by different producers, the price to be calculated, as well as may be, by the value of the damage done by growing and marketing the different batches. Damage to the grower—an estimate of the labour costs involved in producing the potatoes—should take into account the topography of the farm (hilly land involves more effort than flat land), the weather conditions in the area (an "inclemency index"), and so on. A traffic congestion charge must be levied against potatoes taken to market during rush hours." Given such a conceptualization of optimum pricing for potatoes, one can imagine the funds that would be allocated to such research projects as "A Computer Simulation of Optimum Management Strategies for Growing and Marketing Potatoes in the Lower Fraser Valley." I do not understand why economists reject such nonsense for potatoes and promote it for water management.

Finally, note that in assessing damage charges against upstream dischargers rather than downstream users, or as well as downstream users, those who believe in damage cost pricing are implicitly making all sorts of value judgments that they probably do not realize they are making. If a downstream user increases his production and uses more of the water fouled by his upstream colleague, thereby increasing "damages," why should the upstream man bear the costs of the downstream man's actions? Why should not the charges be levied against the downstream "pollutee" rather than the upstream "polluter"? After all it takes two to create damage—and according to the "damage cost" principle, the damage could be reduced by the downstream man's installing a water treatment plant as well as by the upstream man's installing a sewage treatment system. Fortunately, economists are beginning to realize that *all* relationships are reciprocal—that the arbitrary designation of one variable as independent and the other as dependent is an invidious business—and that the cry that "the polluter must pay" is meaningless because he cannot be identified. Damage cost pricing, with all its computational complexities, questionable logical foundations, and dubious moral connotations, may be on the way out. "None too soon!" is my sentiment.

ESTABLISHING DISCHARGE LIMITS

Having ridiculed others' conceptions of the water quality management problem, I must now reveal my own conception of the problem and expose it to the ridicule of others. First and foremost, I view the problem of water quality management as one of allocating a scarce resource that I shall call "the waste disposal capacity of natural water systems." Resource allocation is an economist's problem, but not a monopoly of economics; governments, legal systems, and sociological systems, as well as market systems, allocate resources. "Resources" is indeed a word that is hard to define, since it includes the many connotations of natural resources, human resources, cultural resources, and so on. There is some advantage in replacing it with the phrase "rights to do things." The water quality management problem would then be defined as "the allocation of rights to discharge wastes into natural water systems." In the past there has been no allocation, or limitation, of rights to discharge wastes into natural waters; the right to do so has been a "common property" right available without charge or permission to anyone who wished to use it. The common property nature of the rights is the institutional arrangement that leads to the water pollution problem and incidentally to the failure to control those "technological externalities" that so exercise economists. Accordingly, any solution to the pollution problem involves removing the right to discharge wastes into water from the "common property" category and "allocating" it. Allocating the right to discharge means (1) limiting the amount of waste that may be discharged, and (2) adopting some rule for distributing this limited amount among dischargers. There are many ways of improving water quality, but they all involve putting less waste into the water. The object is to improve water quality, not to assess damages, internalize externalities, punish public malefactors, make polluters pay, create employment for engineers, or preserve ecosystems.

The first principle of any water quality management system is that the allocational decision of how much waste may be discharged into natural waters—of the extent to which the right to do so is to be limited—must for all practical purposes be made by a government. The reason is that a natural water system is an integral whole that admits of only one owner; and only the owner can decide whether the use of water for waste disposal is to be limited and, if so, what the limit shall be. There is no known system of deciding what the optimum capacity of a water system to carry wastes is, mainly because the "product" of a given level of abatement activity—the quality of the water and the types of ecosystems associated with that water quality—are what economists call "public goods." There is no practicable method of determining the demand for a "public good" and therefore no way of determining its optimum production. In practice only a crude trial-and-error political process determines the amount of goods and services such as schooling, miles of highway, courts, police protection, and national defence that are provided on a "public good" basis (whether or not there exists an alternative to collective supply). Inability to determine the optimum level of water quality is, of course, no reason for not raising quality above the existing level if it is judged to be unsatisfactory, any more than inability to determine the optimum number of courtrooms is a reason for not supplying any.

The decision about capacity and the decision about how the capacity is to be distributed among users are quite separate. The second problem can often be solved by allowing *decentralized* decision making to operate. Thus if a municipal government owns a swimming pool of a certain capacity, it can set a user charge that is high enough to ensure that the capacity will not be exceeded and then let those individuals who are willing to pay the fee use the pool; it need not set up a commission to decide who may use it. The capacity question *must* be answered by a government; how to distribute that capacity is a question that has many solutions, each characterized by a different set of managerial operating procedures.

There is, therefore, a clear analytical distinction between the two questions of capacity and the distribution of capacity, and logically the first question should be answered first since the capacity limit should provide the constraint within which the solution to the second problem is formulated. In practice we have put the cart before the horse. I know of no government in Canada that has announced a waste discharge limit for the waters in its jurisdiction. Unwillingness to do anything that may seem to check "economic growth," readiness to avoid making a decision until the "experts" can determine what the optimum capacity is (which as we have seen will be never), and an ingrained political preference for avoiding issues are possible reasons. The result has been that governments have tended to concern themselves with the second allocational problem and have allowed the answer to the first to emerge as a by-product of various "solutions" to the second. Effluent standards on an industry-by-industry or plant-by-plant basis expressed as pounds of discharge per unit of production, for example, establish *relative* discharge rights among industries or firms; their effect on total discharge capacity is a function not only of the standard but also of output decisions by the industry. Even if the immediate effect of the standards is to reduce total discharge by, say, 5 per cent, growth of the industry by anything more than 5 per cent will, with the established standards, result in a fall in water quality. Water quality can *only* be improved and the improvement maintained by setting a total discharge limit that is less than present total discharge and *then* arranging for the distribution of this capacity among dischargers under the constraint that the sum of individual discharge rights must not exceed the established limit on total discharge.

In discussing the first principle of water quality management I have been careful to say that "a government" or "some government" must provide an answer to the first allocational question. What government? The answer depends on the answer to the regional, or zoning, question. In my view, the second general principle of water quality control is that large national or provincial areas should be divided into several regions (perhaps watersheds) for management purposes. The basic justification for a regional approach, in my opinion, is not to facilitate management, but to make it possible at least to preserve the existing variety of ambient water qualities and perhaps to increase it. In other words, regions are desirable so that the stringency of total discharge limits may vary; to increase variety in water quality the most stringent limits should be applied in regions that now have relatively high qualities and the least stringent in regions that now have relatively low qualities. So far as I know there is no "scientific" way of identifying regions. The regional decision, like the capacity decision, must be arbitrary, and it must be made by government. There is no shortage of arbitrary, government-defined regions in Canada for all sorts of activities ranging from voting through schooling to fishing, but so far as I know neither the Canadian government nor any provincial government has yet established a water management region.

The minister of the environment for Canada opposes regional water quality management, fearing what he calls "pollution havens" if some regions were to impose less strict controls on discharge than others. He is therefore in the process of setting effluent standards for industries and sections of industries that will apply across the country. These he refers to as "national standards," though sometimes he talks of "minimum national standards." If some provinces were to apply higher standards than the minimum, they would presumably become "pollution deserts" rather than making the others into "pollution havens." It is most unlikely that differential costs of water quality control among regions would have any significant effect on the location of population or industry. The world is full of geographical price differentials—there are wage havens, tax havens, rent havens, milk havens, vegetable havens, and beer havens—and the effect of one more would make little difference. Locational decisions involve a net balancing of dozens of price differentials; there is no reason whatever to think that differential pollution costs between regions would be so large as to dominate all other geographical differentials. The fear of "pollution havens" reveals deep respect for economic growth and comparatively little concern for environmental quality.

It should be noted that management of water quality on a regional basis, as I have outlined the problem, implies *no* management at individual sites within a region, that is, no attempt to control locational decisions and no differential in effluent charges or effluent standards on a locational basis within the region. With a fixed total discharge limit and no locational control, discharge might very well increase in any one part of a region—but if it did there would necessarily be a corresponding decrease in other parts of the region. Management by site would lead to all the complexities of damage-cost pricing. No administrative structure, I feel sure, could cope with the problems of site-by-site management either effectively or efficiently.

Consider briefly the national effluent standards now being developed in Canada as a good example of a procedure that fails to control water quality in Canada or in any part of Canada. The pulp and paper standards, for example, differentiate between old and new plants. The standards for new plants are the more stringent; they have been promulgated and affect one plant in Canada. The weaker standards for old plants have not yet been promulgated and therefore are not in effect. The standards are specified in terms of "pounds of pollutants per unit of production." The amount of waste discharged into Canadian waters by the pulp and paper industry will therefore depend not only on the standard but also on the output of the industry. The amount of discharge into various regional waters will depend on the locational decisions of the industry. There should be some immediate reduction in discharge when, and if, the regulations for existing plants are promulgated; after that, future changes in discharge from the industry will depend entirely on output decisions of the firms in the industry. It is intended that such a "control" system will be developed for all major industry groups and for municipalities. Once they are in effect, future changes in Canadian water quality will be determined by industrial and municipal growth, as they have been in the past; and changes in regional water quality will be determined by locational decisions of industry and differential rates of population growth—as they have been in the past. Plus ça change ....

I now summarize the argument so far. My main contention has been that no institutional arrangement for water quality management has any chance of working well until the nature of the problem is properly understood and the objective of management clearly expressed in operational terms. It seems fatuous to say that the quality of water in Canada, or in any region of Canada, can only be raised by reducing the amount of waste that is dumped into it; but in fact endless debate about assimilative capacity, optimum discharge, responsible behaviour, income distribution, and jurisdictional authority has effectively obscured that simple and obvious point. Almost equally obvious is the second point, agreed to by all, that the only possible "owner" of any significant natural water system is a government and that only a government, therefore, can establish and enforce a total waste discharge limit for that water. My third point is that discharge limits by regions are desirable; and it is obvious that only governments can establish jurisdictional regions. I have also argued strongly that there is no scientific way of establishing either water regions or waste capacity limits for any given region; governments must do the best they can. But only when they have defined regions and established waste discharge limits for those regions will it be possible to give managers an operational objective that will ensure an improvement in water quality. To the best of my knowledge, no such objective has been given to any water quality control agency in Canada. Instead, agencies have been told, in effect, to do something about water quality, which is the sort of instruction that is guaranteed to produce much frustration for the managers and little in the way of improved water quality for the public; managers do not have the power to make the political decisions that are prerequisite to effective management. Water quality control depends not only on the technocratic ability to manage but also on the political will to control; in Canada, as in many countries, it is the political will that is the weak term in the equation. Where there is no will, there is certainly no way.

TECHNIQUES FOR DISTRIBUTING DISCHARGE CAPACITIES

Under the (unrealistic) assumption that a government has set a total discharge limit for a particular water region, I now pass in review various techniques for making it effective. It will be seen that the main task of management agencies is to solve what I called above the second allocational problem, namely, to establish a system to distribute the total discharge limit among dischargers. I assess the various techniques in terms of their effectiveness, their ability to do what they are intended to do, their efficiency, and their relative costs. I specifically exclude any criterion of distributive justice; if it is possible to achieve any desired income distribution, only a government can achieve it. Income distribution is clearly a different problem from water quality control, and any attempt to use water quality management as a means of affecting income distribution will reduce either the effectiveness or the efficiency, or both, of water management. The effectiveness of any water management technique depends in a crucial way, as we shall see, on the ability to measure the variables that the technique operates on. The efficiency of a scheme depends on how closely it achieves the marginal conditions for cost minimization, as established by economic science.

If preaching in its various forms—publicity campaigns, informational programmes, and propagation of some particular code of ethical behaviour—may be considered an institutional arrangement for water quality management, it may be summarily dismissed as almost completely ineffective. It misconceives the nature of the pollution problem, for it does nothing to change the common property nature of the right to use water for waste disposal purposes. As Garrett Hardin has demonstrated beautifully, it sets up a tension between conscience and rationality, and since rationality usually wins out in the long run, preaching about the evils of pollution produces guilt, not an improvement in water quality. Preaching has clearly led some dischargers to reduce their waste discharge—thereby creating opportunities for others to increase *their* waste discharges without worsening water quality! Even if preaching in fact reduces the marginal propensity to pollute for all dischargers taken together, the gain will probably be short-lived, since economic growth will erode the effect of any given individual ethic as surely as it will erode the effect of any given set of individual effluent standards.

Living necessitates discharging wastes, and the social problem involves the questions of how much waste is to be discharged, in what forms, by whom, and in what places. No environmental ethic can programme a discharger's conscience in such a way that he will know how much waste he "should" discharge in any given situation or what his response should be to the constantly changing conditions of his and others' operations. Judicial processes are also very poorly adapted to the control of a collectively supplied good such as water quality. Riparian rights have proved unworkable except in socially insignificant cases involving private parties of roughly equal power; no state can be expected to protect the quality of a stream flowing through private property against the interests of an upstream municipality of half a million people that discharges effluent from a sewage plant into the stream. Nor can the present fascination with court cases utilizing badly-worded old or new laws that "forbid pollution" be taken seriously; attempts to bend bad (because unworkable) laws to virtuous purposes, like attempts to bend good laws to evil purposes, smack of deviousness.

More important than these "strict interpretations" of the law is an attempt, through "class action" or "public trust" cases, to adapt the judicial process to environmental problems. Courts are asked either to protect assumed rights of individuals, or classes of individuals, to a certain supply of a collective good (water quality in this case) or to assert such rights if they do not exist. Proponents of this solution, a group that probably includes only a minority of lawyers and judges, always seem conveniently to ignore the fact that everyone, including the plaintiff, both gains and loses something by *any* change in water quality and the further fact that on balance some individuals and groups of individuals will in all probability be net gainers, and others net losers, as the result of any change in water quality. If those who advocate judicial remedies recognize these facts and still maintain that judges are in a better position than legislators to decide what level of water quality best serves "the public interest," let them defend the proposition in print before they assert its validity in court. Suppose they make their case; the second allocational problem is still left dangling. The courts decide that present total discharge into a certain river is too large; but there are a hundred dischargers using the river. Should they all be hailed into court? How will the judges decide how much each should abate? Should some be prosecuted and not others? If so, why? The idea that courts are capable of providing satisfactory solutions for the management of a collectively-owned resource, like the idea that individual consciences can magically provide the answers, reflects either a misunderstanding of the problem or an attempt to avoid it.

Statutory control of pollution is the best form of control in those few cases when it is decided to ban the use of a substance either completely or with a few stated exceptions. The ban is appropriate when a substance is known to be dangerous, though not exactly *how* dangerous; when there is no practicable way of preventing its entrance into water systems; and when the risk of using it is judged to outweigh the benefits of using it. DDT fits the first two requirements, and in a growing number of jurisdictions it is deemed to meet the third. Such cases are rare, but whenever they arise a law banning the substance in question is obviously the cheapest and most effective way of dealing with the problem. (By comparison, appeals to conscience or to courts would have been a slow, uncertain, and expensive method of dealing with the DDT problem.)

We have nearly exhausted our list of institutional arrangements for allocating discharge capacity and so far have succeeded in doing nothing except ban DDT! The regulatory board, commission, agency, department—call it what you will—must obviously be the institutional home of our water managers. But the board, as I shall call it, is perhaps the most protean institutional form that political man has ever invented. It defies definition and reduces one to the circular comment that it is what it does. In the remainder of this paper I shall set down in a simple and thoroughly dogmatic form how I think managers in a water quality control board should operate. You will recall that I have assumed that their political bosses have already given them an areal jurisdiction and an instruction—which I shall now suppose reads "Reduce waste discharge by at least ten per cent." The managers' task is to come as close as possible to this target by a combination of means that involves the lowest possible social cost—including their own salaries in the cost calculations!

Let them start by dividing waste into two categories: discharges that can be measured (usually in terms of mass) and those that can only be roughly estimated. Not knowing total discharge, they cannot, obviously, reduce it by exactly ten per cent. They can reduce the measurable portion by ten per cent, and they can take measures that they think will probably reduce the other discharges by at least ten per cent—and if they miss the mark, neither they nor anyone else will know it!

To regulate the measurable discharges (pounds of suspended solids; the oxygen consumption of biodegradable effluents; ounces of mercury; calories of heat; pounds of salt; and so on), an economic mechanism must be used. There are two of these—effluent fees and discharge warrants— and both are so superior to any form of effluent standard, subsidy, tax break, or negotiated "deal" that there is really no comparison. The superiority comes in the efficiency dimension. The economic costs of achieving a given amount of discharge reduction by one or the other economic technique are minimized, which is not true of any other scheme; the "transaction costs" of operating an economic scheme—and here discharge warrants have a definite edge over effluent charges—will almost certainly be much less than for alternative schemes; and the "enforcement costs," the costs of ensuring the effectiveness of a scheme, are no more for economic techniques than for the alternatives.

Let me add a word about measurement and enforcement. If a discharger promises to meet an effluent standard or to pay for the effluent he discharges, the only way to know whether he is fulfilling his promise is to measure his effluent. The measurement is commonly performed by some combination of regular sampling and irregular inspection. It is possible that the liability for payment under the economic schemes may be more cheaply determined by self assessment (as in the liability for income tax) plus spot checks. Each discharger might be required to draw up a "materials balance" statement for his operation, to file a statement of the production processes he uses, and to calculate a figure for "materials discharged per unit of production." Such a statement could be certified by a "chartered engineer" (on the model of the chartered accountant), filed with the board, and, along with an annual statement of production, used to calculate either effluent fees or the number of discharge warrants required to be bought. Changes in production processes leading to reduced waste output would permit the discharger to submit new statements, again certified by a chartered engineer, in order to qualify for a reduced assessment. It should be noted, finally, that any "market" sort of system is to. a large degree "self-enforcing." Checks on effluents under an effluent standard scheme would not, presumably, be made public, but the fees paid by a discharger could easily be published; under a warrants scheme the number of warrants held by a discharger could be routinely published, or it could be required that the warrants themselves be displayed in the office of the plant. Competitors, journalists, or busy-bodies would do the rest!

Managers would not have much discretionary power in operating the economic schemes—which must be considered a major advantage—but we must give them direct, discretionary, decree-promulgating powers when it comes to discharges that cannot be measured at any reasonable cost. Here there are two sets of situations. As an illustration of the first, let us assume that it is known that run-off from farmland is a significant source of water pollution, that it is either impossible, or unreasonably expensive, to measure the discharge for any one farm, but that the conditions that are likely to lead to heavy discharges are understood. Then all that the managers can do is to manage by direct decision and decree; for example, they may require that no more than a certain amount of fertilizer be used on fields with a certain slope that lie within three hundred yards of a watercourse. The technique is almost certainly non-optimal by Pareto standards, may not be very effective, and will certainly be difficult to enforce. But is there a better alternative?

The second "unmeasurable" situation is the analogue of the farm situation in an industrial setting. A substance in the effluent from a plant is known to be harmful, though its amount is not measurable; on the other hand, a technique is available that is known to be effective in transforming the substance into an innocuous form. In such cases, the managers should have some cost-benefit analyses performed and, depending on their results, require that some or all dischargers of the noxious substance install the corrective technique. Again, the "solution" cannot be Pareto-optimal, but it may nevertheless be very much worthwhile.

CONCLUSION

I now summarize very briefly my understanding of how water quality may best be controlled. The politicians, by whatever process of decision making they wish to employ, must first decide on regions, jurisdictions, and discharge limits. As to the discharge limits, let me emphasize that nothing drastic or dramatic is either necessary or desirable. A political decision to improve water quality by ten per cent, or five per cent, or one per cent, or even to freeze it at its present level would almost certainly represent an improvement over our present situation. Let governments do *something* and later do a little more if the results of the first move prove desirable; let them make progress slowly. So much for the objective. As to means: no preaching; modest use of the judiciary; statutory prohibitions in special cases; regulatory boards which are required to use either effluent fees or discharge warrants when effluents are measurable (but always to use them on a "zone" basis and never on a discharger-by-discharger basis) and to use their discretionary powers when effluents are unmeasurable.

7

Environmental Protection: The Complexities of Real Policy Choice*

Marc J. Roberts

INTRODUCTION

The economics literature on environmental problems has not fully confronted the great complexity either of natural systems or of the policy options available for altering man's impact upon them.[1] To help fill this gap, this essay considers the practical merits of various pollution control strategies. The focus is on all those nasty problems of information and decision costs, uncertainties, and imperfections, which simple price-theory exercises too often ignore.

The root issue is illuminated by Schelling's discussion of the traffic light as a resource allocating device.[2] Such lights make many wrong decisions. A man with an important errand is held up while someone without pressing business (or no one at all) passes the other way. But the costs of operating the process are low. One need not, indeed cannot, hire a lawyer to plead his case at each intersection. The resources thus saved more than make up for the allocative inefficiency. In addition, special exceptions (fire engines) and the availability of a more sophisticated and costly procedure when needed (a policeman) improve the functioning of the system.

The neo-classical model portrays the economy as a complex, perfectly balanced Swiss chronometer. Change an adjusting screw one degree, and

* The work underlying this study was initially supported by the Workshop on the Regulation of Economic Activity, Harvard University, with funds provided by the Brookings Institution and later by the Environmental Protection Administration. Earlier versions were presented to a seminar of the Committee on Urban Public Economy (C.O.U.P.E.) in Madison, Wisconsin, the Applied Microeconomics Workshop at Harvard University, and the Seminar on Water Quality Management at the University of Victoria. The helpful comments of the participants in these meetings are gratefully acknowledged.

the whole mechanism precisely responds. Alternatively, consider the easterner, walking down the street of a small Texas town who sees an old prospector hit his burro over the head with a two-by-four. The dude intervenes, protesting, and the grizzled sourdough replies, "Jus' tryin' to get his attention." Is the economy more like a watch or a burro? Are finely detailed adjustments or crude tactics called for?

In the course of the analysis, I will try to show that the economists' usual enthusiasm for the use of special prices or taxes for environmental protection purposes is not fully warranted. Compared to effluent standards, such schemes have fewer virtues and more difficulties than has generally been acknowledged. In so far as we wish to employ any decentralized method, mixed schemes are generally superior. In particular, marketable pollution rights, in conjunction with fees and subsidies, have some very desirable features. But given the limits of all decentralized methods, the centralized provision of clean-up services also is an attractive option in certain circumstances. On the other hand, judicial remedies are mainly valuable as a supplement to, not a substitute for, administrative process. Input subsidy schemes are also considered and found to be of limited value. As a preliminary matter, we shall have to define (indeed redefine) "the environmental problem" in order to provide a framework for the discussion of policy options. Only when we realize why the current situation is inadequate and what a "solution" to the "problem" might look like can we judge alternatives effectively.

WHAT IS THE PROBLEM? A FIRST STATEMENT

To begin, note that an "externality/public good" is any output of any economic activity that matters simultaneously to more than one consumer.[3] Neither the physical nor the psychic effects have to be the same for everyone (nor even different from zero for most). The Strategic Air Command and a neighbour's obnoxious barking dog raise the same "problem": the "correct" level of production can only be discovered by "adding up" and equilibrating the marginal costs and benefits that accrue to *all* affected parties. For the sake of argument, in this context by "correct" I mean the traditional Pareto-optimum criteria; namely, that no mutually beneficial gains from trade remain unexhausted.

Production and consumption processes which affect the environment clearly generate such externalities. But what "problem" do such externalities present? Should we worry that a market economy, on its own, might not arrive at "Pareto-optimality" when such goods are present? As Coase has argued, if all trades were "costless" and all participants "rational," by definition all mutually beneficial transactions would occur.[4] As a result, we can conclude, tautologically, that *in a perfectly frictionless world the economy must wind up in a Pareto-optimal situation, regardless of externalities.* For example, in such a world, if the harm caused by a smoking factory were greater than the cost of cleaning up, those harmed would organize to pay the factory to limit its emissions to the "correct" level.

In the real world, there are two main reasons why perfect, voluntary bargaining about externalities does not occur. First, the "game" of bargaining over the externality might be structured so as to give rise to perverse incentives. As a result, the players find it difficult to arrange agreements which would make everyone better off. Second, high transaction costs could prevent otherwise mutually beneficial trades from being negotiated. This latter possibility raises some problems in the definition of "optimality," to which we return below.

The first of these difficulties is a type of "prisoners' dilemma" problem and is known in the public choice literature as the problem of "the non-revelation of preferences," or the "logic of collective action" problem, or the "free rider" problem—depending on whom one reads.[5] The argument depends upon four assumptions: (1) there are a large number of beneficiaries of the good, all of whom assiduously seek their own self-interest; (2) the provider of the good cannot deprive any one person of benefits except by changing total output and thus depriving everyone else; (3) clean-up is financed by voluntary contributions or taxes based on what is known about how much different individuals benefit, and (4) no one consumer, by his own consumption choices, can alter the benefits derived by other consumers.

In such situations each person might expect to gain by claiming to assign a low (or negative) value to a good like pollution abatement. If his fellow citizens provide clean-up anyway, the understater gains and yet does not pay. If enough people behave this way, their calculations will turn out to be incorrect; no action is taken and everyone winds up worse off: the classic "prisoners' dilemma" outcome. Large numbers are crucial. Otherwise, each individual will know that his expressed valuation can be expected to affect the level of externality control.

While such phenomena do help to explain why it is so hard to organize *private* bargains to control widespread environmental effects, they cannot explain all of our environmental difficulties. In the real world, one or more of the pre-conditions of the argument are not infrequently violated. First, people do not always behave on the basis of narrow calculations of self-interest as opposed to following cultural norms about what is "good" or "right." Many individuals vote, help strangers, voluntarily curtail water or power use in a crisis, or contribute to charity.[6] Such phenomena suggest that, were it not for other difficulties, voluntary efforts might not be totally futile, if such action were deemed socially appropriate. After all, many do contribute time and money to environmental lobbying organizations and receive only "ideological" satisfactions in return.

A different assumption of the model is violated in cases where those who claim not to care about cleaning up the environment (and do not contribute) can at least partially be deprived of the benefits of any action which results. Such situations contradict Samuelson's classic formulation of the "public good" problem, in which he considered a single parameter commodity for which only the level of expenditure/output could be varied.[7] On such assumptions, each level of output of such a good produces a *fixed* distribution of benefits. It maps to a point in the space defined by the utility levels of the various beneficiaries. What I am suggesting here is that the distribution of benefits might be *variable* for any given expenditure level. Each level of expenditure would then map to a frontier (or a set of points) in utility space—depending on the technology of production.[8] For example, a co-operative mosquito-spraying programme undertaken by the households around a lake could at least partially slight the lands of a non-participant.

Thus, in the real world, an individual who duplicitously claims not to care about a public good cannot always expect to "get away" with it. The likely outcome depends upon a number of features of the situation. Can any one person's benefit be easily denied him or must others also be affected, and, if so, how many and to what extent? In addition, what resources can be saved by such action? Without presenting a full formal argument, we can hypothesize that the greater the potential savings and the more separable the benefits to individuals, the more likely it becomes that those who claim not to care will receive little or no benefits, lowering their incentives to understatement.

There are clearly some environmental issues where the distribution of benefits can be varied significantly, for example, the location of roads, power plants, and oil refineries. Perhaps as a result, in such instances widespread lobbying and public protest (if not exactly voluntary bargaining) has often taken place. If you do not complain, the "public bad" winds up distributed (located) in a way that injures you particularly.

Note that the whole game theory argument is typically not applicable to the case of goods provided by the government, where the non-revelation problem usually does not arise. Such goods, environmental and otherwise, are not usually financed either by voluntary contributions or on the basis of expressed individual valuations. The members of the Sierra Club or Friends of the Earth do not face higher tax bills when they successfully lobby to keep the Colorado River wild or for a new national park. Why then not state, even overstate, one's preferences? (The latter actually seems more characteristic of our public choice processes than non-revelation.)

In addition to these game theory problems, the information and decision costs of arranging voluntary transactions for environmental goods do help to explain why more such trades do not occur. Environmental externalities usually affect large numbers of individuals. This greatly increases the costs of reaching an agreement. The complexity of various options and the multiple uncertainties involved also raise the costs of bargaining. So does the fact that the benefits to any one individual are often small and difficult for the individual to determine, even for himself.[9]

Under such circumstances, an investment in bargaining—or even in defining one's own position—might well not seem worth the expected returns. As a result, no one tries to arrange bargains which could be in everyone's interest—if only the transaction costs were lower.

In practice, transaction costs are often the relevant obstacle to voluntary arrangements. In contrast, the static inefficiency that results from charging fees to customers who can be served at zero marginal cost is widely tolerated. We charge for seats on uncrowded airplanes and in half-empty movie theatres—perhaps in order to generate information that will help guide long-run capital investment decisions. It is not so much the fact of non-rival consumption (zero marginal cost) but rather the technical difficulties of excluding non-payers (a type of transaction cost) that has hindered the creation of certain kinds of environmental markets.

There is a theoretical difficulty, however. Once decision and information costs are considered, it is possible to argue (tautologically) that the world is always in a Pareto-optimal situation—from an expected utility viewpoint. Is everyone not always "intendedly rational," trying to do the "best" he can, "all things considered"? For any unmade move, then, at least one of the participants must believe that in view of the likely decision and transaction costs, the change is not desirable in an expected utility sense. Otherwise the move would be made. Even obvious inefficiencies that result from decisions which are clearly mistaken *ex post* may not indicate non-optimality. Such choices could easily have been made on the basis of optimally imperfect decisions rules and information, which inevitably lead to error some of the time. (This is quite apart from the "bad luck" of drawing an unfavourable outcome from a known stochastic process.) But perhaps these were errors whose expected costs *ex anti* were believed to be lower than the costs of avoiding them. How then can we call *any* outcome "inefficient"?[10]

To understand the definitional problem more clearly, consider a group of men who (wrongly) chose to cease bargaining when there were still unachieved gains from trade. Perhaps they believed (mistakenly) that such gains were less than the costs of continuing or that they had exhausted such gains. Suppose too that a little more investment in information gathering and decision making would have revealed the desirability of further negotiation. They did not undertake such an effort, however. Each of them had a "rule of thumb" which said (1) detailed analyses of whether additional bargaining is beneficial will not "pay off" on average in the long run, and (2) it is not profitable to spend too much time worrying about possible exceptions to the previous generalization. If these rules were reasonable—and note that they too were chosen "imperfectly"—in what sense is the outcome "Pareto-optimal" or not?[11]

To answer this question, we must realize that a Pareto-optimal outcome can only be defined in terms of a given information state, a given set of decision costs, and a given set of objectives for each of the participants. In order to characterize an outcome as non-Pareto-optimal, the observer must proceed from an evaluative position which in some respect differs from that of the actual participants. How can we identify the "best guess" choices of others as "mistaken" unless we know more than they, or can make better (cheaper) decisions, or have different objectives?[12]

In addition to perverse incentives and transaction costs, two other explanations of environmental market failure have been offered which I consider less important but wish to discuss briefly. First, believers in the efficacy of free markets have argued that environmental "property rights" are not clearly defined.[13] How can the necessary transactions occur, they ask, when ownership is unclear? The state—which defines property rights—is thus at fault, not the market processes themselves.

In my view, this contention is not well taken. Most environmental property rights are quite clear. Firms and households have effectively "owned" the air, land, and water for waste disposal purposes. It was not any obscurity in the system of property rights which prevented the citizens of New York from banding together to pay Con Ed to emit less sulphur into the air. Environmental property rights often are non-exclusive and are shared by large numbers of individuals. Many others can also dump waste into the stream I use. But joint rights are still rights, as buyers and sellers of non-exclusive patent licenses and property with rights to the use of community facilities will attest. By defining "defect" appropriately, one can assert tautologically that all transaction costs and incentive problems are really "caused" by "defects" in the system of property rights. But it is not clear what insight one gains as a result of this terminological manipulation. (The relationship among property rights, liability rules, and transactions costs is complex to say the least—see below.)

Second, Arrow has suggested that when only a small number of individuals are involved in bargaining, the imperfect markets that result do not guarantee a Pareto-optimal outcome.[14] In such cases, participants might make strategic moves (for example, all-or-nothing offers) in order to capture most of the gains from trade for themselves. Threats, mistakenly perceived as bluffs and "called," may in fact be carried out. Participants in a good position might be unwilling to negotiate further when there are still gains from trade. They might be fearful that social or cultural pressures—or a coalition of other participants—will force them to give up what they already have won. Non-Pareto-optimal outcomes seem distinctly possible. This is especially so if the participants are playing an ongoing series of games, environmental and otherwise. In that case, their credibility in each depends on their behaviour in others.

In environmental problems, however, large numbers are generally involved. In practice, transaction costs and perverse incentives usually are the more relevant difficulties. Yet on occasion the many participants have been effectively aggregated into a small number of actors through political processes. When this occurs such bargaining problems can arise. For example, the relevant states could not agree on any Columbia River Basin Compact after twelve years of negotiation. Yet that was a situation in which almost undoubtedly there were some gains from trade that might have been realized.[15]

The conclusion of all this is that our current system of markets for allocating environmental resources is not making the "correct" allowance for external effects because of incentive and transaction cost difficulties. Now, however, I want to take the argument one step further and contend that in general it is not possible to know what that "correct" allocation would be. Instead of seeking the "best" situation, we must be content with simply trying to achieve a "better" outcome than the one we currently experience.

WHAT IS THE PROBLEM? A SECOND STATEMENT

The usual economist's tactic of depicting social choice problems as seeking the maximum for a known, well-defined, single period opportunity set just does not capture critical features of real environmental problems. First of all, our opportunities are uncertain. Environmental systems themselves are generally stochastic. Furthermore, the behaviour of business and government agencies in response to various policies cannot in fact be perfectly predicted. Those entities have limited information and respond on the basis of imperfect decision rules which are imperfectly adjusted. Such "satisficing" processes (while globally rational) do not yield determinant outcomes.[16]

It is not even clear what choices various actors have open to them in responding to policy choices. The notion of what is "technically possible" is simply not well defined in practice. There is no unambiguous point in the development of a process at which it suddenly becomes "available."[17] In addition, the set of policy options that are relevant in the light of social and political constraints also cannot be delineated with perfect clarity. Samuelson's suggestion that we think of the "politically feasible" set of out-comes[18] seems an unsatisfactory way to characterize the complex uncer-tainties of the process by which policies are selected. And beyond all this, our knowledge of these systems is highly imperfect, which adds an element of subjective uncertainty to all our predictions.

For all these reasons, *the "boundary" of our opportunity set is a fuzzy and ambiguous region.* There is no way to distinguish exactly between what we can and cannot accomplish with respect to environmental protec-tion. For any one period we might think of our opportunities as described by a probability distribution over the set of outcomes. Some are impossible and have zero probability. The decision problem of any actor in the social choice process then can be posed by asking how that probability distribu-tion alters as a result of his actions, such as the expenditure of different amounts of the various resources he commands (time, money, and so forth).[19]

Yet even this is much too simple. Real decisions are multi-period and involve complex strategic questions. Programmes, institutions, and in-vestment decisions are only partially and imperfectly reversible. Informa-tion, opportunities, and attitudes will all be affected by experience. Policies pursued in the short run change the transaction and transition costs among alternative future outcomes and the probabilities that they will occur under various circumstances. Choices are so complex, decision making so costly, and information so limited that it is not very useful to conceive of current policy choices as selecting from the set of complete, detailed, multi-period strategies. Instead, we must proceed sequentially, where policy is successively redefined as information accumulates.

This viewpoint does not lead one to think of policy as trying to fulfill, one by one, the "optimality conditions" of static social welfare maximization. The argument for this conclusion goes beyond the well-known fact that in an imperfect world, piecemeal efforts will not necessarily lead to optimal outcomes.[20] The conventional approach to that difficulty has been to specify formally the more restricted opportunity set and then to seek the maximizing conditions for such "second-best" situations.[21] Instead I urge that we recognize that fuzzy boundaries do not have partial derivatives. We face a very complex incremental search process. And we have reliable knowledge about both our opportunities and our preferences only for situations that are similar to those which we have already experienced. It is neither possible nor rational to try to consider "all" options. Instead, a globally rational strategy requires us to use various simplifications and rules of thumb as we make choices among a limited set of alternatives.

Because our opportunities do depend upon the magnitude and distribu-tion of the transactions costs, they also depend on the institutional ar-rangements and culture of the society. Coase noted that without transaction costs or other constraints, the outcome of bargaining over externalities is independent of how we assign the property rights.[22] *In the real world, however, the pattern of resource allocation we actually experience depends very much on where we begin and on the processes we use to arrange transactions. The initial assignment of property rights in externality situations is thus very important.* If high transactions costs lead to the system being "stuck" at the status quo, the initial distribution of rights plays a large part in determining the outcome.

In our own society we have generally assigned rights to the would-be polluter. It is not fully accurate to say that the relevant markets in property rights for use of the environment as a waste sink do not "exist." Rather the high transactions costs and game theory problems have made it impossible for those harmed to organize an effective attempt to buy up such rights. As a result, the "price" we observe for the use of the environment for waste disposal purposes has been effectively zero. When the price paid for a resource is so low—even low value uses are encouraged. Waste has been disposed of through the environment even when it might have been cleaned up very cheaply and where the damage that results is large.

Because our opportunity set cannot be precisely defined, it is not very interesting to ask if the current situation is or is not Pareto-optimal in an expected utility sense. *The policy problem is simply to develop a strategy for getting to a situation that is more desirable than either the current one or than the outcomes of various other alternative moves* (keeping in mind the implications of each policy for possible future options). The "problem" is not simply that the environment is "dirty." In this, my exposition differs from that of some ecologists who insist that natural preservation should be an end in itself. Instead, I have posed the question in terms of the economist's traditional homeocentric viewpoint which accepts individual experience as basic to making judgments about alternative outcomes. *Thus our task is to devise a set of institutional and cultural arrangements for allocating environmental resources which leads to an outcome where enough individuals are sufficiently better off to make us prefer it to current circumstances.*

Furthermore, in my view, we should not only consider changes from which everybody gains. Information and decision costs and social constraints limit our choices. It may *not* be possible to make everyone better off as we improve environmental quality. Or we might choose not to do so for distributional reasons. Schematically, in figure 1, suppose we begin at point A, in individual utility space, with B and C unattainable. If new arrangements now make them possible, we might choose B, even though C is Pareto-superior to A and B is not. The gains to one man might be large enough to make the losses to the other an acceptable price to pay. Note that putting it this way does not amount to reviving the old "compensation test"

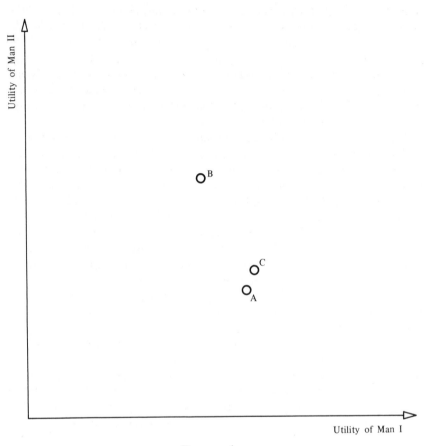

FIGURE 1

once urged by Kaldor, Hicks, and so on, although the incremental spirit is similar.[23] Here we are comparing the social value of actual changes in individual circumstances, not the money payment each party potentially would make to accomplish or avoid the proposed change.

Admittedly, this is not a precise statement. How much better is the outcome we seek? What alternatives do we examine? These questions do not have general answers. Rather they can only be resolved in some specific context on the basis of various strategic simplifications. Social choice itself, to be globally rational, is a "satisficing" process. In order to devise and choose among such policy options, however, we need a better understanding of the substance of these matters. What are environmental systems like? What opportunities and potential benefits do they offer?

ENVIRONMENTAL OPPORTUNITY SETS

Environmental systems are stochastic, non-linear, non-separable, and not infrequently in disequilibrium. Our information about them is imperfect and uncertain, and better data and analysis are very costly. Relevant policy suggestions must respond to these characteristics. In contrast, the aesthetic sensibilities and training of economists usually lead them to formalize the policy problem as a static choice under certainty with perfect information, where all resources are mobile, homogeneous, and divisible.

The limits on our information introduce substantial elements of subjective uncertainty into all forecasts and analyses. We know surprisingly little about many of the relevant biological and chemical processes. Exactly how will various levels of temperature or dissolved oxygen in a stream affect various fish species? What are the health effects on plants and humans of air-borne sulphur, particulates, and nitrous oxides? When is water safe to drink and swim in? The scientific data on such matters are surprisingly skimpy.[24]

Ecosystems also are objectively uncertain. Rainfall and hence stream flows will vary from season to season and year to year.[25] In some years there will be few atmospheric inversions, and in others they will be more frequent. Similarly changes in animal populations are determined by uncertain reproductive processes. In sum, we are uncertain about the shape of the probability distributions that generate our options.

Natural systems also can be imperfectly reversible. The damage done by waste sometimes depends on the slowly decaying stock of the material in the environment (for example, DDT). Often, we cannot modify these situations at all or else can do so only slowly, imperfectly, and at great cost. The bottom deposits in an estuary (which use up oxygen in the water) can only be removed by making very large expenditures for dredging. Some strip-mined land can be at least partially reclaimed. But the costs are high, and there are severe limits as to what can be done in various climatological and topographical circumstances. More young redwood trees can be planted, but the stock of mature ones cannot be expanded in our lifetimes.[26] And some would say that "purity," by definition, cannot be recaptured, that a restored system is never the same as, and is always less valuable than, one which has never been contaminated.

Limitations on "reversibility" make it harder to seek out a good position. Since mistakes cannot be fully corrected, the value of policies designed to preseve options and avoid risks is enhanced. If we guess wrong about the steady state population of eagles, the birds could become extinct. Unfortunately, the harm caused by a "stock" of environmental bads may not become apparent until the stock has grown (irreversibly) to dangerous levels.

Many environmental systems also exhibit non-linearities and non-convexities. To survive normal climate variations, they must be able to absorb shocks of less-than-critical magnitude. But ecosystems can also be pushed too far—past a threshold—which can then lead to large effects. For example, some decline in the dissolved oxygen in a stream caused by the addition of organic wastes may have very little impact on the fish. To the fish it is just like a hot day in a dry summer. But if just a bit more waste is added, the dissolved oxygen level can then fall below a critical point, and many members of certain species will suddenly die.[27]

Such "thresholds" lead to non-linear damage functions. Consider the certain, simple, full-knowledge case for expositional purposes. Suppose we have a number of ecosystems with the same linear damage functions as in figure 2 (that is, constant marginal damages). This means that the distribution of any given amount of pollution among the systems does not matter. Marginal damages are always the same everywhere. On the other hand, threshold effects imply some region of increasing marginal damages (figure 2b). Here the marginal value of clean-up does depend on the final outcome. In this situation a given amount of pollution should be spread around as evenly as possible among a number of such systems if we wish to minimize total damage. Alternatively, if additional waste loads do not matter very much beyond some point (an open sewer is an open sewer), marginal damages are decreasing (figure 2c). Then waste loads should be concentrated in one system. The policy problems raised by such non-linearities are considerable, as we discuss below.

Obviously, not all environmental systems are the same. Real damage functions vary with the receiving medium, the geography, the waste products, the surrounding pattern of human activity, the ecology, and so on. Yet it is not unusual to find multiple non-convexities. There can be increasing marginal damages as we push past some environmental threshold, then decreasing marginal damages until we push through yet another critical area where marginal damages again increase (figure 2d). In water pollution, for example, this might happen as we successfully lost additional species and uses. Faced with such non-convexities, a simple marginal decision criterion might not be sufficient. There might well be more than one point at which marginal costs and benefits are equal! Consideration of *total* as well as *marginal* conditions is then required.

Of course, these diagrams are deceptive. In most relevant ecosystems a great number of parameters matter, and their damage functions usually are not "separable" (cross partial derivatives are not zero). Both particulate and sulphur oxide air pollution, for example, appear to make the effects of the other more severe.[28] Algae growth in lakes depends simultaneously on nutrient levels, oxygen, and water clarity (here clear water creates problems!).[29] The diagrams also do not indicate that the particular shape and

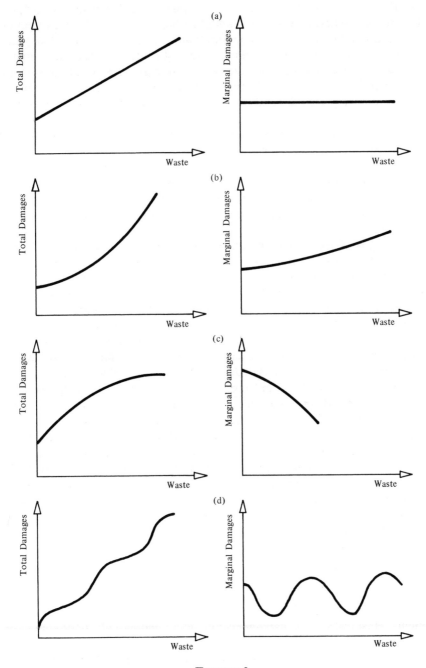

FIGURE 2

position of those damage functions at any one time will depend in turn upon the stochastic natural processes noted earlier. For example, the effect of air pollution will depend on (uncertain) atmospheric conditions like wind directions, thermal layering, and so on.[30] In addition, the value many people will place on any one ecosystem will depend on what happens in other situations. For example, the value of preserving clean air in a smog-free desert may well depend on whether there are twenty or zero other unspoiled areas.

The social systems whose responses help to define the opportunity set for environmental policy are also known only imperfectly. Who ultimately pays for property taxes? How will manufacturers respond to various pollution control regulations? How will local governments adjust taxes or services to pay for environmental programmes? These processes too may be stochastic, and their behaviour is a matter of substantial professional controversy.[31]

As a way of seeing our ignorance more clearly, consider how difficult it is for us to measure, or even conceptualize, the benefits of environmental protection. We might sort these into five categories: (1) materials damage, (2) health, (3) recreation, (4) direct aesthetic pleasure, and, less usually considered, what could be called (5) ideological benefits or the value of the unexperienced environment. Damages to materials are probably the easiest effects to measure and the least important. In contrast, the difficulty of gathering direct, self-report data on consumers' willingness-to-pay for recreation opportunities has led to the use of conceptually more ambiguous surrogates like the time and money devoted to recreation purposes.[32] Health benefits, from a consumer sovereignty viewpoint, should also be based on willingness-to-pay. Yet the existing studies employ expected treatment costs and income losses, which make no allowance for pain and suffering or attitudes toward risk and death.[33] Aesthetic benefits are even more troublesome. What parameters of an ecosystem matter to individuals from an aesthetic point of view, and can potential beneficiaries place monetary values on these? The few existing studies suggest that citizens typically judge an environment by those parameters which are observable unaided: colour, clarity, smell, and so forth. Yet scientific studies and policy decisions are often made on the basis of quite different measurements.[34]

Ideological benefits are the most difficult of all to compute. Many care about keeping the Colorado River wild or the Alaskan North Slope unsullied who do not and will not come into direct contact with those environments. Besides any altruistic pleasures, many individuals no doubt enjoy simply knowing that these systems are preserved, regardless of what people ever see them. Such non-experiential benefits greatly enlarge the set of individuals who must be considered when making choices about any one ecosystem. Asking those directly along a river what they might be willing to pay to clean it up is not enough. In theory everyone who might care "should" be consulted. Perhaps everyone in the nation is relevant, or even everyone in the world! If we take the councils of utilitarianism seriously, we cannot ignore such a potentially significant source of "utility" simply because it makes decisions more difficult.

Benefits (tastes) and costs (technology) are not just difficult to discover. They also change in response to experience and hence in response to policy. Although we frequently assume otherwise, the value people place on environmental outputs often depends in part on their experiences.[35] The future technology of production and waste control also depends on the research we support and the requirements we impose in the interim. All these magnitudes and relationships are known very imperfectly. And even significant investments in forecasting frequently will offer only very modest improvements in predictive accuracy.

The available analytical techniques for dealing with such complex systems leave many fundamental issues incompletely resolved. There is surely no agreement about how we should make choices about changing our own tastes and values or about how we should "count" the satisfactions of citizens yet unborn.[36] Similarly, there is no consensus on how to place a social value on the various objective and subjective "risks."[37] Many economists—to their and our peril—have self-confidently suggested that they know how to "solve" the environmental system for "optimal" policy outcomes.[38] In fact, neither the data nor the theory support such an optimistic position. At every step we should ask if more complex policies and an additional investment in making choices is worth the cost. Since we are involved in a search process, institutional flexibility and policies which have learning potential are especially valuable.

But how shall we conduct that search process? How shall we pose the policy question in a way that facilitates our analysis of it? That is the question to which we now turn.

AMBIENT STANDARDS AND ENVIRONMENTAL CHOICE

For both analytical and practical purposes, it is useful to distinguish between two (interdependent) aspects of the problems of environmental policy: the condition of environment we achieve—the ambient state—and the techniques we use to achieve that outcome. As a way of dealing with the first choice, several writers have suggested, I think correctly, that we begin by setting—and then iteratively adjusting—a system of ambient environmental standards or targets.[39] Such standards specify quantitative goals for a number of the parameters that reflect the "quality" of each ecosystem. These levels can and should be readjusted as information about costs and benefits accumulates. In effect, ambient standards are a formalization of the "aspiration levels" that are, as Simon noted, a part of sequential, "satisficing" choice processes.[40] Such a formulation is attractive because, given our steadily developing, but still highly uncertain information about both costs and benefits, the usual economist's maxim to equal marginal costs and benefits is simply not "globally optimal." However, defining satisfactory and consistent ambient standards does involve some difficulties, which I propose to review briefly before going on to consider the techniques which might be used to achieve them.

To use ambient standards effectively, we must be willing to readjust them as experience accumulates. Any such standard is at best a very crude approximation to our views about costs and benefits; it can be taken to imply that clean-up beyond the standard is of no value, while violating the standard causes infinite damage. Where there are significant threshold effects, it is easier to set such standards and defend them as plausible. Under a wide variety of circumstances we might well want to avoid such a major increase in damages. In contrast, where marginal damages are more nearly constant (and small), it is difficult to justify choosing any specific quality level as the standard. For example, the language of the Clean Air Act concerning ambient standards appears to presume the existence of some air quality level beyond which the marginal impact on air pollution on human health will be negligible. Unfortunately, it is not clear from the data that there is such a level.[41]

The stochastic nature of the environment makes it still more difficult to set ambient standards. Any given pattern of waste emissions will give rise to a probability distribution of ambient conditions. Both the law and some economists have not faced squarely the complications of formulating a standard in such a context. Should the standard apply to the mean outcome, or should it be stated as a "chance constraint," a level which can be violated only with a certain low probability? The problem is made more difficult because the probability distribution of ambient conditions that result from any given pattern of emissions generally has quite a long "tail." That is, even low levels of waste discharge can be expected to lead, albeit infrequently, to quite low environmental quality when unfavourable natural conditions occur (droughts, severe inversions, and so forth). As a result, it is difficult or impossible to develop a pollution control programme which can ensure that any reasonable ambient standard will *never* be violated.

Unfortunately, a probabilistic rule is almost assuredly not administratively feasible. Determining when such a rule is violated is a matter of statistical inference. One can just picture the experts and lawyers employed by various parties trying to agree on what tests to use in different circumstances! Perhaps the best we can hope for is a rule with some allowed *frequency* of violations—together with some administrative procedures for granting exemptions in special cases (the policeman in place of the traffic light when needed). Determining what routine and non-routine violations to allow involves, among other things, considering the costs and consequences of trying to meet ambient goals even when nature confronts us with circumstances which make that quite difficult.

Current U.S. air quality standards more or less ignore these complexities. They simply specify levels which are presumably not to be violated.[42] The problem of adverse conditions is handled by allowing higher levels to prevail for various shorter time periods, compared to the allowable annual average. At the same time, the mathematical models widely used to relate air-borne discharges to ambient conditions are oversimplified. These typically present only the expected level of ambient conditions—and not the full probability distribution of possible outcomes. Thus, even if the models were accurate and used with precision (which is surely not the case), emissions limits set by using them would periodically fail to satisfy ambient targets.[43]

How should ambient standards actually be determined? A referendum? A legislative choice? An administrative choice on the basis of legislative guidance? Should we limit those whose opinions are considered by making it a state or local decision, or should everything be done by national (or world-wide) institutions? Are new political institutions required for special environmental jurisdictions? To develop and defend an acceptable set of procedures for various circumstances would require an exercise in normative political engineering well beyond the scope of this essay.[44] In making these choices however, we must remember that the government is a device for reducing transaction costs. The costs, as well as the likely outcomes of various procedures, have to be important considerations.

A related issue is whether ambient standards should be the same across the country. This decision is interdependent with the choice of a mechanism for environmental decision making, since a national decision-making body is more likely to produce national uniformity. The U.S. experience with respect to water pollution is interesting in this regard. Before 1972, there was a complex system of non-uniform stream standards, proposed by the states and approved by Washington. In contrast, the 1972 legislation proposed a very high "minimum" ambient goal for all streams—a formulation that seems difficult to defend even as a "crude simplification" for policy purposes. Surely rivers of all sizes, with all varieties of waste loads, all types of river bank development, and in all locations should not necessarily be at the same quality level.[45]

In contrast, the current national uniformity of ambient air quality standards is not totally indefensible from the "traffic light" perspective. It is not clear that marginal health benefits of cleaner air vary very much with ambient concentrations.[46] Such benefits do vary with the population near a waste source, which would seem to imply a need for stricter standards in urban areas. At the same time, aesthetic and ideological benefits are likely to be highest in some of the currently cleanest areas—for example, the southwestern deserts. Given the additional possibility that some air-borne materials may travel substantial distances and the desire to avoid creating relocation incentives, uniformity is not obviously inappropriate. At least this follows for those who would place a high value on keeping wilderness areas unspoiled.

Recent U.S. experience also reveals that ambient standards alone do not constitute an environmental programme. When an ambient goal is violated, all waste sources have contributed and so all are responsible in some sense. Which source should clean up further to meet the goal? This difficulty plagued the enforcement of U.S. water pollution control laws which were based, as noted previously, on ambient standards. An administrative guideline, requiring uniform levels of *effluent treatment,* was soon promulgated to resolve this ambiguity.[47] The same problem has not arisen in air pollution control because each state's implementation plan specifies the particular effluent standards to be met by each existing stationary source. On the other hand, "new source" emissions are controlled by national uniform effluent guidelines.[48]

Complexities aside, for the rest of the paper I do wish to pose the problem of environmental choice in the context of trying to meet a given set of ambient standards. This both simplifies the argument and gives us a realistic setting in which to compare alternative policy techniques. Assuming we can resolve the conceptual and procedural difficulties, how shall we go about achieving such objectives?

OPTIONS: A TYPOLOGY

Given the environmental problem as we have described it, some form of government action would appear to be called for. The alternative is to continue to rely on private bargaining. But unless we alter the structure of that process, there is no reason to believe that it will not suddenly begin to produce more satisfactory outcomes.

Government action helps to circumvent the two major obstacles to private agreements identified previously. Since the funding for a particular project is seldom based on the apparent distribution of benefits from the project, the "free rider/collective action" problem tends to disappear. Furthermore, governments can be effective devices for lowering social bargaining and decision costs. They embody a standing resolution of otherwise expensive arguments over how to conduct the bargaining process. They also spread the fixed (start-up) costs of bargaining over a number of issues. Only once, for example, must we go through the process of choosing representatives actually to undertake the negotiations. Furthermore, if we want to change property rights or liability rules, government action is generally required. But what shall government do?

To see the alternatives, note that each firm or household can be seen as using and producing three interdependent sets of commodities: conventional inputs, conventional outputs, and waste flows with an impact on the environment. The most obvious point of attack for altering these choices is to change the prices the economic unit confronts for one or another of these sets of commodities. Taxes on high sulphur fuels, or on electricity generally, or on sulphur emissions from power plants illustrate in turn policies designed to alter each of these three types of prices. All of these measures can be expected to have some, albeit different, effects on both sulphur emissions and the use of other inputs and outputs.

Alternatively, instead of acting on prices, we could seek to alter directly the quantities involved. Regulations limiting lead in gasoline, driving downtown, or automobile exhaust emissions are examples of such quantity controls on inputs, conventional outputs, and environmental outputs respectively. Again, we should expect all of these policies to have both environmental and non-environmental repercussions. Third, rather than acting directly on either prices or quantities, we can act indirectly to alter the balance between supply and demand for inputs and outputs in the hope that this will affect prices, which will in turn influence the pattern of activity, which will in turn alter its impact on the environment. Programmes to train sewage treatment plant operators or to support research to discover how to lower electricity use by appliances would be in this category. Fourth, we can act directly on the ecosystem. Examples here include adding chemicals to streams injured by acid mine drainage or programming water releases from dams to keep up stream flow and dissolved oxygen levels and keep down water temperature during critical periods.

Each of these four basic approaches might be implemented by using any one of a number of techniques. While some have been mentioned, a systematic list would include at least eight major policy devices:[49] Regulations; Taxes/Subsidies; Public Production; Artificial Markets; Rationing; Moral Incentives/Persuasion; Private Bargaining/Liability Rules. Not all of these methods can be usefully employed in every context. But the number of possibilities is very rich indeed. For example, some states require waste treatment plants to employ only licensed operators. This is a regulation to control a labour input. In contrast, relaxing import quotas on low sulphur fuel is using regulations to influence indirectly supply and demand conditions and price in an input market. On the other hand, allowing accelerated depreciation for pollution control investment is a subsidy for a capital input. Setting allowable radiation releases from an atomic power plant is simply directly regulating an output, while municipal garbage collection is public provision of a waste control process and so on. Clearly we might do many things.

SOME CRITERIA

Concluding that one or another of the various policy measures just reviewed is a "good" alternative in certain circumstances ultimately depends on unprovable ethical commitments. I have argued that social choices are sequential, but what criteria shall we use to guide our search? By way of some brief background, I would argue that the usual form of both individual and group choice is to be guided by some maxims or "moral rules of thumb." Examples are very varied, for example: "Stop at traffic lights" or "Administrative procedures should be impartial and incorporate procedural safeguards." In most cases, such statements are not themselves fundamental moral commitments. Rather, they can only be justified by invoking a number of predictive and normative generalizations which serve to link them to more basic moral principles. Like all "rules of thumb," they are imperfect and incomplete but serve to economize on scarce mental capacity. It is not optimal to spend too much time refining our criteria when that time might be better spent on directly achieving our goals.

This view implies that an argument for the use of certain social choice criteria involves two tasks—neither of which can be fully undertaken here. The first is to describe and defend a set of statements about how the world works. These allow one to say what is likely to result from using a given maxim to guide choices in a particular set of circumstances. The second is to explore the consistency and acceptability of these results in terms of a set of (perhaps incomplete and not perfectly coherent) basic ethical positions.

In the "satisficing" spirit of the analysis as a whole, I propose to avoid such discussions. Instead I will simply list a set of qualities which, I suggest, it would be desirable to have in order to characterize any policy which we do select. These derive from the utilitarian definition of the problem, the common wisdom of public policy making, and my own personal position. They are quite vague and obviously the critical normative judgments come in making the language more specific and in assigning relative weights to different criteria. They are offered here as little more than a checklist of potentially relevant considerations to provide some guidance for the specific discussion which follows.

Reliability. The policy should work as intended. The resulting institutions should function adequately in the hands of the kinds of individuals who can actually be expected to operate them. The risk of major departures from planned outcomes should be reasonably low.

Implementation Costs. The costs of gathering the necessary data and of planning and administering the policy (for example, billing and enforcement) should be acceptable given the scale and probable accomplishments of the proposed programme. These functions should be appropriately divided between public and private sectors to ensure that accurate and informative data are developed.

Efficiency. The policy should avoid short-run technical and allocational inefficiency. It should respond to differences in the costs of clean-up at different locations and for different sources; to variations in the impact of discharges on ambient conditions, and to variations in the value of improving ambient conditions. All relevant technical alternatives should be employable within the administrative framework.

Stochastic Flexibility. The policy should respond to variations in the state of the ecosystem, to the extent that such flexibility is valuable given its costs and gains.

Dynamic Adaptability. The programme should not become entrenched but rather have the capacity to be self-correcting. Some potential for learning and improvement should be designed into the policy.

Technological Implications. The development of new waste treatment technology and new production methods that minimize waste generation should be fostered.

Distribution Equity. The gains and costs of the program, and its net benefits should be equitably distributed both within and among income, occupation, cultural, and geographic groups.

Social and Political Effects. The scheme should foster the development of desirable social and political arrangments and processes. It should be perceived as fair and appropriate and not injure the vitality of other desirable programmes or institutions.

Psychological Impact. Insofar as the programme has an effect on tastes for and perceptions of the environment, it should serve to make individuals more sophisticated about and better able to appreciate both their options and their own responses to them.

Environmental Risk Aversion. The policy should resolve borderline cases in a manner that tries to minimize major long-term, imperfectly understood, environmental risks.

In advancing such a broad set of criteria, I am explicitly departing from the view articulated by Bergson.[50] He suggested that economists can and should worry only about maximizing economic welfare narrowly defined, as opposed to social welfare more broadly considered. His argument was that the socio-economic system was more or less separable, that manipulating economic outcomes left the other variables and parameters of interest largely unaffected. In the environmental area, this traditional view is simply not accurate, its analytical convenience and popularity notwithstanding.

EFFLUENT CHARGES AND EFFLUENT STANDARDS: AN INITIAL COMPARISON

The two environmental policy techniques that have been most discussed are (1) regulations concerning waste output, usually called effluent standards, and (2) schemes for putting a price on the use of the environment for waste disposal, typically termed effluent charges. A comparison between these provides a useful place to begin our study of policy options.

Effluent standards have appealed to both legislators and environmentalists by offering the promise of "getting the job done," and they have been widely employed. Such standards may simply specify the amount of waste each source may discharge into the environment. More usually, rules have required some specific percentage reduction in waste output—compared to a base period—or limited waste output per unit of primary production.

Economists, on the other hand, have generally urged the creation of special taxes or fees based on waste discharges.[51] Such fees, proponents claim, will lead to minimum abatement costs, since each source will clean up until marginal waste control costs are equal to the fee—and hence equal for all sources. It is also claimed that consumers will be encouraged to buy less of those goods which use more environmental resources in their production, since the prices of such goods will rise to reflect the fee.

Fee schemes come in three varieties. When effluent standards are also used, fees are merely fines to promote compliance with the standards. Used in conjunction with ambient standards, fees become a mechanism for allocating the clean-up burden to meet those standards at least cost. Alternatively, it may be that no standards are set, and the fees alone act to balance the marginal costs and benefits of abatement.

Despite the vigour of some discussions, the differences among these approaches should not be exaggerated. Waste sources comply with standards because violation carries some penalty such as fines or jail terms. Thus both "effluent fees" and "effluent standards plus sanctions" confront the discharger with a schedule of penalties as a function of his waste output. For discussion purposes we can make the simplifying assumption that all penalties can be reduced to monetary equivalents. This allows us to portray the distinction between the approaches in terms of differences in the shapes of those penalty schedules. A firm that pays an effluent fee of so

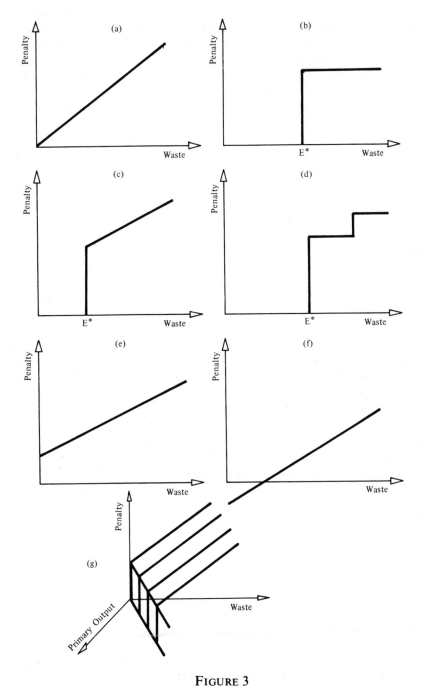

FIGURE 3

much per unit of waste discharged faces a linear penalty schedule as in figure 3a. In contrast figure 3b illustrates what happens when the firm faces a set discharge standard (E*) with a penalty for violation that does not vary with the magnitude of the violation. Penalties that were higher for more serious violations of a standard might imply penalty functions like those in 3c or figure 3d. Fee schemes too can be varied. For example, they might have a positive or negative fixed charge as in figure 3e or figure 3f. Although marginally equivalent to the scheme in figure 3a, such variations could alter the total conditions—that is, whether a waste source operates or not. Notice the similarity between figure 3f, a "fee approach," and figure 3d, a "standard approach." Figure 3g illustrates a standard set in terms of an allowable rate of discharge per unit of primary output, where for any level of primary output the waste source confronts a penalty schedule like that in 3c. Regulations restricting capital or labour inputs cannot be analyzed in this way—which emphasizes their greater difference from the fee approach.

Of course, fee schemes ultimately do depend on still other sanctions (fines, jail) for their operation. In effect, then, a fee scheme confronts the waste source with two different penalty functions, depending on his behaviour. If the enforcement system were effective, however, the penalty function for non-compliance would offer the waste source only inferior options.[52] Since we discuss enforcement problems separately below, to simplify the argument here we will assume that the relevant penalty schedule for a fee scheme is the one generated by having the waste source make the fee payments.

Before using the "penalty function" analytically, I want to stress that it should not be taken too literally. It could serve to suppress relevant differences among various schemes. In practice, for example, fines for violating standards *might* be more uncertain than fees. The judge who administers the first may well have some discretion while effluent fees would be generally fixed in advance. In such cases the issue is, how does this uncertainty affect the likelihood of various responses by the waste source? In addition, the diagrams portray one-period outcomes, while real waste sources confront multi-period decisions. If the penalty for repeated violations of a standard rapidly increased, non-compliance might only be attractive as an interim strategy. Thus, whenever we are trying to understand long-run behaviour, we need to consider as the "penalties" the present value (corrected for risk) of the cumulative sanctions that would result from each continuing waste discharge level. Finally, it may not be easy to reduce the multi-dimensional consequences of violating a standard to a simple money equivalent. Different sources could easily assign divergent weights to various dimensions of the enforcement package so that we could not legitimately write down a unique penalty function.

Despite these limitations, the penalty function does provide a useful way to contrast effluent standards and effluent charges. The key difference is the coercive discontinuity characteristic of the penalty functions typically associated with effluent standards which gives waste sources a strong incentive to clean up just enough to meet the standard. In contrast, linear effluent fee schemes say to the waste sources, clean up until the marginal cost of clean-up is equal to the fee and no further.

The meaning of this discontinuity can be explicated in a stylized manner by asking how the profit maximizing firm would respond to various penalty functions. We can draw a marginal cost of waste reduction curve which begins (with positive marginal cost) at the waste output level characteristic of profit-maximizing production.[53] The cost minimizing firm will contract waste output until the marginal costs of doing so are equal to the marginal penalty avoided. A constant effluent fee implies a marginal penalty function like AB in figure 4a and gives the waste source two options: to adjust to marginally optimal waste output, E, or to move to a corner solution and do no abatement at all (E/M) thereby avoiding any fixed costs. Final choice can be made by looking at the total conditions (that is, net profit) under each option.

The total penalty functions associated with effluent standards do not generate neat marginal penalty functions since the latter derivative is not defined at the point of the standard. For example, figures 4b and c give the marginal penalty functions associated with the total penalty functions in figures 3b and 3. In figure 4b, the marginal penalty is equal to zero except at the standard, E*, where it is undefined. In figure 4c the marginal penalty function is OE*BCG.

In these cases there are two "corner solutions," E/M or no clean-up and E*, compliance. There also can be a marginally optimal partial compliance strategy E, provided the marginal cost of clean-up function intersects the marginal penalty function. (This possibility does not arise for penalty function MC/2 in figure 4c nor for any cost function in figure 4b). In making choices among these local optima, the waste source again needs to look at total conditions, that is, net profits, which depend upon the change in clean-up costs (fixed plus variable) plus penalties at various points. The need to consider such total costs is evident when we realize that penalty functions 3e and 3f give rise to the same marginal penalty functions! (See figure 4d.)

Given that effluent standards do provide an incentive to achieve a particular discharge level, they are relatively attractive when, owing to the nature of either costs or benefits, we know reasonably clearly what waste control we want each source to undertake. In particular, they are most attractive when there are major damage thresholds we want to avoid or possibly large (if poorly known) risks we want to minimize. Why try to find

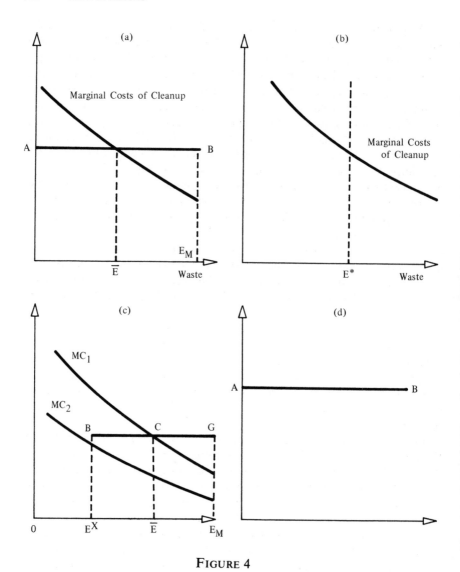

FIGURE 4

the "effluent fee" which will lead to a zero output of mercury discharges as opposed to simply prohibiting such emissions?[54] Standards can also be used more effectively when the technology of waste control is well known and involves only a few options that are similar for all waste sources subject to the policy (for example, municipal sewage treatment).

However, if we are unsure what the marginal cost of clean-up is for each source at each control level, we run the risk that our effluent standards will produce substantial technical inefficiency. That is, we might coerce some firms to undertake very high cost clean-up at the margin, while others achieve the standard while their marginal costs of abatement are still quite low. To put it another way, effluent standards provide no incentive for clean-up beyond the standard, even if that costs little. Fee schemes, in contrast, put both a ceiling and a floor on the marginal cost of the waste treatment activities that any one firm will undertake. This avoids the waste of resources that could come about from incorrectly set effluent standards. However when our knowledge of waste control technology is most limited and fees appear most attractive, we also face the greatest uncertainty about how firms will respond to them. Will we then meet our ambient standards or not? *Thus the choice between the approaches turns to a great extent on a comparison of the risks of inefficient input use and the risks of not achieving environmental targets.*

We can identify several circumstances which do serve to increase both the risks of inefficiency in waste control and the attractiveness of fees as a policy measure. These include uncertainty as to control costs for each source, variety in the nature and technology of those sources, and highly varying marginal costs for different waste control levels. Fees also have an advantage in those cases where ambient standards are most arbitrary and difficult to set, that is, where marginal damages are small and nearly constant. In such cases there are smaller risks from moderate variations in ambient quality levels.

On the other hand, fees do not seem to be useful where the "outputs" are hard to summarize in a few measurable dimensions or where the resulting "damage" surface is quite irregular. Design and locational problems are obvious examples. Take the issue of controlling power plant locations. By heroic aggregation, we could try to summarize the total costs of any one location in a two-dimensional "damage surface" defined over real map co-ordinates. But such a surface will have many local maxima. Given such a non-convex opportunity set, it is hard to see how we could usefully construct a fee scheme which would communicate to the "locator" enough information to lead him to the overall "best" outcome. For design problems like aeroplane or nuclear reactor safety, the same issues arise; and there the definition and measurement of the appropriate parameters of the "outcome" seems difficult indeed.

The relative virtues of fees and standards suggested by these simple comparative-static comparisons is only the beginning of the story. We now need to go further and ask about their relative virtues in the presence of "satisficing" waste sources, costly information about a stochastic environment, and an imperfect political and administrative apparatus. The next three sections are devoted to some of these issues.

COMPARATIVE EFFICIENCY FROM SEVERAL PERSPECTIVES

Although it has been argued that, unlike standards, fees will lead to any given level of environmental quality at least cost, this contention is subject to significant objections and limitations. These arise in part because at best we have imperfect information about (1) the costs and benefits of pollution control and (2) the likely responses of waste sources to various policies. Such imperfections are the essence of the problem, since an omniscient administrator could easily either proclaim rules that would lead to the "correct" outcome or else impose the "perfect" fees which would lead to this result.

There are a number of simulation studies of pollution control options on various rivers that claim to show that fees are a superior tactic.[55] In general, these have compared the costs of achieving a given level of ambient quality via rules that require all firms to cut back waste by the same percentage, with the costs of the least-cost approach. But little is proven simply by contrasting such simple rules with fees which are presumed to be so sophisticated as to lead to the optimal result. In the abstract, either fees or regulations could be designed to achieve the low cost solution. To do this, either scheme would have to take into account variations in the costs and benefits of waste treatment for different sources at different points along the river. The questions are: what can we expect each policy to be like realistically and what effects do they seem likely to produce in the real world?

Note, in this context, that even "perfect" effluent fees will only lead to least cost pollution control if two additional conditions are met: namely, waste sources must be effective cost minimizers, and the minimization of private costs must also lead to a minimization of social costs. Unfortunately, one or both of these pre-conditions may not be met in real situations.

Many waste sources are not business firms at all, but households with only a limited capacity to make optimizing decisions. In addition, the local government agencies that operate waste treatment plants are also often less-than-perfect cost minimizers—especially since their survival and growth may not always be fostered by cost-minimizing behaviour.[56] And for all waste sources, including conventional business firms, when information is limited and expensive and the best strategy very uncertain, actual choices will be quite imperfect. The response to any fee scheme will be both non-linear and not fully determinate. It will depend on whether managers notice and how much effort they put into formulating a response.

Cost-minimizing behaviour cannot be assumed, especially in the short run. Even in the medium to long run, firms with market power could have enough "slack" resources not to clean up but rather to pay effluent fees instead—even if it would be cheaper to curtail pollution. Such choices would allow their managers to avoid the private and organizational costs that a major pollution control effort could entail. In more competitive industries, we can hypothesize that firms will have less choice about deviating from least-cost operation. But even there, surely all firms will not invariably act as if all information were free, and all markets perfect. Indeed the process of pollution control itself—especially if it is done efficiently—will tend to create rents for those firms that happen to be located favourably, thus creating additional discretionary funds for some enterprises. Politicians have sometimes suggested that big corporations might unfairly "buy their way out" of an effluent charge scheme, making it a "license to pollute." While economists have generally scoffed at such statements, the existence of "managerial" enterprises with market power does raise the possibility of such outcomes under an effluent fee scheme.

The least-cost property of effluent fees is also undermined when social and private costs diverge elsewhere in the economy. This is just another specific manifestation of the "second best" problem.[57] At most, effluent fees lead firms to minimize their *private costs* of waste control. This is not always the same as minimizing *social costs*. For example, we simply cannot say *a priori* that an effluent fee on air-borne sulphur emissions—a notion which has been widely discussed—will lead to an efficient allocation of resources. Today the private costs of different energy alternatives with different sulphur content (for example, coal, oil, atomic, solar) do not reflect the full social costs of their production and transportation. In addition to various environmental problems, other distortions are introduced by government price regulation, special tax treatment, import and production controls, private monopoly power, and so on. Thus we will not achieve Pareto-optimal fuel use simply by adding a "sulphur tax," since even with the tax, the prices for various forms of energy will still diverge significantly from marginal social costs. Indeed the major point of the second-best argument is that we cannot be sure, unless we examine the specific situation, whether making one more price equal to marginal costs will even move us in a desirable direction. The use of effluent fees can thus only be justified by an analysis of the case at issue.[58] Do note, however, that the same objections apply to performance-oriented (as opposed to input-restricting) standards. Defenders of such standards have argued that firms will seek to meet them at least cost. But even if firms are cost minimizers, they will seek to minimize the private costs of meeting such standards, which does not imply that they will minimize social costs.

Another efficiency claim made for fee schemes is that they alone will lead to "correct" prices for final goods in light of the latter's relative use of environmental resources. This too, however, is not easy to establish. First, imperfect firms in imperfect markets may not set prices equal to marginal costs. And there are also second-best problems here. In addition, standards will bring an increase in both long-run and short-run marginal production costs, perhaps even higher increases than fees for some firms (depending on exactly how the standards are specified). On the other hand, standards, might result in different, and perhaps very different, average and marginal costs for various producers in an industry. With competitive forces limiting price differences, substantial effects on profits could occur. Such losses could in turn generate significant political forces—examined further below.

Another aspect of efficiency broadly considered is the effect of alternative policies on the technology of production and waste control. Both fees and standards encourage technologic change because, under either system, waste sources gain by cleaning up at lower cost. But standards only foster new methods which lower the costs of meeting the standards. Unlike fees, they would do little to encourage a new technology whose main impact is to lower the costs of treatment levels more intensive than those the standard requires.

A final aspect of efficiency is the ability of each method to cope with variations in the condition of the receiving ecosystem. Such stochastic adaptability can be difficult to arrange. Perhaps as a result we have only a few examples of such programmes, for example, power plants that switch fuels or curtail operations under adverse meteorological conditions and paper mills that lower production during the annual salmon run.[59] The root policy issue is how to distribute the unavoidable costs associated with the inherent unpredictability of nature. Fees or rules based upon *actual* conditions shift the cost of variations in natural processes to waste *sources*. With *constant* policies, in contrast, the *users* of the environment bear the risks of natural variations. There are also intermediate arrangements. For example, if fees or rules were based on seasonal average conditions, the cost of normal variations would be borne by waste sources and the costs of abnormal variations by users.

Short-run variations in policy are obviously most useful when the technology allows short-run changes in waste output at relatively low cost. In unfavourable circumstances, the character of the capital equipment determines the nature of the waste output per unit of primary production, and the only way to lower waste output is to lower primary output. On the other hand, where waste output depends on material inputs like fuel, there is more to gain by giving waste sources an incentive to respond to changing conditions. This is especially so when natural variations can shift damage functions so that we can suddenly find ourselves in danger of crossing a major damage threshold. The additional monitoring and implementation costs are also a factor in deciding how sophisticated to make our policy measures.

Unfortunately, neither fees nor standards are especially effective in achieving such "on-line" responsiveness. Both approaches decentralize the administration of pollution control. As a result, under either system, responding to changing natural conditions would be cumbersome, expensive, and probably not very effective.[60] Furthermore, fees or standards based on either average or actual conditions would greatly complicate the decision problems of all waste sources. They would find it difficult to compute the "optimal" response, and we would find it difficult to predict their "optimally imperfect" behaviour. Do note, however, that where stochastic variations are significant and where there are significant thresholds in the relevant damage functions, the greater indeterminacy of outcomes under fees implies some special disadvantages.

CHANGES, STANDARDS AND INFORMATION

Some have contended that unlike "correct" standards, it is possible to arrive at the "correct" set of effluent prices without knowing in detail the waste treatment and production costs of all waste sources.[61] The argument is that we can only set standards at the cost-minimizing level if we know everyone's costs. In contrast, charges allow one to decentralize decision making, lowering the information needs at the centre. I want to argue that this claim too is not easy to support except in special circumstances.

To pick the "correct" effluent fee, we need to know how waste sources will respond to such fees, and there has not yet been much experience with such policies. Instead, we must find other means for discovering the underlying production functions that govern waste output and waste treatment. But knowing this much would also allow us to set correct standards. Thus, in general, to set either "perfect" fees or "perfect" standards, we require the same knowledge. The only exception is in the case of a linear damage function. Only there, where marginal benefits are constant, can the correct fee be known in advance—regardless of where the system winds up. Alas, as argued previously, the world does not often exhibit constant marginal damages.

A more complex informational argument on behalf of fees is that one can adjust them sequentially in order to search out the desired solution.[62] The suggestion is that effluent charges can just be raised or lowered until a previously chosen ambient standard is met, and met at least cost, without data on source-by-source waste treatment costs. In the real world, however, there is little reason to believe that such an iterative adjustment process would reach the "least-cost" outcome. Real capital goods are not composed of a homogeneous and malleable "jelly," but rather of poured concrete and welded pipe. Once in place, equipment cannot be costlessly transformed to other uses if changes in effluent fees were to make previous plans no longer optimal. In addition, many types of facilities and equipment are not available "off the shelf," but instead take a substantial amount of time to design and construct. Thus any charge schedule would have to be enforced for three to five years (or more) before one could hope to observe the equilibrium response. And the response to all successive policies will be heavily influenced by the capital stock put in place in response to previous schemes. The system equilibrium would depend on the route taken, even for adjustment periods on the order of twenty to forty years. With costs, benefits and policy changing as rapidly as they do, it is not clear that the system would ever converge.

In addition, if fees were being sequentially adjusted, waste sources would undoubtedly be aware of that fact. It would be foolish to assume that they would act as if each price schedule were permanent, when they knew very well it was not. A complex strategic situation would result, which would make it difficult to interpret the response of waste sources to each set of fees in order to specify policy for the next iteration.

Even where waste control does not require new capital goods but can be influenced by switching inputs, iterative tactics face similar difficulties. Changing effluent fees will alter the demand for various inputs, resulting in transitional, disequilibrium prices in those makets. Only once supply has adjusted to its new long-run level, will prices and the use of various inputs also reach equilibrium. Yet this too will often require durable, imperfectly reversable and time consuming investment projects. Suppose we put a tax on sulphur emissions to the atmosphere. How long would it be before the supply of low sulphur energy readjusted to the new long-term level? It takes seven to ten years to produce a nuclear power plant, three to five years to bring in a new refinery, and so on.

When it comes to the costs of data collection, however, fees do seem to have some advantage. In principle the same data is required under both programmes—namely, full information on what everybody discharges. And, in principle, under either approach some of these costs could be shifted to the private sector by requiring firms to report their own waste emissions. We could use selective check-ups and high penalties for discovered violations to operate such a system (like the income tax). Thus, under either policy, if the waste sources would undertake at least some data gathering (as only seems plausible), we could save resources, provided we could make private monitoring operate reliably in place of public efforts.

The information-cost advantage of fee schemes is quite subtle in the context of such self-reporting. It comes about because waste sources may well face lesser incentives for cheating when they report on their own activities under fee schemes than under a similarly enforced effluent standards programme. The discontinuity in the penalty function with standards implies that the gain to the firm from underreporting could be greater in such cases (where the firm avoids a major penalty) than under fees. Furthermore, it is not clear we will be able to create penalties for failing to self-report which would have a deterrent effect under standards comparable to that under fees. Under standards, the penalty for primary violations might be so high that we could not credibly impose differentially higher ones for failing to self-report such violations. Also our cultural norms do not make failure to self-report a violation as inappropriate as dishonesty in payment of a fee. Indeed, waste sources might wish to avoid the disapproval that could follow if they were labelled as rule-breakers, even if they "turned themselves in." Consequently these reasons for self-reporting to achieve a given level of accuracy might require fewer resources for "checking up" under a fee system than under a standards system.

Under any scheme, data for enforcement could be costly. Some localities with sewer service charges report that it costs over one hundred dollars to do the grab sampling and laboratory procedures required to perform a spot check of an industrial source.[63] Costs are higher for batch processing activities because samples must be collected over an entire production cycle. And such industries are important pollution sources. Some continuous monitoring devices are now available, but they are expensive and not especially reliable. Enforcement is easier where waste output is independent of operating practices and instead depends on capital equipment and material inputs. Then the plant can be inspected once; from then on only production levels need be monitored. But such short cuts are generally not reliable since methods of operation and equipment maintenance typically make a major difference in waste outputs.[64]

In summary, effluent fee schemes may have some information-cost advantages over effluent standards when it comes to the costs of enforcing a self-reporting system. On the other hand, the data required to set a correct policy seem to be quite similar. It is not clear that information-cost differences are large enough to make this a dominant consideration in policy choice.

RELIABILITY AND IMPLEMENTATION

What will fees and standards be like in practice? In particular: (1) what will the reliability of enforcement be like under each scheme? (2) how are politics likely to affect the details of each programme? (3) what impact will price instability have on each programme? and (4) how well will each approach handle the problems raised by continuing economic growth?

Enforcement costs and reliability depend not only on logic but also on culture. For example, the procedural requirements for imposing penalties for violating standards could involve more "due process" than we would insist upon when collecting fees (which also rely on additional fines or jail to coerce firms to comply). *The procedures do not have to be any different,* since either could be handled as an administrative matter. But we might well expect them to be different in practice. As a result, waste sources might well believe that the possibilities of successful delay and the likelihood of having to pay up ultimately will be different in the two approaches. And they could be right.

In general, the possibilities for corruption or simple maladministration do not seem dissimilar for fees and standards. Local building code enforcement is often corrupt (standards) but so is local parking ticket collection (fees). The I.R.S. does reasonably well on collecting money—although cheating, corruption, and expensive court proceedings are not unknown. Yet the F.A.A. too does fairly well in enforcing safety and maintenance standards on aeroplanes and skill standards on pilots. In contrast, federal meat inspection is far from perfect, and the Interior Department has had difficulty in collecting fines for violations of the new coal mine safety law. The efficiency of the enforcement process seems to depend on the details of the particular situation. The career patterns, incentive structures, opportunities, training, and norms of the individuals and organizations involved are all relevant.[65]

However, as in the case of self-reporting, effective outside administration is made more or less likely by the shape of the penalty function itself. Very high penalties can provide a special impetus for violators to buy off enforcers. When such penalties are also widely perceived as "unfair," these transactions raise fewer moral qualms on both sides and become that much more likely. Since everyone will pay some fees under a fee scheme, "confiscatory" fees seem unlikely. Put another way, with fees, the marginal cost of small variations in reported behaviour is likely to be small. Thus the costs that waste sources suffer as a result of honest enforcement are likely to be small. In contrast, a "get tough on polluters" attitude could easily yield very high penalties for violating standards.[66] These could be so severe as to be unemployable (for cultural, political, or economic reasons). Alternatively, they could be somewhat less severe but still high enough, given expensive compliance, to make cheating and corruption of enforcers attractive. Thus, the very discontinuity of penalties which characterizes a standards scheme could help to diminish the reliability with which those penalties are imposed. This is essentially the same argument we used previously about self-reporting.

Another aspect of reliability is the impact of price level changes on various schemes. This seems likely to be a particularly difficult problem for fee systems exactly because they put a limit on the level of the waste treatment costs that will be incurred. The problem is especially serious when the character of inputs has a major impact on waste output and when waste sources find it technically possible and economically desirable to respond to changes in the relative prices of alternative supplies. Suppose, for example, we have a tax on sulphur emissions, and the price differential between high and low sulphur fuel were to rise. Then firms might find it in their interest to buy fuel with a higher sulphur content and to pay effluent fees on their increased sulphur emissions. This will be the socially correct response only if the fee is equal to marginal damages at extant levels of ambient quality—which will not necessarily be the case where fees are being used to achieve a predetermined ambient standard. Similarly, in recent years the economy has observed a steady secular increase in all prices. This means that if the price of waste disposal is fixed in money terms, the real price will steadily decline and with it the scheme's incentive effects.

Political and cultural constraints will also influence the detailed structure of any pollution control scheme. In particular, correct effluent fees may *appear* to be more nearly "fair" than correct effluent standards. Suppose that two plants are located close together on a river and produce similar products via different processes. Suppose also that at any given treatment level, the costs of waste control from the first plant are higher than those of the second. Least-cost abatement would require the plant which can clean up more cheaply to undertake more intensive waste control. The appropriate effluent fee scheme would charge them both according to the *same fee schedule*. However, to minimize costs, they would have to be subject to *different effluent standards*. Such standards may not be "politically acceptable" because of their apparently discriminatory character. Thus the nature of political bargaining and of our particular social conventions could make it easier to institute a "good" fee schedule than a "good" standard system. However, both appropriate fees and appropriate standards would have to vary with location, since neither the physical damages caused by emissions, nor the value of changes in ambient quality are the same everywhere.

Recent American legislation and administrative practice hardly make one optimistic that either sophisticated fees or sophisticated standards will be developed. In the new Water Pollution Act, the bureaucracy is required to create nationally uniform effluent standards for each type of industrial process, based on the "best available" technology, and the "best practicable" technology. Furthermore, the act proclaims the goal of moving the nation to a system of zero waste discharges as well as an interim goal of making all streams "safe for fish and shellfish."[67] Similarly, the water pollution effluent fee proposal that has been considered most seriously in the Congress would have instituted a nationally uniform charge system for water-borne wastes.[68] There have been two main proposals to tax airborne sulphur discharges. One of these would also have set uniform fees. The other would have imposed lower charges in cleaner areas (which may be quite incorrect).[69] None of these fee schemes has made significant legislative progress.

Once an initial programme is established, how can we expect each control strategy to handle the increasing waste loads that time, higher GNP, and larger populations will produce?[70] Maintaining a given ambient level in the face of more waste will require ever more intensive treatment. Standards will have to become tighter or fees higher (beyond any increase needed to compensate for inflation). Will prices prove easier to adjust upward than standards? One might argue that people are accustomed to the former phenomena, while higher standards may be perceived as particularly "unfair." After all, waste sources will already have made investments based on the earlier rules. However, there are reasons to be uneasy about the long run with either scheme, since ambient quality will decline unless someone regularly takes what would be a very unpopular initiative.

Note, however, that certain kinds of effluent standards have been defended exactly as a response to such long-range problems, for example, requirements that all waste sources use the "best" technology. What seems like a nonsensical policy from the viewpoint of short-run allocative efficiency may be less unreasonable when one confronts the prospect of ever-growing wasteloads, uncertain risks, and the fact that retrofitting often costs much more than original construction. Similarly, standards so tight as to be unattainable with current technology have often been justified by their proponents as the best way to spur the development of new methods and devices.

Obviously making such claims for a policy does not mean that those claims are correct. Although in my judgment recent U.S. legislation in several instances has gone too far in this respect,[71] a relevant policy analysis must respond to these concerns. The society could obviously be overly stringent and try to do too much too soon. But discovering whether that has in fact happened requires a detailed analysis of options and probabilities that opponents of recent legislation have not always undertaken. We also need to be sophisticated about the incentives we create in the course of the implementation process. By telling an industry that they will have to use the "best available" technology, we may encourage them to make overly conservative estimates as to what is "available"!

MARKETS IN TRANSFERABLE POLLUTION RIGHTS

An intriguing policy option that combines some of the desirable features of both fees and standards is the creation of new, artificial markets in transferable waste discharge rights. The quantity of rights, and hence the ambient quality level, would be controlled by some public agency. The scheme assumes that it is possible to distinguish more or less independent ecosystems, since the dumping rights in question would be rights to discharge waste into a particular system.

The most notable exposition of this scheme is given by Dales,[72] who clearly had a lake in mind as the example. He presented the plan as an avowedly crude device, designed to short-cut the analytic and administrative problems of other approaches. For each "region" a special agency would prepare a "table of equivalents" that would serve to reduce all wastes to a common denominator. The water control board would then put up for sale transferable rights that allowed the holder to discharge so much waste, as measured by the "table of equivalents." After an appropriate transitional period, all waste sources would have to keep their discharges below the amount allowed by the rights that they had purchased. Presumably, in deciding how many rights to sell, the board would be guided by its understanding of the impact of wastes and its goals for ambient environmental quality.

The special virtues of a rights scheme can be seen by comparing it to a programme of non-transferable effluent quotas that specify the quantity of waste each source may discharge. Either scheme would limit overall waste output and preserve ambient quality even with economic growth and administrative inaction. However, transferability does lessen the possibility of an inefficient allocation of waste control efforts. With rights, voluntary transactions will tend to minimize control costs. Only in so far as waste control is relatively expensive will sources find it in their interests to buy such rights. As with fees, if clean-up is "too expensive" under a rights scheme, a firm will not undertake it but will buy additional rights instead. Like standards, the firm would still face a discontinuous penalty function, once it had bought a stock of rights. But now it has the opportunity of choosing from among a family of such functions.

In principle, the costs of implementing a rights approach would not appear to be very different from those of any other decentralized scheme, since in all cases comprehensive monitoring and an administrative agency would be required.[73] The only advantage of marketable rights is the possibility that violating a standard one has to some extent chosen will seem less legitimate than violating an externally imposed rule. This might make the sociology of the enforcement process more conducive to effective implementation.

Transferability does have political and procedural advantages in coping with the effects of economic growth. If rights are transferable, new waste sources would, and could, simply buy a share of the existing stock of permits. The resulting increase in the price for dumping rights would be the outgrowth of impersonal market forces. this would in turn provide increased incentives to all waste sources to limit their discharges. Such a situation might well be accepted more gracefully than if an administrative body imposed ever tougher standards or ever higher fees over time. The resulting adjustment would be "fair" in the sense of being non-discretionary, which would not be the case under a non-transferable quota scheme. It would also avoid the creation of a potentially very powerful planning authority. Like the traffic light, the process would save on decision-making resources since there would be no role for hearings and arguments over who should bear the burden of clean-up.

The rough-hewn simplicity of Dales's particular scheme is both a virtue and a source of some difficulties. For example, why reduce all substances to a single common denominator?[74] One could, at little administrative cost, require separate certificates for each material since this would require no more data than that needed to evaluate the discharges of each source in terms of the "table of equivalents."

Similarly, we could go beyond Dales' suggestion that we not allow for locational variations in the impact of discharges. Jacoby et. al.[75] have discussed how to construct an effluent rights scheme for a river basin with the following characteristics: (1) only one substance matters; (2) ambient standards exist for only one point on the river; and (3) the marginal impact on ambient quality at the critical point, for waste discharges at various locations, is different for different locations but constant at any one location. Given this "linear environment," they construct a scheme of freely transferable dumping rights that both promote least-cost abatement and also guarantee meeting the quality standard at the critical point. The key is to establish a set of transfer prices which allow certificates for discharge along each distinct "reach" of the river to be converted into those licensing waste output along another reach. The relevant "exchange rates" depend on the relative impact of waste discharged at each location on ambient conditions at the crucial point.

This approach however is limited by the assumption that ambient quality only matters at one point of the relevant ecosystem. This may be plausible for dissolved oxygen problems along some rivers, but it is hardly the general case.[76] Yet the existence of a single set of transfer prices among all certificates depends critically on this assumption. As Montgomery has shown, if we care about ambient quality at several points, there is no way to create a single set of locationally transferable licenses which will both limit waste discharges just enough to meet ambient standards and do so at least cost.[77] Instead, there must be as many distinct yet simultaneous systems of licenses as there are locations whose quality we wish to guarantee. Then we allow each firm to emit only as much waste as is permitted by the smallest stock of licenses it holds.[78]

If more than one substance matters, we might, in theory, create separate licenses to control the impact of each substance at each location we care about. Yet there might not be enough participants in each of these markets to produce competitive results. Wherever market imperfections did develop, the price of licenses could either be too high or too low from the viewpoint of correctly influencing the prices, profits, and outputs of various firms. Furthermore, the "second best" condition of the real world and the fact that actual waste sources may not be perfect cost minimizers both imply that even complex dumping rights schemes might not lead to a Pareto-optimal outcome.

In the spirit of Dales's initial presentation, the dumping rights approach can be defended by claiming that it is intended to be nothing more than a sophisticated "two-by-four," designed to move a reluctant waste-producing animal a few small steps in the right direction. Even from this perspective, however, the administrative and bargaining costs of operating many thin markets (one for each substance at each point of concern) is a potentially significant problem. Alternatively, if we are content with a simplified set of rights, we either might not meet ambient goals or else might not do so at minimum cost.

The fact that such licenses might become expensive over time raises several political and economic questions. Do we want to require local government entities, like sewage or incinerator departments, to buy licenses? This would have regressive distributive effects and might not have the desired effect on such non-cost-minimizing organizations. But avoiding this difficulty is not easy. If we try to omit the domestic waste component of their outputs from licenses, how do we deal with the fact that such entities often also treat industrial waste? To require licenses for the latter and not the former would involve a cumbersome double system with standards for only part of the output. Similarly, if small firms, with poor access to capital markets are unable to compete for licenses, political as well as economic problems might arise, and there might be a need for special programmes for hardship cases (see below). Finally, some may worry that creating a new scarce resource could raise entry barriers in some industries. But in a world of dumping rights, widely held in various industries, this would not seem a serious problem.

The administrative costs of a rights scheme, like those of other policies, would vary with the pollution problem under consideration. Such methods would seem to be too costly when we confront very many small sources, as in automobile air pollution or household heating systems. In such cases, carefully drawn regulations or fees can be cheaper to implement. For example, regulations limiting the sulphur content of fuel available for home use are now widely enforced at the wholesale level—limiting the number of points one need check for compliance.

In operating a license scheme, specifying the penalties for discharging more than one's purchased quota is a tricky matter. If the stock of licenses is low relative to the demand and the price high, paying penalties could be less costly than trying to obtain licenses, at least in the short run. On the other hand, increasing penalties to avoid such a possibility could lead to their being set "too high" for effective enforcement. Diagramatically, in choosing to buy a given quantity of licenses, the firm is choosing its own penalty function. In Figure 5, the market price of a license to discharge one unit of waste is P/L and the fine for violating the license is $UY = XY$, the same regardless of the size of the violation. If the firm buys an amount of licenses E/1, it confronts the penalty function BXYZ, where E/1X equals the total amount spent for licences. If the firm had bought only E/2 in

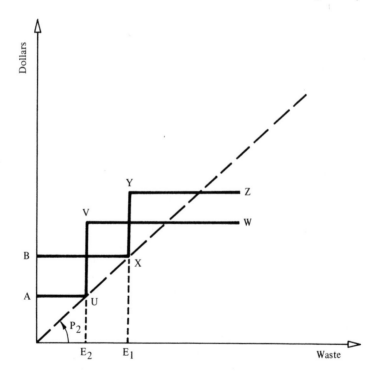

FIGURE 5

licenses, it would face AUVW. The line OUX (whose slope is the market price of licenses) represents the locus of outcomes a firm can reach if it buys exactly as many licenses as it uses. But the locus of such points is only the set of least-cost options for the source if the penalty functions themselves do not intersect it (note that they do intersect it in the diagram).

This discussion implies that penalties for enforcing a discharge rights scheme should increase both with the size of any one violation and with repeated violations, in order to make the "pay the fine" tactic unattractive. In addition, decreases in the stock of licenses should come slowly and with advance warning. Otherwise short-run, transitional scarcity prices and the incentives to cheat could both become very great, undermining the whole system. To smooth the "adjustment" caused by a new plant trying to buy up dumping rights, Dales suggested that the authority should have a stock of "issued but unsold" short-term rights on hand which could be put on the market under such circumstances.

There are obviously many details to be worked out for any marketable pollution rights scheme. For example, what term will the licenses be for? Perpetual licenses would limit the flexibility of the authorities in altering ambient conditions. On the other hand, firms might be reluctant to invest in long-lived capital facilities if they only possess a license for a few years of operation. Similarly, should non-waste sources be eligible to buy such licenses as a way of improving environmental quality? One could argue that the ambient standard implicit in the available stock of licenses is the outcome of a social judgment as to the desired target level of environmental quality. Should we allow this to be overturned by private action? On the other hand, social judgments are not infallible. Given the transactions costs and incentive problems facing would-be "public interest" buyers, their demand for licenses would probably be quite limited. This is especially so if licenses are not perpetual, if a real improvement in quality is being achieved (implying license prices), and if the scheme is being used in a number of locations simultaneously.

Note too that marketable license schemes are not well adapted to responding to stochastic variations in ambient conditions. Conceivably one could sell rights that licensed seasonally varying discharges. But on-line responsiveness to actual conditions does not seem feasible— implying that at best the beneficiaries of clean-up would bear the risks of "abnormal" seasonal variations. And since the distribution of meteorological experience has a significant variance, those risks are not negligible.

SUMMARY AND SYNTHESIS: THE POSSIBILITY OF MIXED SCHEMES

The real world is very much more complex than the one economists habitually draw on their blackboards. The relative virtues and deficiencies of various decentralized schemes arise in part because of differences in their ability to cope with such complexities. Fees have an advantage over standards because they provide incentives even for relatively "clean" sources to go further, if costs are low enough, and hence they also give incentives for the development of new waste control technology. Insofar as sources are cost minimizers, fees also help to avoid the inefficient distribution of clean-up costs possible with standards; especially when sources are heterogeneous and marginal clean-up costs are highly uncertain and highly variable both for each source and among sources. Fees also are potentially easier to enforce, especially via self-reporting, because they produce lower incentives either to lie or to corrupt enforcers. And politically correct fees seem slightly more feasible than correct standards. Standards, on the other hand, offer greater security in attaining ambient targets, especially in the face of non-maximizing behaviour and cyclical or secular price variations. And in theory they could be just as efficient as fees, if enough information were available. Indeed even very crude measures can be made to seem somewhat plausible in the light of long-run strategic considerations and major uncertainties about costs, benefits, and opportunities. Unfortunately, like marketable licenses, neither fees nor standards do very well in coping with stochastic variations in the environment.

Unlike standards, but like fees, transferable rights allow individual waste sources a "safety valve" if their particular abatement costs are high, by allowing total-cost-reducing transactions to occur. Unlike fees, however, they do simultaneously constrain waste discharges as a whole. When the proper conditions are met, marketable rights thus seem to have much to offer. One of those conditions is the existence of an appropriate intermediate number of waste sources; enough to enable the market to function smoothly but not so many as to make administration costly. Another is that the number of pollutants and the structure of the natural system should be such that by using only a small number of different kinds of certificates we can still do quite well in meeting our ambient goals. If we are very concerned about the distributional question, we could arrange to give away some amounts of licenses for a transitional period to hardship cases— licenses which they could resell, however.

Using either "waste quota" type standards or transferable rights does mean that we must predetermine the aggregate amount of waste output. If waste sources have either higher or lower treatment costs than we expected in setting those limits, the only way to adjust treatment levels up (if costs are low) or down (if costs are high) is to alter the stock of rights (transferable or not) outstanding. This in turn involves paying the cost penalties of not designing initially for the final pollution control configuration. To put the same point another way, even if control costs turn out to be less than expected, like standards but unlike fees, marketable pollution rights do not provide any automatic incentive to clean up beyond some predetermined point. Unfortunately for all decentralized schemes, monitoring, enforcement, and organization costs can be expected to be high—especially as the number of sources, substances, and locations of interest all increase.

There are also serious environmental problems for which no output-oriented scheme (fees, effluent standards, or marketable dumping rights) seem appropriate. Problems like land use and aesthetics would seem to require restrictions on, or standards for, inputs. Input standards may also be best for some residuals which are hard to monitor or to attribute to specific sources like stormwater run-off. Here we might be better off, for example, by directly regulating the structure and hydraulic performance of sewage systems.

However, perhaps because they seem easy to administer, input standards have often been used in the U.S. in situations where they are not appropriate. For example, the requirement that municipalities construct secondary sewage treatment plants was accompanied by very little effort to monitor the output of such plants or to enforce performance standards on them. Their actual performance has often been very disappointing as a result. Similar events have taken place, in part because of cost-saving underdesign, where electric utilities have been required to install electrostatic precipitators to remove smokestack fly ash.[79] I would contend that in fact such input standards should only be used very cautiously because of their potential for limiting technologic progress and reducing the incentives to control waste via changes in the design and operation of production processes.

If someone is determined to use standards, there are several types to choose from: effluent quotas or performance rules based on previous waste emissions or regulations on waste as a function of the level of primary production. Of these, only effluent quotas automatically guard against long-run ecological deterioration as waste loads increase. They also focus attention on the "bottom line", namely, what waste is being produced. However, their potential for inefficiency, the economic power they give to the pollution control agency, and their failure to provide incentives for clean up beyond the quota remain serious objections.

To push our discussion further, we have to discard the assumption that the question is "Which one of the available policy approaches should we use"? In fact, there is much to be gained by constructing a mixed strategy which can realize some of the advantages of more than one scheme simultaneously. For example, if we have effluent standards, using effluent fees in addition would serve to provide a floor under the marginal waste control costs incurred by each waste source. If costs turn out to be low, sources will clean up more than the standard to avoid the fees. At the same time, the standards provide some insurance against high levels of damage. Indeed, it is difficult to see why some fees should not be used almost everywhere that standards are employed to provide additional incentives for current clean-up and for the development of new technology. At the same time, any fee programme could be improved if we also instituted special standards for special conditions (such as air pollution emergencies) where avoiding a damage threshold becomes of major concern. This is not quite the police-man in place of the traffic-light, but more like the use of special one-way streets at rush hour.

A similar argument can be made in the context of marketable licenses. We could institute a flat subsidy per unit of waste for any producer who cleans up more than his stock of licenses. This would have the effect of causing additional clean-up if clean-up turns out to be less expensive than was anticipated when we specified the stock of licenses. In effect, it would set a lower bound to the license price. For those who are concerned with such matters, it is easy enough to demonstrate that such a system would imply a cost-minimizing allocation of treatment burdens among waste sources. Either the license constraint would be binding for all sources (with the price of the license above the subsidy) or it would be binding for none. In either case, all would confront the same marginal cost for additional discharges.[80]

Indeed, it is possible to go further and also impose a flat fee per unit of waste output for discharges greater than that allowed by a source's stock of licenses. Such fees serve to put an upper bound on the price of licenses, just as the subsidies considered above impose a lower bound. Hence, if the costs of abatement turn out to be greater than anticipated, firms will all violate the terms of their licenses and, at the margin, pay fees. (Each firm will be indifferent as to the stock of licenses it holds since the license price will equal the fee.) Such a scheme also is cost-minimizing on the usual idealized assumptions.

Regardless of whether one believes that the theoretical least-cost prop-erties of such mixed schemes are of interest in the real world, they do have the pragmatic virtue of allowing the pollution control agency to insure itself against extreme outcomes. The parameter values that define the various fee and license schedules need not be "optimal" for the measures to be useful in actual situations. Yet, despite their desirable features, all such mixed schemes share two weaknesses common to all decentralized ap-proaches. First, they do not ensure that all economies of scale in waste treatment will be exhausted, and, secondly, they do not provide for the use of treatment processes that operate directly on the ecosystem. Are there policy choices which might be used to surmount these deficiencies where they are significant?

PUBLIC PROVISION

The deficiencies of all decentralized approaches provide some argument in favour of centralized public provision of waste treatment and environmental clean-up services. Appropriate public entities might well be in a position to exhaust economics of scale, to operate treatment devices that directly affect the ecosystem, and also to respond directly to changing environmental conditions. Clearly, further discussion of these possibilities and their limits is called for.[81]

The cost savings possible with centralized provision in part accounts for the existence of municipal sewage systems and garbage collection. Some of this savings is not caused by economies of scale (on the *extensive* margin) but rather by what might better be termed "economies of universality," which develop on the *intensive* margin wherever significant fixed costs are required for distribution facilities (for example, water, sewers, gas, electricity). Much the same logic applies to "universal" service functions like police, fire, and garbage collection.

Traditional economies of scale are also relevant in environmental problems, for example, in the construction and operation of sewer treatment plants. These savings may be large enough to dominate the increased costs of transporting waste longer distances so that a least-cost system of sewage treatment will transcend local government boundaries. In many areas, local governments have agreed among themselves to create special joint sewer authorities exactly for these reasons.

The argument for public provision in the face of both these kinds of economies turns on whether the waste sources themselves will reach agreements that allow them to exhaust the available cost savings. In my view, we cannot assume that such private bargains will generally be made. If there are only a small number of waste sources, the possibilities for strategic moves and imperfect outcomes would be quite high. If there are many potential participants, transaction costs would be a significant obstacle. In addition, firm managers might be willing to spend discretionary resources either to maintain their independence of "entangling alliances" with other waste sources or else to get rid of all waste treatment responsibilities. In either case, cost-minimizing arrangements might not arise. We would probably find it necessary to regulate the rates charged by private waste control companies to their customers in order to be sure these reflect marginal costs. Otherwise participating waste sources would not have the right incentives to make internal process changes. Yet the need for such regulation is an unattractive prospect. Unfortunately, we cannot just assume that "correct" effluent fees will in fact bring about socially optimal agreements among waste sources.

Because many of the activities of a public agency would be co-ordinated by administrative and not by market or regulatory processes, it could potentially be able to respond better to stochastic changes in environmental conditions. As Coase and Williamson have discussed,[82] there are cases in which it is easier to transmit information and influence behaviour within an organization than across organization boundaries. That is why ongoing business firms exist at all, instead of constantly shifting sets of contracting participants.

Within an organization, subordinates have an incentive conscientiously to implement conscientiously complicated instructions that it would be both expensive and difficult to transmit and enforce via a system of decentralizing signals to independent profit-making entities. Suppose the waste treatment plants along a river were all operated by a single public agency. When river flows were very low, a central office could simply ask the various plant superintendents to implement additional waste abatement measures. It would be substantially more difficult to achieve the same results via a change in effluent fees or in the stock of available dumping rights, or in the specifications of a set of effluent standards.

Finally, public agencies could operate treatment programmes or facilities to act directly on the ecosystem. To do that, we need an entity which is responsible for the system as a whole. Under a decentralized scheme, no one waste source has any incentive to undertake such activities.

These arguments apply most clearly to certain kinds of water-borne and solid wastes. It is difficult to see how air-borne pollutants could usefully be collected by a public agency and transmitted to a central location for treatment. Similarly, we do not yet have well-developed technologies for operating directly on airsheds (for example, fans to break up thermal inversions). In contrast, techniques like bubbling oxygen into streams and regulating stream flows are already important options in achieving enhanced water quality.[83] It is one of the ironies of U.S. pollution control policy that manipulation of river flows, a potentially very helpful approach to both thermal and dissolved oxygen problems, has been legislatively restricted in its use as a policy tool.[84]

Some environmentalists have gone further and argued that where production activities have important environmental effects, for example, offshore oil drilling, these too should be directly carried out by public agencies. Without going too deeply into this suggestion, we should realize that getting one public agency to respond to the regulations set by another can be every bit as difficult as getting a comparable private entity to respond.[85]

In some special cases we could make a single private entity directly responsible for ambient quality. For example, some electric utilities operate plants in rural locations where no other major emissions occur. T.V.A.

in particular has experimented with adjusting plant operating rates and fuel characteristics when daily meteorological observations indicate atmospheric conditions might prevent adequate dispersion of the smoke plumes from their generating stations. This is a sensible approach provided we are sure that marginal damages from emissions are low under certain conditions. If it were to turn out, for example, that some sulphur components have a significant health impact even under "good" conditions, there would be little point to using such operational controls.

In calling for centralized public provision of clean-up services, we must carefully consider how to organize and control such agencies. In earlier papers I have discussed such matters at some length in the context of water pollution control.[86] There are many complex issues about the responsibilities, geographic extent, financing, and structure of such an agency, too many even to list here. The relevant point for this discussion is that "public provision" itself is not a well-defined policy suggestion—but only a broad strategic approach within which much variation is possible. Indeed, calling for public provision without doing the detailed institutional engineering needed in a specific context makes little sense, since the mere fact of public operation tells us very little about what outcomes to expect.

It is worth reiterating one detailed point about the financing of public waste treatment. I believe that industrial waste sources should face service charges for such treatment which reflect the costs of all actions taken by the agency because of that waste discharge (including more intensive treatment at other locations). Such a system would provide many of the same incentives as an effluent charge for waste sources to modify production methods to curtail waste output. In contrast, I would also argue that the costs to a public agency of treating household wastes should be financed by taxes and progressive taxes at that. Service charges on households would be quite regressive and also would lead to very high monitoring costs. Furthermore, given the household production function for waste, they are likely to bring about little waste reduction. In addition, since households do not resell their output, underpricing their use of environmental inputs does not have the effect of distorting final goods prices, the way comparable policies would in the case of industrial firms.

However, in making these choices, we should not get too carried away by the appeal of bureaucratic integration. Since everything is related to everything else, we cannot internalize all externalities in any organization below world-wide scale. Some other principles have to guide us in reaching a workable administrative compromise. Perhaps fortunately, there are many other ways beside full administrative amalgamation for distinct organizations to co-ordinate their activities. These range from tacit reciprocity, through market transactions, to complex formal bargaining—as Scott has emphasized.[87]

Public agencies, then, are not a magic solution. Both in the U.S. and elsewhere, such entities have been inefficient or inflexible or both on more than one occasion. Ensuring that they will operate properly will require a more systematic approach to the problems of organizational design than we have yet taken. Every student of public policy has his favourite example of a government programme which now appears to have been worse than the problem it was designed to correct. There are also formidable problems in effectively integrating any new entity into the existing political structure. Yet in water pollution control in particular, the arguments for cost saving technology and stochastic flexibility seem substantial enough to make movement in this direction quite attractive.

POLICIES DIRECTED AT INPUTS

We have yet to consider many of the policy options suggested by our earlier typology. While a comprehensive review of all those still un-examined is not possible, we cannot properly ignore the many proposals and programmes which have been directed at the *inputs* into pollution control. These include special tax treatment for qualifying capital invest-ments, grants for research and development efforts, the support of training for sewage treatment plant operators, and many more. In most cases, such policies have been used in conjunction with ambient or effluent standards, with the avowed aim of increasing the speed and effectiveness of private efforts to meet those standards.

Since most of the programmes that have been proposed, notably the many suggestions for special tax treatment, would not lower the costs of waste control by even 10 per cent, it is hard to see why they would have much impact on waste control. After all, waste control would still be a money-losing operation, and the profit-maximizing firm would not volun-tarily undertake such activities. In the standards context, it seems unlikely that such a programme would push any substantial fraction of the heterogeneous waste sources in an area over the dividing line into choosing compliance rather than non-compliance. Furthermore, any input subsidy would alter both the total and the marginal costs of all control efforts— which could in turn serve to distort whatever response waste sources do make by encouraging them to use more of the subsidized input. Recogniz-ing the imperfect character of actual firm decision making does little to change this conclusion. Even if we include the "penalties" of community disapproval and poor public relations, the sort of programmes that have been proposed or implemented for private firms do not seem likely to lead to major changes in firm strategy or expenditures.

Input subsidies in conjunction with fees create a slightly more compli-cated situation. Lowering the marginal costs of compliance will expand the treatment undertaken by maximizing firms which have continuous production functions for waste control. But if we really want additional waste treatment, why not set the fees higher to begin with rather than expand subsidies? The latter device can lead to an inefficient choice of abatement techniques and will have a varying impact on different sources. Indeed, in some cases the available technology offers only a few alternative waste treatment processes, and hence the outcome chosen in response to effluent fees might not be altered *at all* by small input subsidies.

Actual waste sources are engaged in making very complex decisions. They must consider the implications of current choices for the future when production, costs, waste loads, and environmental policies may all be different from what they are today. Such decisions will surely be made "imperfectly," which lessens the extent to which they will be readjusted by small amounts when public policy succeeds in changing costs by a small amount.

Input subsidy schemes also distort final goods prices because they lower the costs borne by waste sources at any given level of waste treatment. This is so regardless of whether we believe prices depend on average or marginal costs. As a result, the signals to consumers to curtail their purchases of products with high environmental impact will be similarly distorted. This problem will be less serious if one believes the previous suggestion that (1) the dollar impact of the relevant input aid programmes is small, and (2) waste sources are imperfect decision-makers, which would presumably include their decision making about prices. However, the larger the input subsidies and the more carefully firms respond to them, the more undesirable they become from an allocational viewpoint.

Using tax breaks to provide aid to firms is especially objectionable because of the "uncontrolled" character of such programmes, as Surrey among others has argued.[88] The legislature has no way to set the total amount of money devoted to the programme or to allocate the funds among recipients according to any priority scheme. Yet such measures are attractive to Congress exactly because the benefit is concentrated and clearly visible to the recipients, while the costs are diffuse and almost invisible.[89]

Input subsidy measures are sometimes justified on the basis of various ethical or distributional arguments. One is the suggestion that it is only "fair" for "the public" to pay part of the costs of waste control since it is "the public" which gets the benefits. On the contrary, I would argue that it is only "fair" for those who purchase goods whose production causes pollution to pay for the costs that their purchases impose upon others. Tax breaks have also been justified as a way of keeping small companies from being forced out of business owing to pollution control expenses. Yet it is hard to see how a programme which subsidizes everyone can be justified as an aid to special cases. Workers or owners of capital can suffer losses when they are deprived of the free use of environmental resources. But this change does not obviously entitle them all to some compensation. If income distribution problems do arise, specific actions might be taken, as discussed below.

In the United States, the largest input subsidy scheme in the environmental area has benefited not industrial but rather local government waste sources; namely the federal sewage treatment plant construction grant programme. These have been partially justified as a matter of equity—an argument I personally find reasonable. Yet incentive effects have also been claimed for this programme. And in this context such suggestions may have some merit. The simple existence or non-existence of certain types of municipal treatment facilities is easy enough for enforcement agencies to check on, which implies that if there are federal requirements for local sewage treatment, local governments can expect to have to comply with them eventually. Furthermore, the federal share began at 50 per cent or more of the capital costs (in 1964) and has since risen. This is large enough to have an impact on local government decision-makers as they contemplate the financial and political costs of compliance versus delay. Unfortunately, it does not guarantee that the plants that result will be properly operated, especially since local governments must bear those costs themselves.

Policies to influence the factor markets for inputs into pollution control could be helpful where those markets suffer from informational or monopolistic imperfections or government-created distortions. However, such problems exist in many markets, environmentally and otherwise. For example, one might argue that the environment in a certain new technology has been "too low" owing to the size and risk of the requisite research efforts and risk adverse attitudes on the part of corporate managers. The implication of such arguments is that more government spending is in order, as some have recently suggested, with respect to the development of environmentally desirable methods of energy production.[90] Similarly, one could act to remove the regulatory restrictions that hamper the production and importation of oil and natural gas. Unfortunately, some of the programmes that have been proposed ostensibly to enhance the functioning of input markets would in fact have the opposite result. They would merely serve to expand the incomes of industry participants, as do many of the existing regulatory constraints or market imperfections which they might more usefully correct.[91]

The rapid implementation of pollution control policies can create temporary disequilibria in input markets. The Clean Air Act for example did sharply increase the demand for low sulphur residual fuel oils. In such instances, governments might try to facilitate the expansion of supply in order to bring about a new equilibrium more quickly. This might, for example, take the form of loan funds (at market interest rates) to assist companies which encounter capital market constraints in trying to increase output rapidly. However, we should be careful in such cases not to reduce the long-run supply price of the input in question. Policies that lead to a permanently lower price for an apparently scarce input only serve to make use of that input larger.

JUDICIAL PROCESS: LIABILITY AND CITIZENS' SUITS

All of the above policies require some *collective* evaluation of the benefits of environmental protection. Given the difficulties of such assessments, several writers have suggested using legal liability rules together with private bargaining and judicial processes to *decentralize* both damage assessment and the implementation of pollution control.[92] There has also been much interest in judicial approaches to improving the reliability of bureaucratic performance. I want to consider both of these issues in turn.

Most participants in the discussion of liability rules have been lawyers. This has led to an analysis which, unlike typical economic reasoning, focuses on institutions and practicality and assumes the existence of imperfections and transaction costs. The discussion has also proceeded from the premise that *any* party to an externality relationship could alter his behaviour to ameliorate the interaction. For example, a factory could clean up its smoke emissions, or the residents downwind could move—or perhaps install air conditioners. This leads to the question, "What is (or should be) a cost of what?"—that is, whose actions should be construed as the source of the problem?[93] This viewpoint is quite different from the perspective of partial-equilibrium economics which has causal assumptions built into the very notion of the production of externalities.

Two main suggestions have been developed. One is to use liability rules and damage suits as a *substitute* for the process of arranging large and complicated environmental bargains. The other option is to use the liability system to *foster,* even coerce, such negotiations. When no negotiation is envisaged, the question is who should be pressured to change his activities by means of the liability rules. The hope is that an effective system of rules could *avoid* the need for a costly bargaining process. The "injured" parties would *not* all have to agree in order to bring about a change in the situation. Instead (while the details vary) at least some of those harmed would just sue those with liability. This should compel the latter to take account of the damages they cause others when they undertake the activities in quesion.

To facilitate this process, it has been argued that the "cheapest cost avoider" should be made liable. He should be pressured to change his behaviour because he can do so at least cost. Unfortunately, this phrasing is not fully satisfactory when clean-up is a matter of degree and not an either/or proposition. In certain continuous cases we have to ask about the costs and benefits of successive *incremental* changes. And in those, I would argue, the rule should be phrased as "Liability should be borne by that party for whom marginal adjustment costs are lower in the initial situation." But that is a small point.[94]

Note that deciding whom to make liable does not involve a comparison of costs and benefits, but of the costs to both parties of altering the situation. As we know from the public finance literature, where they are called "alternative costs," such adjustment costs (say, to the householder for achieving clean air) are *not* in general the same as the benefits an actor will derive from such actions.[95] The balancing of costs and benefits comes once the liability system has been instituted. Then the liable party has to face the choice of paying damages or bearing the costs of altering his behaviour.

Having identified the "cheapest cost avoider," there are many additional details to be worked out. As we make it more difficult for the injured party to prove that he has been damaged, the lower are the probable liabilities of the party we have chosen to make liable. Do we, for example, require independent proof of injury, or do we presume that someone has been injured once certain actions by the liable party have been shown to have taken place? As the evidence we require increases, the number of claims and their total amount can be expected to decline, while their average value will rise. As we raise the cost of proving injury, more of those who suffer sufficiently small harms will not act, since the costs to them of doing so are larger than the likely gains. Similarly, can claims be made only on behalf of one's own injury, or will class actions be allowed?

Michelman has taken this line of argument still further. He contends that ignorance is one of the main reasons we have difficulty in formulating environmental policy. We simply do not know enough about the relevant causes, processes, and consequences. He suggests, therefore, that we might make liable (or responsible) those who will find it least expensive to develop better information about the ecosystem and our options for altering it.[96]

Liability rules can also be used to promote negotiation by allowing injured parties the right to obtain an injunction (removable by mutual agreement) to bar the offensive activity. This compels the party who is enjoined to arrange an agreement with all those who might enjoin him if he wishes to continue his activities *at all*. To do this, it is argued, one should place the liability on the party that can most easily arrange for the appropriate negotiations, that is, on the shoulders of "the best briber."

This analysis has its subtleties. Zerbe has asked why the likelihood of bargain should depend on who owns the rights to the environment, that is,

on who is liable.[97] Suppose there are gains from trade and that one participant could arrange the requisite transaction at a low enough cost to have
some benefits left over for himself. Why should he not proceed with such
arrangements regardless of his liability status? This would seem to imply
that there is no reason to make the "best briber" liable, since transactions
will occur independently of the distribution of liability or property rights.

This contention is mistaken, however, because the incentives which
individuals confront and the associated transactions costs are *not* independent of their ownership and liability positions. For example, suppose that a
business is "liable" for any damages it causes to homeowners in the area of
its plant and needs their unanimous agreement in order to operate. Alternatively, suppose the homeowners were "liable" and must either suffer,
move away, or else raise voluntary contributions in order to pay the factory
to clean up. In the first case, every individual has an incentive to "be
reasonable," since each person's gains cannot be realized without
everyone's consent. The same problem does not face the would-be "free
rider" when the homeowners must raise the payment. If enough others *do*
contribute, his non-co-operation and the resulting non-unanimity will not
be decisive.

Furthermore, the existence of cultural norms and accepted decision
strategies and modes of behaviour means that some proposals are more
likely to arise in the context of one set of property rights than in another.
Suppose that a previously operating firm needs consent from its neighbours
if it is to continue to function or, alternatively, that the firm has the right to
pollute. The firm must have an agreement in the first case but not in the
second. Of course, in the second case, the management, in pursuit of profit
maximization, could conceivably organize a bargain by which the
neighbours pay more than the costs of clean-up (and negotiation) in return
for pollution control. Yet, as recent history suggests, the strategies and
attitudes of managers and citizens make it much more likely that the firm
will act in the first case and not in the second. Contra Zerbe then, the
likelihood that the "best briber" will try to initiate negotiations does
depend on the distribution of real-world property rights.

All proposals to use liability rules in this way do have several deficiencies. First, it would seem difficult to capture aesthetic and ideological
benefits by such a process. Many of the "recipients" of such gains receive
only small benefits from any one ecosystem. Hence they are not likely to
assume the costs of bringing a legal action. And on any reasonable "proof"
criteria, they will have difficulty establishing the magnitude of the harm
they have suffered. On the other hand, trying to coerce bargaining by
allowing negotiable injunctions seems unpromising. The high transaction
costs that have limited agreements in the past will remain. All the injunction can do is to force everyone to incur those costs anyway, in order that

the negotiations might take place. Nor is it obviously wise to let judges use injunctions and very detailed decrees to strike the balance between costs and benefits in particular situations. I would argue that judges are neither expert enough nor possessed of the appropriate political legitimacy to make such decisions. And such a trend would only add still further political pressures to the judicial selection processes.

These same difficulties lead Michelman to abandon decentralization via liability rules as a solution to the problems of air pollution control. He sketches out instead an effluent permit system, perhaps operated in conjunction with effluent fees. Citizens could sue for injunctions against permit violators (although not receive damages in addition) and could also challenge the permits themselves in court. In general this pessimistic view of the possibility of decentralization seeems to me to be warranted. The complexity of the options, the low level of public knowledge, the large numbers involved—all these argue for a less decentralized approach to environmental protection.

Michelman's proposal, however, does raise additional issues, specifically the role of citizens' litigation in the enforcement area. In suggesting that we use citizen suits to keep the bureaucracy honest and conscientious, Michelman is taking a position similar to that of a number of others.[98] These proposals have arisen in a legal context in which citizens ordinarily lacked standing to challenge agency decisions unless especially affected by the action in question. In a number of recent pieces of environmental legislation, however, widespread standing has been explicitly granted for just these reasons.[99] As a result, a number of actions won by "public interest" litigants have had a significant impact on the formulation and implementation of environmental policy.[100] Some of these cases do support the view that such litigation can be a useful corrective to the tendency for an agency and its "clients" to arrange a mutually acceptable agreement. The problem with such agreements is that they often do not give appropriate weight to more diffuse interests that are not effectively mobilized to influence the administrative bargaining process.[101]

Such litigation, however, does have costs as well as benefits. These costs are of two kinds. First, such suits may help to bring about wrong, as well as right, decisions. An agency which seeks to avoid the resource and political costs of a contested action could make mistakes in trying to appease an especially litigious segment of the public. Second, these actions can use up a good deal of expensive technical, legal, and management resources. We have to ask at what point the costs we incur by making such legal actions more attractive begin to outweigh the increased benefits we can expect from doing so.

To help answer such questions, I want to explore the various circumstances that might provoke such actions, albeit in a very stylized way, recognizing that the real world will seldom be so unambiguous. Suppose a citizen complains about what he believes to be a violation of an agency's own rules or of its authorizing legislation. The agency either "acts" or "does not act," meaning that it either does or does not change its behaviour as the complaining citizen asks. As a first approximation, let us suppose that the courts will be able to decide whether the agency's response is "correct" or "incorrect," even though the agency itself does not necessarily know infallibly which is the case in advance.

Discussions of this issue sometimes assume that there are only two outcomes to a complaint—either the agency, properly, acts on it or, improperly, fails to do so. In fact, in addition to these two outcomes, which we could label act/correct and do not act/incorrect, there are two others, act/incorrect, do not act/correct. And these results could come about in various ways. A fuller picture of the complicated possibilities is given in the flow diagram in figure 6.

Four outcomes are straightforward: the agency agrees with the complaint and acts, either correctly (1) or incorrectly (3), or disagrees and does not act and is either correct (7) or incorrect (9). The other outcomes are the results of two possible switching processes. One I have labeled "appropriate switching." Here the agency does *not* do what it believes correct, but for good reasons. The most obvious example is insufficient resources to follow up a legitimate but small complaint. Again, since the agency might be mistaken, even if well intentioned, the final choice could be either correct (10) or incorrect (8). Similarly, one can imagine an agency pursuing a case which it expected to lose, for incentive effects or to clarify the law. The final outcome could be either losing as it expects (4) or, to its surprise, winning anyway (2).

In contrast, "illegitimate switching" has to do with changes made by political influence, the interests or convenience of agency personnel, and other forms of malfeasance or misfeasance. Examples include incorrectly dropping a case to avoid industry pressures, or revoking what is believed to be a just variance in order to appease the ecological activists (5). Note that the agency could wind up doing the right thing for the wrong reasons (inappropriate switching), by acting (6) or not acting (12), or the right thing for defensible reasons (appropriate switching), even though it thought it was doing the wrong thing in acting (2) or not acting (8).

Advocates of citizens' suits appear often to have in mind the case where the agency (correctly) agrees with a complaint but does not act for one or another "inappropriate" reason and as a result makes the wrong decision (11). The notion is that instead of such outcomes, the threat, or fact, of litigation will produce correct action (1). But when the agency does act on a complaint, it is possible that both the agency and the plaintiff are incorrect in believing the complaint valid (3) or else that the agency sincerely disag-

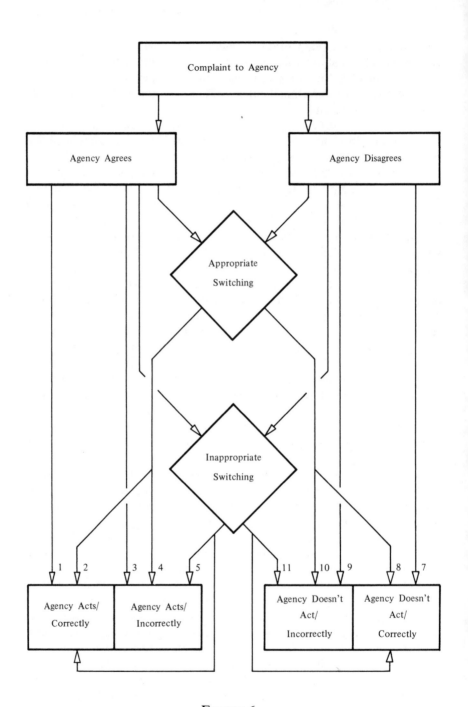

FIGURE 6

rees with the complaint, but instead of not acting (7 or 9), it wrongly acts on it anyway, perhaps to satisfy the protesting group. This would give us outcomes (5) or (6). Note that whether it acts or not, it could be either correct or incorrect. The cost of making suits more attractive includes not only the direct costs, but also whether on balance "correct" outcomes are made more or less likely. Incorrect positive actions on complaints (perhaps for inappropriate reasons) can be expected to increase if changes in the rules make suits from one "party" substantially more likely than those from another.

A different case, but one also clearly in the minds of advocates of citizen suits, is one where the agency sincerely but mistakenly disagrees with the complaint, on scientific or legal grounds, and hence refuses to act. The point of allowing suits here, I take it, is to guard against such incorrect rejections (9). It is not obvious that the court will always be the best place to settle such a disagreement—especially if it turns on divergent scientific opinions. In practice, however, there will be no way to avoid such issues, especially since, even in cases of malfeasance (11), those accused will often defend themselves by contending that what is really at issue is a difference of scientific or legal opinion (9).

The more generously we treat interveners and litigants, the more actions we can expect. But given the philanthropic and ideological nature of many of the organizations involved, it is not at all clear how the level and the distribution of actions would respond to such possibilities as the ability to recover legal costs if successful.[102] Since a litigant will not always win, even if successful suits lead to full cost recovery, the expected returns of any action will still be negative. Only some bonus scheme could make public interest litigation even potentially profitable. And in a regulatory proceeding, there is often no way to proclaim a "winner" that would allow public interest or citizen groups to claim cost reimbursement even if that were a general policy. Especially now, when costs cannot be recovered, it is clear that such actions are not being brought on the principle of profit maximization, since that notion would imply zero activity which would guarantee zero loss.

These issues become even more difficult when we confront the possibility that agencies with limited budgets will make "correctly mistaken" decisions—for example, refuse to consider a complaint in order to conserve on scarce administrative resources. If it were only injured parties who brought actions to overturn such "mistakes" and if they did so despite their inability to recover costs and their unsureness about winning, then we should clearly allow them to do so. If the plaintiff found the data, analysis, and legal costs of such an action worth the potential gains to him, that would tell us to spend more on administration in such situations, since the gains from better decisions are apparently greater than the costs. (This assumes that the initial costs of doing a better job would have been less than litigants' costs in bringing the action—a safe assumption.)

However, under most proposals to expand "standing," plaintiffs would not just be injured parties. This raises a significant problem, because *an optimal administrative system will almost invariably leave some violations unnoticed and some decisions incorrectly made.* Sufficient "public" intervention could thus conceivably force the administration to devote too many resources to decision making in one area. Indeed, some have alleged that this has already happened in the operations of the environmental "impact statement" required by the AEC under the National Environmental Policy Act and in the process of licensing nuclear power plants by the AEC.[103]

Determining the "correct" scope for citizens' and public interest actions depends in part upon predicting how administrative organizations will respond to the resulting pressures. Such concerns as the smooth running of agency affairs, budgetary politics, and public image already provide outside groups with various levers for influencing policy. How will that balance of forces be altered by introducing additional channels and processes? A fuller analysis of these proposals can only be provided by means of a detailed discussion of a particular institutional context, which we cannot offer here.

The substantial enthusiasm for legal remedies among environmentalists seems based in part on the belief that judges are more likely to give a "pro-environmental" answer than a regulatory or administrative body, which often has long-standing industry ties. Nor is it obvious that this conviction has been mistaken. In a number of cases administrative decisions have been overturned by litigation in part because the relevant agencies had not taken environmental concerns very seriously. Within a regulatory or administrative agency, the desire for a quiet life, the lure of industry recognition and approval, and later employment prospects can all lead an individual to take a "reasonable" view of the problems of those with whom he deals. Judges, in contrast, confront quite a different set of options and pressures.

When we look at the matter from a broad perspective, however, the same questions arise about judicial enforcement of agency rules as they do about judicial rule making as discussed earlier. The former, after all, will often turn into the latter in practice. Are judicial mechanisms really the best way for solving complex disputes which often turn on technical issues? Given the sources of judicial authority, there is some tendency for courts to transform an issue from one of morality or policy into one that apparently turns on procedure, on the correct interpretation of statutory language, or on the proper application of constitutional principles. Such a process can surely serve to confuse individual citizens by not making it clear what values underlie alternative choices. Furthermore, having the bureaucracy more assiduously carry out what the judge says the legislature has written will not always be an unmixed blessing.

In all, however, much of the increase in citizen suits and public interest intervention, and the legislation which made them possible, has had a desirable effect. Making policy choices within the context of a close relationship between agencies and interests is a practice open to obvious objections. Opening up these processes can provoke better, or at least more examined, decisions—whose higher costs would seem to be worth the resulting benefits on average. Indeed, decision-making costs should decline over time as new procedures and expectations become established. Given that public interest litigation will always have to rely on philanthropy to some extent, allowing some cost recovery in successful actions would provide more secure funding for such activities. At the same time, we also need to examine the structure of incentives within rule-making and enforcement agencies to diminish our need for such groups to act as "watchers to watch the watchers."

EQUITY: DISTRIBUTION AND HARDSHIP

All of these policy proposals raise issues about income distribution which cannot be avoided simply by claiming that others should make these judgments or by assuming that they will be taken care of elsewhere in the political system. A policy must be judged on its actual results. Since the redistributive mechanisms in the society are imperfect, we cannot avoid the fact that the distribution of welfare will be influenced by environmental and other policies.

Current professional thinking tends toward the view that the U.S. tax system as a whole is slightly progressive, while being proportional over much of its range. Regressive state and local taxation is counterbalanced by the progressive burden of federal taxes. On the expenditure side, state and local expenditure is generally more "pro-poor" than federal expenditure. Such results, however, do depend on the assumptions one makes about several controversial questions, for example, who pays the corporation income tax.[104] Furthermore, for policy purposes the relevant issue is not the total burden of current taxes and expenditures but rather the likely incremental burden as these are adjusted in response to new fiscal pressures.

In particular, most local governments have only two options for financing new programmes: to raise property taxes or to cut back on other spending.[105] Thus, having local governments finance pollution control expenditures (or pay effluent fees or buy disposal rights) means either higher property taxes or lower local services; both of which hurt lower income individuals relatively more than upper income ones. Furthermore, using financial incentives to alter household waste output, like a price on household effluent, would also be regressive, perhaps markedly so.[106]

These distributional problems are made more serious because environmental protection generally will have a broad regressive effect—like a sales tax. The prices of many goods will rise because of pollution control costs. While most such increases will not be large, some consumer goods are quite environmentally intensive—for example, energy. These often are also necessities, that is, lower income individuals spend a higher proportion of their income on them. As a result, the overall effect of environmental protection efforts will probably be to make any given degree of apparent income inequality *more* unequal in terms of the relative command over resources it represents. As I.M.D. Little pointed out, the meaning of an income distribution in a society is not independent of the relative prices of luxuries and necessities.[107]

The likely pattern of benefits from environmental protection may well exacerbate these distributional problems. There is some scattered empirical research to suggest that willingness to pay for environmental gains rises more rapidly than income. For aesthetic and ideological benefits this may be especially the case.[108] Such findings do not necessarily mean that lower income individuals have different preferences; they might just have lower incomes. Yet, because of their financial position, upper income individuals may well also have more opportunity to experience and appreciate the environment; this could increase their willingness to pay for its preservation, relative to those with more limited backgrounds.

Additional light on these matters is provided by some preliminary results drawn from a study of water-based recreation in the Boston metropolitan area, carried out by the author in the summer of 1973.[109] In the study more than 1,000 interviews were conducted at fifteen different recreation sites scattered over the region. The data show that although travel distances are generally small, upper income/education/occupation individuals tended to use higher quality recreation sites and to travel further distances on average. Yet at any given site, travel distances were quite similar for users in different income/education/occupation classes. Users of low quality sites were aware of that quality, although the characteristics they most frequently complained about were those more directly evident on casual observation (for example, trash on the beach).

Since the opportunity costs of travel time for upper income individuals would not in general be below those of those with lower incomes, differences in preferences would seem to play some role in inter-income variations in recreation patterns. That is, upper income individuals are willing to pay the higher access costs of higher quality sites. But differential oppportunities also are involved here. For example, few people with incomes above the median used one particularly crowded suburban picnicking site—with poor quality swimming. Yet this site was heavily used by working class inner-city people of varied ethnic backgrounds. Unlike the users, however, the upper income residents who lived in the immediate vicinity of the site, did have the option of cooking out in their own backyards.

There are also other studies which show that willingness to pay for environmental quality rises with income. And, in particular, participation in esoteric and wilderness activities is even more closely related to income and education (for example, backpacking or white water canoeing.)[110] Again, both taste and resource differences would seem to be at work.

Such patterns of use and attitude imply that the distribution of benefits of environmental protection will depend in great measure on exactly what kind of programme is undertaken. For example, the recreation facilities provided will be a major factor in determining who will benefit from water pollution control. Some people will value highly moderate quality swimming beaches downtown; others will place more weight on the preservation of a scenic lake in a state park twenty-five miles away. Keeping a mountain stream wild, and hence accessible only by canoe, will have different distributional results than opening up camping sites on its banks complete with trailer hook-ups and hot-water showers. For distributional reasons, the "preserve or develop" choice promises to be a particularly vexing one for environmental policy.

This is not to say that environmental protection will only benefit rich people. Much urban air pollution is worse in central city areas with lower income residents.[111] But considering ideological gains and the middle class's higher willingness-to-pay for health, even here the question of who will gain most does not have an obvious answer. At the same time, benefits to upper income households are still benefits. The interests of future citizens in preservation, give the pervasiveness of irreversibilities, are also extremely important. Thus we should not abandon wilderness preservation simply because most backpackers are upper middle class. Furthermore, even regressive financing and progressive (pro-rich) benefits do not insure that the lower income groups will be made worse off by environmental policies. It might be, as a recent study of water pollution control along the Merrimack River has suggested, that *everyone* gains, even though the rich do gain more than others.[112] The complexity of the arguments and judgments involved here only serves to illustrate that a more than cursory concern with distribution does need to be a part of any environmental decision.

A different distributional issue involves the effect of environmental protection efforts on particular firms, industries, or regions. Not infrequently it has been alleged that environmental protection efforts were forcing a plant to close, injuring the workers (and the owners) in the process. As noted above, that possibility has been used as an argument in favour of extensive public outlays for environmental protection. There is a real issue here since whether or not a plant should be kept open may not be a question which the market will answer correctly. Suppose that some of the workers in a plant that closes would be unemployed as a result. This implies that the social opportunity cost of their labour is in fact below their current wage. In such circumstances, closing the plant because private costs are too high might not be socially optimal, since the social costs of that output could be considerably lower.

It is difficult to know exactly what is occurring when a plant closes ostensibly for environmental reasons. In some cases the environment is just a handy excuse for a managerial failure. In others, the firm might be viable in the long run, if only it could raise the necessary capital for waste control equipment. In still other cases the plant would soon close anyway, and pollution control only serves to accelerate that date. There seem to be few situations where pollution control costs are the margin of long-run survival—if only factor markets operated effectively. After all, if nothing else, the firm could go through bankruptcy, and the production facilities could be resold at a price low enough to make them attractive even after pollution control expenditures. Furthermore, a company will only have serious competitive difficulties if it faces especially high pollution control costs compared to the rest of its industry. In a growing economy it is unlikely that price increases caused by pollution control would bring about a decline in demand for the industry as a whole sufficient to force some firms out of operation.

There are cases where some plants in an industry do face much higher pollution control costs than others (for example, kraft process paper mills).[113] Where such plants are old and have short expected lives, their pollution control costs are still higher because any capital investment must be depreciated more rapidly. Larger and newer plants (in paper and elsewhere) also gain from economies of scale in pollution control and have often incorporated some waste control features in their initial construction. In such cases environmentally influenced plant closings appear to have occurred—although perhaps a shutdown would have taken place in the near future.[114]

In deciding how to respond in such cases, we should pay special attention to the composition of the work force involved. Immobile, isolated, elderly workers are more likely to be unemployed following a plant closure than young and well-trained ones in the midst of a tight regional labour market. To facilitate the transition, temporary variances from pollution control regulations could be appropriate in selected cases—provided they were really temporary. Loan programmes too might be considered to overcome capital market imperfections. But even in serious situations, a programme of direct subsidy is not obviously desirable. It would provide an incentive to companies to claim financial troubles (or actually perform badly) in order to obtain funds. And some "endangered" plants should in fact close because the purchasers of their products are not willing to pay the full true social costs (environmental plus production) of the goods in question.

From a distributional viewpoint, the owners of a plant are less likely to be of critical concern than the workers. Indeed, many of the facilities in question are part of large corporations whose owners will not even be able to notice the impact of such closing on their own asset positions. In such cases, programmes directed at the individuals involved rather than the company may be the answer. Yet in saying this, one should recognize the limited success of retraining and relocation efforts in comparable cases in the past.[115] Aggregate economic prosperity, effective regional development programmes, and a significant negative income tax are really the best answers to the difficulties we have been discussing. But in the absence of such programmes there will be some distributional costs of environmental protection, among producers as well as consumers. These costs, in my view, imply a particular need to avoid waste and to proceed efficiently with environmental protection efforts. Furthermore, we should seek to minimize distributional effects insofar as that can be done at acceptable financial and environmental costs.

POLICY DIRECTIONS: SOME TENTATIVE CONCLUSIONS

At the end of such a lengthy discussion, some sort of summary is in order. The arguments that have been presented fall in two categories: conceptual and substantive. Some are suggestions about the nature of the problem and how we should approach it. Other parts of the discussion have been specifically aimed at explicating and evaluating various policy techniques.

On the conceptual side, certain broad conclusions emerge. The first is the complexity of real environmental choices. We are dealing with highly interdependent and variable systems that continue over time. Comparative static models that assume perfect certainty and focus on only one period can at best be very approximate guideposts to policy in such a world. Crucial issues like what environmental risks we should tolerate and how do we evaluate the possibilities of irreversible damage cannot be formulated without using a more complex analytical framework.

Given this complexity, social choices about the environment will inevitably be imperfect and sequential. There is no way to "solve" for "the optimal solution." We are too ignorant of the world and too limited in our ability to influence it for that to be a useful way of portraying the problem. We are simply trying to discover and arrive at a set of arrangements which make enough people enough better off to make those conditions preferable to current circumstances. Formal analysis is helpful, indeed essential, in many specific instances. And the overall approach of decision theory provides a useful framework within which to clarify our alternatives and focus our attention. But the structure of the decision process is clearly a "satisficing" and not a "maximizing" one.

In evaluating any policy proposal we would like to know how we might expect it to operate in actual practice. When we ask such questions, however, the limitations on our ability to do institutional engineering and the gaps in our knowledge of bureaucratic behaviour become especially evident and painful. We need a better understanding of the probable administrative and political dynamics of any given policy. Furthermore, evaluative complexities like income distribution, the vitality of the political and social system, and the development of individual tastes and attitudes should be considered in making any choices. The economic world is simply not separable from the world of non-economic phenomena.

We have to deal with the world as it actually is. We cannot legitimately ignore "second-best" problems simply because it is easier to do geometric and algebraic exercises when we assume them away. If business firms are not accurate cost minimizers, if consumer decision making has substantial habitual or random elements, if local government agencies are not precise calculators—then these facts should be taken into account in our analysis. Incorrect assumptions about the underlying social and economic processes should never be other than an unavoidable evil, brought on by mathematical frailty.[116] Building our analysis on fantasy instead of fact only serves to diminish the accuracy, completeness, reliability, and heuristic value of our results.

The problems of environmental policy making are admittedly not easy to resolve on these terms. There is no one "right answer" that transcends wide variations in circumstances. Instead, in each case, one needs to undertake a detailed investigation of the technology, the natural, economic, and political systems, and the effects of various choices on man and nature. Yet, our review has produced some conclusions that can serve as useful guideposts in such more specific studies.

All decentralized approaches to pollution control have their limits when economies of scale, the ability to operate directly on the ecosystem, and on-line stochastic flexibility are important considerations. The two most commonly discussed decentralized schemes, fees and standards, have competing virtues and deficiencies. In particular, fees can help achieve an efficient allocation of clean-up efforts, while standards tend to ensure that desired ambient targets are reliably met.

Negotiable pollution rights are an attractive alternative when there are a moderate number of sources and few enough substances and points of concern that the necessary markets can be organized at reasonable cost. Such rights combine both the discontinuous penalty functions of standards and the price-guided flexibility in allocating pollution efforts characteristic of fees.

If we do proceed with a decentralized programme, there is much to be said for some kind of mixed system. This could mean fees to provide an incentive to waste sources to clean up beyond standards or subsidies for those who discharge less than the stock of pollution rights they hold. Or it could involve emergency standards to ensure that fee payers did not move an ecological system across some major threshold given variations in ambient conditions. The creative possibilities in this regard remain relatively unexplored.

Long-run incentives to technology are important, and fees may have some value in this respect. However, fees are subject to erosion and unreliability due to secular and cyclical fluctuations in various prices. Even very crude and apparently unreasonable regulations can be given an intelligible (if not always convincing) rationale in the context of increasing waste loads, large risks, and the need to provide incentives for technology. Both fees and standards that specify discharge rates per unit of primary output can be expected to have difficulty in dealing with growing waste loads over time, since continuing readjustment of such schemes will be required to maintain ambient quality.

The informational requirements for creating and enforcing various decentralized systems are not very different. In particular, an iterative search for "the optimum" fee schedule by an ignorant pollution control authority will usually not be a feasible option. On the other hand, fees may have some cost advantages over standards in the operation of a self-reporting monitoring and data-gathering system. And their lack of discontinuous penalties could make for easier enforcement.

Some problems are very difficult to deal with via any decentralized mechanism, especially land use issues—where decisions about different areas cannot intelligently be made independently. Problems of irreversibility and the distributive impact of the "develop for recreation/preserve wild" trade-off are especially vexing.

While litigation has promise as a tool to increase the effectiveness of enforcement processes, it is not obvious that manipulating property rights and liability rules is an effective way to solve the problem of formulating environmental policy. The transaction costs and perverse incentives that lie behind the current unsatisfactory outcome of private action often make more direct government action necessary.

Policies directed at the inputs to pollution control mainly have value if they serve to overcome existing market imperfections or to facilitate the transition to a new situation. Special aid to plants that might close because of the burden of environmental protection should be primarily directed at smoothing such adjustment processes. Distributional considerations are important in making choices about how to finance the abatement of household wastes and whether to use local or federal funds for various purposes.

In the midst of these complexities, it is tempting to follow the academic impulse toward agnosticism and proclaim the question "unsolved" pending further research. But implicitly or explicitly, society will have an environmental policy. Inaction is action. This is not an exercise on a blackboard, and substantial amounts of resources are at stake.

Unfortunately, the prospects for obtaining complex and sophisticated policies—at least in the U.S.—are not overwhelmingly bright. Indeed, the problems of environmental policy making are in a sense the problems of democracy. How does one devise a political system that relates the imperfectly analysed preferences, goals, feelings, and attitudes of the public to detailed, esoteric, technical questions? Citizens, faced with limited time, will—appropriately—remain "rationally ignorant" amateurs when it comes to the problems of government. Even the professional legislator will inevitably be an "amateur" about most issues on which he must make decisions. Environmental protection clearly involves some questions of value on which a technician has no particular wisdom, and a legislature is just the right instrument to resolve such issues in a democratic society. But there are also questions of fact—both social and natural—about which the available information and analytical techniques simply do not offer definitive answers. It is all the more difficult for an outsider to know what expert to trust when a certain judgment and craftsmanship is required in order to use our simplified, heuristic models to explain and understand complex actual phenomena.

In this spirit, having come to the end, one might well go back and at least notice a critical assumption which we passed over rather quickly in the beginning: that it is only how individuals view the environment that ultimately matters. We have noted that this "moral rule of thumb" is ambiguous in a context in which policy affects values—as environmental policy surely does. Furthermore, there is the vexing question of how to treat the views of children and individuals yet unborn. As we try to do better in resolving "the problem," we need to consider whether the definition of that problem itself ought not, at least marginally, to be modified also.

Notes

1. See, for example, W.J. Baumol, "On Taxation and the Control of Externalities," *American Economic Review* 62 (June 1972): 307-22; J.M. Buchanan and W.C. Stubblebine, "Externality," *Economica* 29 (November 1962): 371-84; F.T. Dolbear, Jr., "On the Theory of Optimum Externality," *American Economic Review* 57 (March 1967), pp. 90-103; J.S. Bain, *Environmental Decay* (Boston: Little Brown, 1973), chapters 1 and 2; R.A. Tybout, "Pricing Pollution and Other Negative Externalities," *The Bell Journal of Economics and Management Science* 3 (Spring 1972): 252-66.

2. T.C. Schelling, "On the Ecology of Micromotives," *The Public Interest*, no. 25 (Fall 1971): 59-98.

3. P.A. Samuelson, "The Pure Theory of Taxation and Public Expenditure," in *Public Economics: An Analysis of Public Production and Consumption and Their Relations to the Private Sectors*, ed. J. Margolis and H. Guitton (New York: St. Martins Press, 1969), pp. 98-123. This paper clarifies the confusion generated by Samuelson's own previous work which suggested that a "pure" public good was one in which all consumers enjoyed the same physical services. See P.A. Samuelson, "The Pure Theory of Public Expenditure," *Review of Economics and Statistics* 36 (November 1954): 387-89.

4. R. Coase, "The Problem of Social Cost," *Journal of Law and Economics* 3 (October 1960): 1-44.

5. The first term is due to Samuelson; the second to M. Olsen, *The Logic of Collective Action* (Cambridge, Mass.: Harvard University Press, 1965); the third to James Buchanan, *The Demand and Supply of Public Goods,* (Skokie, Ill.: Rand McNally, 1969).

6. Two Harvard professors of Political Science once had an animated faculty club lunch discussion about the rationalty of voting. One, a man of cool and sceptical temperament, insisted that no calculating individual would ever vote in anything but an obscure primary for a local office. Under all other conditions, he contended, the chance of influencing the outcome was so small that voting was a waste of time. His companion remained unconvinced, and in a rejoinder that is

deeper than it seems, said, "My mother always taught me that it was my duty to vote and so I do."

7. See Samuelson, "The Pure Theory of Public Expenditure." A similar point has been made by Buchanan, *The Demand and Supply of Public Goods.*

8. If the production processes did not allow continuous variation in the distribution of services, the "frontier" would only exist as a set of points.

9. See M.J. Roberts, "Comment," *American Economic Review* 61 (May 1971): p. 173-77.

10. Note that this same question applies to Leibenstein's well-known notion of "X-efficiency." Is anyone ever not being "X-efficient" when we write down the "full" production function (including information and decision costs) and all the objectives of all participants? See H. Leibenstein, "Allocative Efficiency vs. X-Efficiency," *American Economic Review* 56 (June 1966): 392-415.

11. On the imperfect choice of imperfect decision rules see W.J. Baumol and R.E. Quandt, "Rules of Thumb and Optimally Imperfect Decisions," *American Economic Review* 54 (May 1964): 44-52.

12. The cases that Leibenstein characterizes as "X-inefficient" seem to include instances of all three kinds. "Inefficient" managers know less, or can calculate as well, or simply put a high value on some unpriced outputs of the enterprise, for example, their own quality of life.

13. R.N. McKean, "Property Rights within Government and Devices to Increase Governmental Efficiency," *Southern Economic Journal* 39 (October 1972): 177-86; and H. Demsetz, "The Exchange and Enforcement of Property Rights," *Journal of Law and Economics* 7 (October 1964): 11-26.

14. K.J. Arrow, "The Organization of Economic Activity: Issues Pertinent to the Choice of Market vs. Nonmarket Allocation," *Public Expenditures and Policy Analysis,* ed. R.H. Haveman and J. Margolis (Chicago, Ill.: Markham Publishing Company, 1970), pp. 59-73.

15. An insight into the controversy is provided by the November-December 1964 issue of *Public Power News,* published by the Washington Public Utility Districts Association, which makes clear that the question of whether public or private power interests were to have access to the most favourable hydro-electric sites was a key

problem. This was confirmed in a private communication to the author by Ken Billington, Executive Director of that Association, May 13, 1971.

16. H. Simon, "A Behavioral Model of Rational Choice," *Quarterly Journal of Economics* 64 (February 1955): 99-118.

17. See Z. Grilliches, "Comment," in *The Rate and Direction of Inventive Activity* (Princeton: National Bureau of Economic Research and Princeton University Press, 1962), pp. 346-53.

18. P.A. Samuelson, "The Evaluation of Real National Income," in *Oxford Economic Papers,* n.s. 2 (June 1950): 1-29. A similar view to that in the text is taken by J. de V. Graff, *Theoretical Welfare Economics* (London: Cambridge University Press, 1967), p. 80.

19. Thus "feasibility" means what is more or less likely to occur if given individuals undertake various efforts; thus it refers to the set of conditional probability distributions that arise from alternative political investments. The "neutral" question is simply what is the unconditional distribution of outcomes and might be better termed simply "probability" than "feasibility."

20. This is the so-called "second-best" problem, the little-known first statement of which can be found in P.A. Samuelson, *The Foundations of Economic Analysis* (Cambridge, Mass.: Harvard University Press, 1948), chapter 8. See also R.G. Lipsey and K. Lancaster, "The General Theory of the Second-Best," *Review of Economic Studies* 24 (1956): 11-32.

21. See, for example, R. Rees, "Second-Best Rules for Public Enterprise Pricing," *Economica,* n.s. 25 (August 1968): 260-73; also W.J. Baumol and D.F. Bradford, "Optimal Departures from Marginal Cost Pricing," *American Economic Review* 60 (June 1970): 265-84.

22. Coase, "The Problem of Social Cost." He also noted, in the second half of his article, that bargaining in real situaions was generally quite imperfect. That part of his argument seems to have made less impression on his readers than the earlier sections which discuss idealized cases.

23. The earlier literature is discussed in Samuelson, "The Evaluation of Real National Income." Kaldor and Hicks sought value-neutral comparisons of efficiency based on what compensation hypothetically might be paid from gainers to losers. Here we seek an explicitly value-relative comparison based on what gains and losses *actually* take place. See, for example, J.R. Hicks, "The Valuation of Social

Income," *Economica,* n.s. 7 (May 1940): 105-24.

24. On the effects of water pollution see U.S., Department of Interior, Federal Water Pollution Control Administration, *Water Quality Criteria* (Washington, D.C.: Government Printing Office, 1968); and G.M. Fair, J.C. Geyer, and D.A. Okun, *Water and Waste Water Engineering,* vol. 2 (New York: Wiley, 1968), chapter 32. On air pollution damages see L.B. Lave, "Air Pollution Damage; Some Difficulties in Estimating the Value of Abatement," in *Environmental Quality Analysis,* ed. by A.V. Kneese and B.T. Bower (Baltimore: Johns Hopkins Press, 1972), pp. 213-42, and W.R. Ahern, Jr., "Health Effects of Automotive Air Pollution," in *Cleaning the Air,* ed. by H.D. Jacoby and J.D. Steinbruner (Cambridge, Mass.: Ballinger, 1973), chapter 7.

25. In many areas of the U.S. the ratio between high and low flows is 3 to 1 and in the West, ranges of 7 to 1 are not uncommon. A good general source on stream flow problems is U.S., Department of Health, Education and Welfare, Public Health Service, *Symposium on Stream Flow Regulation for Quality Control* (Washington, D.C.: Government Printing Office, 1965).

26. On pesticides see M.R. Langham, J.C. Headley and W.F. Edwards, "Agricultural Pesticides: Productivity and Externalities" in *Environmental Quality Analysis,* ed. by Kneese and Bower; also U.S., Department of Health, Education and Welfare, *Report of the Secretary's Commission on Pesticides and their Relationship to Environmental Health* (Washington, D.C.: Government Printing Office, 1969). On coal mining problems see Michael Baker, Inc., "Analysis of Pollution Control Costs," prepared for the Appalachian Regional Commission, February 1973, which gives data on Eastern mines; and E.B. Peterson and H.M. Etter, *A Background for Disturbed Land Reclamation and Research in the Rocky Mountain Region of Alberta,* Canadian Forest Service, May 1970, which discusses reclamation in arid, Western conditions.

27. J.R.E. Jones, *Fish and River Pollution* (London: Butterworth, 1969).

28. L. Lave, "Air Pollution Damages"; also L. Lave and E. Seskin, "Air Pollution and Human Health," *Science* 169 (21 August 1970): 723-33.

29. G.M. Fair, J.C. Geyer, and D.A. Okun, *Water and Wastewater Engineering,* 2: 33-41, 33-45.

30. J.M. Leavitt, S.B. Carpenter, J.P. Blackwell, and T.L. Montgomery, "Meterological Program for Limiting Power Plant Stack Emis-

sions," *Journal of the Air Pollution Control Association* 21 (July 1971): 400-405.

31. For example, on property taxes, see H.F. Ladd, "The Role of the Property Tax: A Reassessment," in *Broad-Based Taxes,* ed. by R.A. Musgrave (Baltimore: Johns Hopkins Press, 1973). On the way local governments adjust to pay for pollution control, see S. Oster, "The Benefits and Costs of Water Pollution Control: A Case Study of the Merrimack Valley" (Ph.D. thesis, Harvard University, 1974).

32. M. Clawson and J.L. Knetch, *The Economics of Outdoor Recreation* (Baltimore: Johns Hopkins Press, 1966). See also J.L. Knetch and R.K. Davis, "Comparison of Methods for Recreation Evaluation" in *Water Research,* ed. by A.V. Kneese and S.C. Smith (Baltimore: Johns Hopkins Press, 1966).

33. See, for example, Lave, "Air Pollution Damages," and Lave and Seskin, "Air Pollution and Human Health."

34. Bruce and Susan Ackerman and D.W. Henderson, "The Uncertain Search for Environmental Policy: The Costs and Benefits of Controlling Pollution along the Delaware River," *University of Pennsylvania Law Review,* 20 (1973): 419.

35. G.F. White, "Formation and Role of Public Attitudes," in *Environmental Quality in a Growing Economy,* ed. by H. Jarrett, (Baltimore: Johns Hopkins Press, 1966); H.G. Fredrickson and H. Magnus, "Comparing Attitudes toward Pollution in Syracuse," *Water Resources Research* 14 (October 1968): 877-89. See also Canada, Department of Energy, *Perceptions and Attitudes in Resources Management,* by W.R.D. Sewell and I. Burton, Policy Research and Co-ordinating Branch, Resource Paper No. 2 (Ottawa: Queen's Printer, 1971).

36. See, for example, C.C. von Weizsaker, "Notes on Endogenous Changes of Tastes," *Journal of Economic Theory* 3 (December 1971): 345-72, and J. Harsanyi, "Welfare Economics of Variable Tastes," *Review of Economic Studies* 21 (1953-54): 204-13. The issue of how to treat the future is longstanding. See A.C. Pigou, *The Economics of Welfare,* 4th ed. (London: Macmillan, 1932).

37. For a review of this discussion, see M.J. Roberts, "Alternative Social Choice Criteria, a Normative Approach," Harvard Institute of Economic Research, Discussion Paper, No. 223, November 1971, pp. 26-30.

38. See, for example, A.M. Freeman III, R.H. Haveman, and A.V.

Kneese, *The Economics of Environmental Policy* (New York: Wiley, 1973), especially chapter 5. Also see the references in note 1 above.

39. See W.J. Baumol and W.E. Oates, "The Use of Standards and Prices for Protection of the Environment," in *The Economics of Environment,* ed. by P. Bohn and A.V. Kneese (London: Macmillan, 1971), pp. 53-65. See also W.J. Baumol, "On Taxation and the Control of Externalities," *American Economic Review* 62 (June 1972): 307-22.

40. Simon, *A Behavioral Model.*

41. Lave, "Air Pollution Damages." See also L. Lave and E.P. Seskin, "Health and Air Pollution: The Effect of Occupation Mix," in *The Effects of Environment,* ed. Bohn and Kneese, pp. 119-38.

42. Some states have adopted ambient standards that do allow for their own violation, typically no more than one year.

43. Indeed, if the model predicts the mean outcome of a given set of emissions and the distribution is approximately symmetric, observed outcomes will be worse than predicted fully half the time!

44. Some of these issues were treated in more detail in M.J. Roberts, "Organizing Water Pollution Control: The Scope and Structure of River Basin Authorities," *Public Policy* 19 (Winter 1971): 79-141. See also E.T. Haefele, "Environmental Quality as a Problem of Social Choice," in *Environmental Quality Analysis,* ed. by Kneese and Bower, pp. 281-332; A. Maass, "System Design and the Political Process: A General Statement," in *Design of Water Resource Systems,* ed. A. Maass et al. (Cambridge, Mass.: Harvard University Press, 1962); and N.E. Long, "New Tasks for All Levels of Government," in *Environmental Quality,* ed. Jarrett, pp. 141-55.

45. In this regard it is interesting to note the use of the Emscher River in Germany as a conduit for a major proportion of the regions' waste discharge, in part to improve the quality of other streams. See A.V. Kneese and B.T. Bower, *Managing Water Quality: Economics, Technology, Institutions* (Baltimore: Johns Hopkins Press, 1968). This tactic obviously pays when marginal damages are decreasing. Actually, uniform quality remains a stated goal under the 1972 act, but it is not a formal requirement since the whole thrust of that legislation is to shift from ambient to effluent standards.

46. Lave, "Air Pollution Damages"; Lave and Seskin, "Air Pollution and Human Health."

47. The rule required "secondary treatment or equivalent" in all cases. See U.S., Environmental Protection Agency, Water Control Office, *Cost of Clean Water* (Washington, D.C.: Government Printing Office, 1971).

48. See Clean Air Act, as amended, sections 109, 110, 111.

49. For other lists, see O.A. Davis and K.I. Kamien, "Externalities, Information and Alternative Collective Action," in *Public Expenditures and Policy Analysis,* ed. Haveman and Margolis; and E.S. Mills, "Economic Incentives in Air Pollution Control," in *The Economics of Air Pollution,* ed. H. Wolozen (New York: W.W. Norton, 1966), pp. 40-50.

50. A. Bergson, "A Reformulation of Certain Aspects of Welfare Economics," *Quarterly Journal of Economics* 52 (February 1938): 310-34.

51. See, for example, Mills, "Economic Incentives"; Baumol and Oates, "The Use of Standards"; Baumol, "On Taxation"; A.M. Freeman III and R.H. Haveman, "Residual Charges for Pollution Control: A Policy Evaluation," *Science* 174 (28 July 1972): 322-29; R. Solow, "The Economist's Approach to Pollution and Its Control," *Science,* 173 (August 1971): 498-503; A.V. Kneese, "The Political Economy of Water Quality Management," in *Environmental Decay,* ed. J.S. Bain (Boston: Little Brown, 1973), pp. 82-109; L.E. Ruff, "The Economic Common Sense of Pollution," *The Public Interest* (Spring 1970): 69-85. A useful review of some issues with respect to such charges is given in E.I. Selig, *Effluent Charges on Air and Water Pollution: A Conference Report,* Council on Law-related Studies, Conference Report, 15 and 16 October 1971, Environmental Law Institute, 1973.

52. In a sense, every penalty function depends upon still other, more severe, penalty functions to compel compliance. After all, why pay a fine for failure to obey a rule, unless failure to do so makes one liable to still more extreme sanctions?

53. This curve represents both direct treatment costs and any change in profits that results from changes in the profit-maximizing level and composition of marketed outputs. These private costs will be equal to social costs if the firm is in a competitive market. See M.J. Roberts and M. Spence, "Effluent Fees and Marketable Licenses for Pollution Control," Institute for Mathematical Studies in the Social Sciences, Stanford University, August 1974.

54. Kneese, a prominant advocate of charges, does say in "Political Economy," "Indeed, the discharge of many substances (primarily heavy metals and persistent organics) should probably be prohibited entirely...", p. 108.

55. See, for example, E.L. Johnson, "A Study in the Economics of Water Quality Management," *Water Resources Research* 3 (Second Quarter 1967): 297ff. Johnson assumes that only one "critical" reach of a stream really matters. See also K.D. Kerri, "An Economic Approach to Water Quality Control," *Journal of the Water Pollution Control Federation* 38 (December 1966): 18-83.

56. After all, political support for their activities—and hence likely future growth—might be positively related to the number and type of employees, which would bias the agency against labour-saving investments and against the utilization of outside experts. For a review of models of local government behaviour see S. Oster, "The Benefits and Costs of Water Pollution Control."

57. See references in notes 20 and 21 above.

58. Discussions of how to do such analysis are E. Mishan, "Second Thoughts on Second Best," *Oxford Economic Papers,* n.s. 14 (October 1962): 205-17. See also some brief remarks by I.M.D. Little, *The Price of Fuel* (London: Oxford University Press, 1953), pp. xiii-xiv, and R. Turvey, "The Second-Best Case for Marginal Cost Pricing," in *Public Economics,* ed. Margolis and Guitton, pp. 336-43.

59. T.V.A., for example, now undertakes quite extensive *daily* meteorological observations around major power plants and plans generating loads accordingly. See Leavitt et al, "Meterological Program."

60. This problem is just a manifestation of the more general issue of where administrative coordination functions better than coordination via market signals. See R. Coase, "The Nature of the Firm," *Economica* 4 (November 1957): 386-405; and also O. Williamson, "The Vertical Integration of Production," *American Economic Review* 61 (May 1971): 112-23.

61. Freeman and Haveman, "Residual Charges."

62. Kneese and Bower, *Managing Water Quality.*

63. ABT Associates, "Incentives to Industry for Water Pollution Control," Report prepared for the Federal Water Pollution Control Administration, Department of the Interior, December 1967.

64. For example, clean-up practices in a slaughterhouse have a great impact on how much organic material is carried off in sewers versus in solid form, ibid., pp. 69-70.

65. See M.J. Roberts, "A Framework for Analyzing the Behavior of Resource-Allocating Organizations," Discussion Paper, No. 264, Harvard Institute of Economic Research (December 1972).

66. The current air pollution control laws fine automobile manufacturers $10,000 per car for vehicles which violate standards, clearly a penalty intended to be effectively infinite. See Jacoby and Steinbrunner, *Cleaning the Air,* pp. 56ff.

67. C. Barfeld, "Environmental Report", *Natl. Journal* 4 (1972): 1871-82.

68. The Regional Water Quality Act of 1970, introduced by Senator Proxmire, section 3181.

69. The various sulphur tax proposals are discussed in Taxation with Representation, "The Proposed Tax on Sulphur Emissions" (Washington, D.C.: Government Printing Office, 1972).

70. This assumes that absent conscious policy, the technology of production will not change sufficiently in the direction of lower waste output per unit of primary production to overcome the effect of increased output. It hardly seems wise to assume the opposite.

71. For a criticism of the 1972 Water Pollution Control Act, see A.M. Freeman III and R.H. Haveman, "Clean Rhetoric and Dirty Water," *The Public Interest,* no. 28 (Summer 1972): 51-65.

72. J.H. Dales, *Pollution Property and Prices* (Toronto: University of Toronto Press, 1968).

73. Full data on all discharges would be required in either case. Dales's suggestion to the contrary does not seem fully accurate.

74. This practice is not seriously in error when damages are linearly additive in the waste parameters being measured. But except for very local approximations, the non-linear and interactive nature of environmental damage functions could make this practice seriously in error.

75. H. Jacoby and G. Schaunberg, "Administered Markets in Water Quality Control: A Proposal for the Delaware Estuary," unpublished. Their proposals are discussed in Selig, *Effluent Charges,* pp. 36-43.

76. It is sometimes possible to use one point along a river as a focus of

concern because typically one point has the lowest quality and is the "critical reach"—see Kneese and Bower, *Managing Water Quality*. However, for a long river there will be more than one significant point, and air pollution almost always diffuses in a more complex manner.

77. W.D. Montgomery, "Markets in Licenses and Efficient Pollution Control Programs," *Journal of Economic Theory* 5 (December 1972), pp. 395-418.

78. One way to set up such a system is to license the firm to cause so much pollution at each point of interest, rather than so much emission, ibid., pp. 403ff.

79. On sewage treatment plant operation see U.S., General Accounting Office, *Examination into the Effectiveness of the Construction Grant Program for Abating, Controlling and Preventing Water Pollution* (Washington, D.C.: Government Printing Office, 1969); on precipitators see J. Greco and W.A. Wynot, "Operating and Maintenance Problems Encountered with Electrostatic Precipitators," presented to the American Power Conference, 20 April 1971, Tennessee Valley Authority.

80. Roberts and Spence, "Effluent Fees," discusses this and related schemes in some detail and demonstrates their properties.

81. The discussion in this section draws heavily on my two earlier papers, "River Basin Authorities: A National Solution to Water Pollution," *Harvard Law Review,* 83 (1970): 1527-56 and "Organizing Water Pollution Control: The Scope and Structure of River Basin Authorities," *Public Policy* 19 (Winter 1971): 79-141.

82. See note 60 above.

83. R.K. Davis, *The Range of Choice in Water Management: A Study of Dissolved Oxygen in the Potomac Estuary* (Baltimore: Johns Hopkins Press, 1968); and L. Ortolano, "Artificial Aeration as a Substitute for Waste-water Treatment"; and D.P. Louck and H.D. Jacoby, "Flow Regulation for Water Quality Management," both in *Models for Managing Regional Water Quality,* ed. R. Dorfman, H.D. Jacoby, and H.A. Thomas (Cambridge, Mass.: Harvard University Press, 1972).

84. Since the Federal Water Pollution Control Act Amendments of 1961 the following language has been part of the ruling legislation. Initially found in section 3.6.1 it is now incorporated in section 102.6.1. "In the survey or planning of any reservoir by the Corps of Engineers,

Bureau of Reclamation or other Federal agency, consideration shall be given to inclusion of storage for regulation of stream flow, except that any such storage and water releases shall not be provided as a substitute for adequate treatment or other methods of controlling waste at the source."

85. T.V.A., for example, has actively opposed the E.P.A., the A.E.C., and various state environmental agencies in an effort to secure less restrictive thermal and air emissions standards from its power plants, and the Los Angeles Department of Water and Power has been involved in a major controversy with the County Air Pollution Control Board over its recently completed Scattergood Unit Number 3. See M.J. Roberts, "The Behavior of Publicly Owned Electric Utilities," *American Economic Review* (May, 1975).

86. Roberts, "Organizing Water Pollution Control."

87. A.D. Scott, "The Economist and Federalism in Environmental Management," pp. 000-000 above.

88. S.S. Surrey, *Pathways to Tax Reform* (Cambridge, Mass.: Harvard University Press, 1973).

89. See James Q. Wilson, "The Politics of Regulation," in *Social Responsibility and the Business Predicament*, ed. James McKie (Washington, D.C.: The Brookings Institution, 1974).

90. Ford Foundation Energy Policy Project, *A Time to Choose* (Cambridge, Mass.: Ballingher Publishing, 1974).

91. G. Stigler, "The Theory of Economic Regulation," *The Bell Journal of Economics and Management Science* 2 (Spring 1971): 3-21.

92. G. Calabresi, *The Costs of Accidents: A Legal and Economic Analysis* (New Haven, Conn.: Yale University Press, 1970); F.I. Michelman, "Pollution as a Tort: A Non-Accidental Perspective on Calabresi's *Costs*," *Yale Law Journal* 80 (1971): 647-86.

93. Michelman, "Pollution as a Tort," pp. 654-56.

94. Actually the situation is still more complicated when there are multiple equilibria and total, not marginal, conditions are relevant. Then we must discover in advance which equilibria are "optimal" and assign liability to the party whose costs are lowest for changing his actions in order to have the system reach that outcome.

95. P. Steiner, "Choosing Among Alternative Public Investments in the Water Resources Field," *American Economic Review* 44 (December 1959): 893-916.

96. Michelman, "Pollution as a Tort," pp. 684-85.

97. R.O. Zerbe, "Theoretical Efficiency in Pollution Control," *Western Economic Journal* 8 (December 1970): 364-76.

98. Most notably, J.L. Sax, *Defending the Environment* (New York: Knopf, 1970).

99. See for example, Federal Water Pollution Control Act Amendments of 1972, section 505.

100. See for example, A.W. Reitze Jr., *Environmental Law*, (2nd ed.; Washington, D.C.: North American International, 1972), pp. one-12 to one-31. See also *Environmental Quality*, the fourth annual report of the Council on Environmental Quality, Washington, D.C., September 1973, pp. 393-96.

101. See Stigler, "Theory of Economic Regulation"; Wilson, "The Politics of Regulation"; R.G. Noll, M.J. Peck, and J.J. McGowen, *Economic Aspects of Television Regulation* (Washington, D.C.: The Brookings Institution, 1973) for an interesting discussion of the Federal Communications Commission; and J.R. Baldwin, "Air Transport in Canada" (Ph.D. thesis, Harvard University, 1973), for a useful discussion of Canadian institutions and regulation in general.

102. We clearly cannot assume that such groups are profit maximizing, since today that strategy would imply zero activity and zero loss. If they were growth maximizing, we should expect them to allocate resources in such a way that provokes additional philanthropic support. In that case, if donors are motivated by substantive goals, we should expect selective public fiscal incentives to have only a small impact on the distribution of effort of "public interest" litigation.

103. P. Joskow, "Approving Nuclear Power Plants: Scientific Decision Making or Administrative Charade," *The Bell Journal of Economics and Management Science* 5 (Spring 1974): 320-32.

104. For a summary of various estimates, see Tax Foundation Inc., "Tax Burdens and Benefits of Government Expenditures by Income Class, 1961 and 1965," (New York, 1967).

105. See Oster, "The Benefits and Costs" for a detailed case study.

106. In general, the water-borne waste output of a household is not closely tied to its consumption levels. The major factor influencing this output is whether or not the household has a garbage disposal. If we believed that the marginal cost of dealing with sewered waste was above that of handling solid waste; we might want to tax or regulate

such devices. Note that some writers on solid waste problems assume that the costs of water-borne wastes are lower and hence suggest encouraging the use of such equipment!

107. I.M.D. Little, *A Critique of Welfare Economics,* 2nd ed. (London: Oxford University Press, 1957).

108. On attitudes toward the environment generally see the references in note 35 above. This pattern is also visible in the generally high income/education/status levels characteristic of the membership of environmental organizations.

109. M.J. Roberts, "Study of the Measurement and Distribution of the Costs and Benefits of Water Pollution Control," Draft Report to the Environmental Protection Agency, November 1973.

110. See Fredrickson and Magnas, "Comparing Attitudes," Sewell and Burton, *Perceptions and Attitudes;* R.C. Lucas, "Wilderness Perception and Use—the Example of the Boundary Waters Canoe Area," *Natural Resources Journal* 3 (January 1964), pp. 394-411. See also U.S., Outdoor Recreation Resources Review Commission, *Research Studies, Number 19 and 20* (Washington, D.C.: Government Printing Office, 1962).

111. A.M. Freeman III, "The Distribution of Environmental Quality," in *Environmental Quality Analysis,* ed. Kneese and Bower.

112. Oster, "The Benefits and Costs."

113. See W. Summers, "Pollution Control in the Paper Industry" (Ph.D. thesis, Harvard University, 1973).

114. *Environmental Quality,* the Second Annual Report of the Council on Environmental Quality (Washington, D.C., 1971), pp. 127-9.

115. See, for example, the studies of job retraining reviewed in J.I. Ribich, *Educational Poverty,* (Washington, D.C.: The Brookings Institution, 1968), chapter 3.

116. This view raises some major issues of social science methodology. For an exposition and defense of this position see my paper, "On the Nature and Condition of Social Science," *Daedalus* 103 (Summer 1974): 47-64.

8

Some Promising Avenues of
Further Research

Neil A. Swainson

Without making the unwarranted assumption that all aspects of a "management" challenge are equally amenable to research investigation, or, indeed, are susceptible at all to institutional, structural, or mechanistic solutions, this short concluding section attempts to highlight some ways in which further investigation may help us with the water quality issue. The comments which follow are really supplementary to those directed to the same end and incorporated in several of the preceding papers.

Perhaps it will be helpful at the outset to restate a point made repeatedly by our contributors. There is no one single basic water quality management problem. Rather there are many of them, and one major contribution which sound research can make is to reinforce or clarify the acts of judgment required if we are to ensure that our investigative effort itself and, ultimately, our policy actions are directed toward the real source or sources of our difficulties as they exist in any one geographic area. Research investigation of technical as well as institutional questions may serve in this way. Consider for a moment a few brief references to the manner in which it has already underscored the variability of water quality management problems in Western Canada.

Recently, it has become apparent that the major threat to water quality in the Lower Fraser Valley of British Columbia is likely to be traceable to toxic discharges from a wide range of sources in the Greater Vancouver area. By contrast, the major difficulty in the Okanagan Valley of the central province is lake eutrophication caused by fertilizer run-off and domestic discharges. And in the Kootenay River watershed of Eastern British Columbia, mining industry and some pulp mill activity appear to be the primary cause of water degradation.

The same point may be made in another way by reminding ourselves of the research-inspired assessment that, for much of Western Canada, including British Columbia, the quality of the water resource has not yet been significantly impaired. Thus, in a fundamental sense, the primary task ahead for this broad region is, fortunately, one of preserving water quality, without, as is the case for so much of the developed world, first having to restore it. The situation faced here, in short, is not at all that which exists on some of Southern Ontario's rivers, or, for example, in the Delaware or Ruhr valleys. Further research effort may well help Western Canadians to determine if there are institutional mechanisms which are particularly useful—or useless—under their circumstances. If, for example, the trans-action costs associated with educing multiple-agency co-operation and the resources required for bureaucratic analysis are great and the decision-making process is thus likely to be tortuous, are there some arrangements or mechanisms—as opposed to others—in which institutional inaction rather than action can be expected to sustain the basic water quality objective of the polity?

The manner in which research into technical and institutional issues may help produce a suitable matching of policy problem and institutional response can be illustrated, thirdly, by referring to the sheer physical extent of so many Western Canadian watercourses. For great stretches of many of them there is little competition with respect to the use of their waste-absorbing properties and not much likelihood of it emerging in the forseeable future. Pulp mills, for example, may be scores or hundreds of miles apart. Under these circumstances, some sets of institutional ar-rangements, such as those involving the use of transferable discharge warrants and the operation of a market in them, may be singularly inap-propriate. Or, if appropriate, their relevance may depend upon hitherto unemphasized considerations.

One of the most effective ways in which to focus attention on the variability of the water quality management problem is to classify the types of decision which governments have to produce as they respond to their perceptions of it. At least four categories of decision can be readily iden-tified.

1. Those establishing how much of an investment to make in a control programme when the consequences of water pollution are reasonably well understood.

2. Those deciding upon the magnitude of a control programme when the effects of degradation, real or threatened, are uncertain. (Two further categories can be identified here if we relate the uncer-tainty involved in categories 1 and 2 to certainty and uncertainty associated with the effectiveness of policy-implementing mechanisms. These categories are not pursued further here in the context of an admittedly gross assumption that it is primarily percep-tions of the *consequences of degradation* which motivate govern-ments to action in the first instance.)

3. Those deciding how much to invest in research and investigation to reduce the uncertainty involved.

4. Those deciding which mechanism or mechanisms to rely on (and which administrative arrangements to utilize in operationalizing these mechanisms) to achieve the desired standard of water quality.

Now if our point is that disaggregating water quality management decisions in this way ought to help focus attention on problems of quite differing orders, it is reasonable to ask ourselves to what extent our public decision-makers do in fact discriminate between the types of problem they have to face. The evidence is far from complete, but much of it suggests that at present they do not distinguish precisely between the first two categories of decision, and have much to learn about adapting the "investment-in-research" decision to specific situations. Careful research into the workings of the existing policy-making process appears to be in order here if we are to improve our performance in the light of the criteria posited in the introductory essay.

Our fourth category of decision—deciding upon implementing mechanisms—seems to pose a somewhat different problem. Clearly we need to know more about the way in which existing institutional mechanisms operate. At the same time, we may be reaching the limits of useful analysis and debate with respect to the relative merits of some of our most theoretically appealing, but largely untried, mechanisms. For them, the time may well have arrived when we should invoke some carefully designed experimentation. The difficulties inherent in such operations are manifest. But, for example, it is not at all clear that there is any alternative means of testing the claims advanced for such pricing mechanisms as effluent charges, of probing the merits of circumstances in which individuals, firms, even governments have the capacity to take individual decisions which reflect true social costs, short of trying them out under carefully controlled conditions.

There is still another question which should not be overlooked as we reflect upon the contribution which further research can make to avoiding misapplied effort. This concerns the breadth or coverage of our definition of water quality as a policy issue. Are we in fact asking the correct question when we make water quality per se the subject of our enquiry? For some, the answer to this certainly is an unqualified "Yes." To them, water quality has become a primary value in its own right. But for many, it is in a sense a subset of still larger objectives—such as the perceptions of desirable land usage, population density, and lifestyle on which the conclusions of the recent federal-provincial study of the water resource in British Columbia's Okanagan Valley appear to have turned. We are back face-to-face with the question raised at the beginning of our introductory essay. There are major advantages and disadvantages associated with approaching policy questions from wide and from narrow perspectives. We factor broad issues into narrower ones to avoid being strangled by complexity. But we need to be careful. How, for example, if we do not tackle the wider issues first, do we allow for the fact that while water quality management lends itself rather well to incremental or iterative decision making, the closely related problem of land-use management does not? We would appear to need to know more here about the wisdom and the means of concentrating concurrently on narrowly and broadly distributed sets of objectives.[1]

A related if difficult matter for research effort to probe concerns our capacity, or our perceptions of our capacity, to pursue consciously a multiplicity of values concurrently within the context of a single policy issue. Obviously we will always do this to a degree, and all decisions affect many values. It would be helpful to know more precisely than we do at present about the possible existence of some point beyond which in one policy "package" we cannot aggregate too much if we wish to keep the attention of the political system focused on a single discrete issue until the difficulty in question has been dealt with to the satisfaction of a significant majority of those strongly interested in it. Do we, or do we not, complicate matters unwisely, for example, if we attempt to pursue an extensive exercise in income redistribution within the context of an effort to improve and preserve water quality?

It seems to be reasonable to assume that our decision making would be improved if decision-makers themselves had a clearer view of their own values concerning matters environmental and a clearer view both of the distribution throughout society of such values, and of the intensity with which they are held. If it be a fact that the political dimension in water quality management is a crucial one, and often—from the perspective of those favouring tough strong remedial preservative measures—a weak one, research effort might also be directed helpfully first to identifying and then to attempting to detemine the accuracy or validity of what appear to be the components, in this policy area, of decision-makers' perceptions of "political efficiency." Is it a fact, for example, that operatively it will be easier to raise prices than standards? Does utilizing the concept of a transferable discharge right/warrant create insoluble problems for decision-makers in the public arena? And, if so, why? In many North American jurisdictions political actors have been convinced that effluent charges invoke unduly high political costs and have favoured approaches which, whatever the inefficiencies they involve, so diffuse the clean-up or protective costs involved as to make them virtually invisible. We would appear to need insight into their "insight" and into the long-range consequences of sustaining illusions of the order referred to here.

An important dimension of political efficiency consists of decision-makers' perceptions of the public's willingness to live consciously with risk and uncertainty. Research effort may help clarify our understanding of the issues here. The viability or nonviability of a deliberately iterative programme of policy development and implementation is often rooted in what the answers to these questions appear to be. The emergence of some risk situations, such as those involving the possible destruction of a fish run or unknown hazards associated with the use of chlorinated hydrocarbons, produce public perceptions of risk and hence thresholds which decision-makers can respond to fairly readily. What we need assistance with particularly, are the public's responses and expectations with respect to situations in which the indications of risk are barely visible and the consequences of the risk are likely to be definable only in the long, as opposed to the short, run. If, as Professor Roberts suggests, in the last analysis we are purchasing not a fixed outcome but a lottery ticket with respect to water quality, perhaps we need some insight into the extent to which public expectations of certainty need to be clarified or modified.

The references already made to the federal setting in which water quality management has to be pursued in Canada raise another set of issues concerning which research-generated information may help. One of these involves identifying the extent of the "problem-shed." As suggested earlier, in some sense there is a national constituency which has an interest in the quality of the water resource in the many regions of Canada. We need insight about how this national perspective can be inserted most usefully into the decision-making process. Should this happen earlier or later in the game? Similarly, we need insight into the feasibility, in circumstances where jurisdiction is shared, of expecting one level of government to be uniquely responsible for injecting an extended time horizon into the decision making. Or are we going to have to expect both provincial and federal decision-makers to move back and forth along the time scale? Perhaps one additional point should be made here. Deciding what constitutes a legitimate national perspective is a crucial problem. Does it incorporate, for example, the right of the federal government to proscribe any region's desire to become, or to remain, by choice, a perpetual residual sink? But the answers to it will not be found in basically institutional considerations, and thus the question is one we leave for the deliberation of others.

We need to know much more than we do about the capacity of various levels of government in Canada to co-operate in policy formation and implementation and, as Professor Scott maintains, about the level of transaction costs associated with various forms of governmental interaction. This appears to be particularly true of situations in which primary decision-making responsibility may be vested at one level of government, but concerning which other levels may possess unique and related capacities. One thinks here, for example, of the federal government's ability to fund, direct, and disseminate the results of technical research and local government's capacity to deal with non-point sources of urban water pollution.

Finally, as has been suggested already, careful research ought to help by broadening our understanding of the decision-making process itself. No thinking observer can fail to have noted some distinctive characteristics of the current scene. One which comes to mind readily involves the wide-spread discounting of the case for generating efficient solutions, or if one will, for avoiding waste. Another, and one which has evoked much latter day concern, is the phenomenon to which Messrs. Graham and Haefele direct their attention in the preceding pages. Far too often in recent years disagreements associated with environmental decision making have de-generated into manifest distrust and thus have called into question those basic rules of the game about which a consensus may well be the foundation of the democratic order.[2]

At a minimum, two categories of research effort into the policy process would appear to be called for. First, we need to know much more than we do now about the comprehensiveness of the decision making currently being pursued. Just how broad is the range of goals and routes to these goals which policy makers consider? How extensive is the investment in assessing the likely consequences of various policy options? How produc-tive is it? Secondly, we need to monitor and examine the consequences of what appears to be a widespread response by government to the distrust referred to above. Admittedly slowly, and with some notable exceptions, the trading-off and synthesizing of mixes of values which is at the heart of environmental (and all) decision making is being moved beyond the confines of executive government, where it has been concentrated for so many years in Canada. As is always the case with structural change, the motives underlying it are mixed. This shift to a more open environment seems partly to be designed to broaden the range of inputs from interested sectors of the public and to permit an ongoing monitoring of the acts of decision and those of implementation. Partly, also, it seems to be the result of a deliberate determination on the part of those currently responsible for final acts of choice to alert the interested public to the realities of the policy formation process and the correlates of its own preferences.

In any case, this general development appears to make sense, not least because in recent years we have been bedevilled by some widespread and simplistic perceptions as to what is really involved in producing socially desirable policy responses to complex problems. It is to be hoped that advantage will be taken of opportunities to test the claims advanced by enthusiasts for public participation in policy making when they present themselves and also some of those advanced by advocates of involving many more of our elected representatives in acts of public choice. In following the latter-day search for improved institutional arrangements, the research-minded are likely to face some other fundamental questions, especially if our response to complexity involves an exended reliance on bargaining procedures. In particular, we are going to need to probe deeply into the consequences of adversary relationships. Are they a necessity, for example, if we are to validate the crucially important results of much of our technical analysis? And how far must they be carried? What costs and benefits are properly associated with them? Can they be made more innovative? Conversely, we need insight into the possibilities for generating information and reconciling viewpoints in circumstances which specifically eschew structured conflict.

Questions such as these require us to face up, as Professor Roberts correctly observes, to what are challenges to modern democracy itself. Answers to some of them may well emerge in a broader context than water quality management, even though their relevance to this subset of general public policy will still have to be proven. Perhaps the reverse may also be true; hard work combined with clear thinking and an inquiring spirit may generate insights with respect to narrower issues which have far wider applicability. It is just this prospect which helps make water quality management as fascinating and challenging as it is to the student of policy formation.

Notes

1. The case is well argued by Amitai Etzioni, "Mixed Scanning: A Third Approach to Decision-Making," *Public Administration Review* 17 (December 1967): 385-92.

2. Henry B. Mayo, *An Introduction to Democratic Theory* (New York: Oxford University Press, 1960), pp. 298-303.

Biographical Notes

David Blair is a practising lawyer in Vancouver, B.C. He is a graduate in Chemical Engineering of Queen's University and of the Law Faculty of the University of British Columbia.

Ron Bozzer is currently articling as a lawyer in Vancouver, B.C. He holds an honours degree in Economics from the University of British Columbia, and graduated from that University's Law Faculty in 1974.

John Dales graduated from the University of Toronto in 1943 and received his Ph.D. from Harvard. A specialist in economic history, he taught at McGill University from 1949 to 1954. Since that time he has been on the staff of the University of Toronto. He is the author of a number of articles and three books: *Hydroelectricity and Industrial Development: Quebec 1898-1940* (Cambridge, Mass: Harvard University Press, 1957); *The Protective Tariff in Canada's Development* (Toronto: University of Toronto Press, 1966); *Pollution, Property and Prices* (Toronto: University of Toronto Press, 1968).

Robert Franson is an Associate Professor in the Faculty of Law at the University of British Columbia. He holds a Bachelor of Engineering Physics Degree from Cornell University and a Jurist Doctor Degree from the University of California at Los Angeles. Currently he is a member of the White Owl Conservation Award Jury and a director of the Sierra Club of British Columbia.

John Graham has spent most of his life in Ontario, graduating from Queen's University in 1967 and from York University in 1969. Successive stints at the Bank of Canada, Ontario's Committee on Government Productivity, and finally Premier Davis's office, in Toronto, convinced him that governments function badly and not at all according to conventional theories. Since writing the paper included in this volume, he has spent a year and a half in the housing field, experimenting with, and refining the set of ideas outlined in his paper. Currently he is living in Ottawa, acting as a consultant to various governmental and voluntary agencies.

Edwin T. Haefele was educated at Illinois Wesleyan University and the

University of Chicago. He has held appointments on the Transportation Center at Northwestern University, The Brookings Institution, and Resources for the Future. He is presently Professor of Political Science at the University of Pennsylvania. He is the author of *Representative Government and Environmental Management* and the editor of *The Governance of Common Property Resources*.

Marc J. Roberts, an Associate Professor of Economics at Harvard University, has been on the faculty there since 1969, when he received his Ph.D. from that institution. During the last four years he has published articles in the *Harvard Law Review, Public Policy, The Public Interest,* and *Daedalus.* He has served extensively as a consultant, and currently is on the Board of Directors of the Public Interest Economics Center and the Federation of American Scientists. He teaches in the areas of industrial organization, public policy toward business, and environmental economics.

Anthony Scott is a professor of economics at the University of British Columbia. Born in Vancouver, he received an A.M. from Harvard and a Ph.D. from London, specializing in the economics of natural-resource conservation. His books and articles on the economics of managing resources and the environments and in the field of public finance include *Natural Resources: The Economics of Conservation* (Toronto: University of Toronto Press, 1955), and, with F.T. Christy, Jr., *The Common Wealth in Ocean Fisheries* (Baltimore: Johns Hopkins Press, 1965).

Neil Swainson has been a member of the faculty of the University of Victoria (and its predecessor institutions) since 1954. After receiving Bachelor's and Master's degrees from the University of British Columbia, he obtained a Ph.D. from Stanford. He is the author of a book on *The Canadian Approach to the Columbia River Treaty,* to be published shortly by McGill-Queen's University Press.

Index